Prais

The Ghost Ship Fire is a brave, deeply moving and enraging book about the sudden death of Colleen Dolan's daughter Chelsea, a talented electronic musician, in the blaze that swept through an Oakland fire-trap warehouse in 2016. Dolan's luminous portrait of Chelsea is the vibrant heart of the book, but the story is driven by her furious mother-love and need to find answers as to why her daughter and 35 other talented, creative young people died. Dolan recounts the agonizing story from the night of the fire and the numb days after, to the exhausting months of trial of the two men who created the hazardous conditions and sublet to artists, to the outrageous, slap-on-the-wrist verdicts, and the lack of accountability at every level of local government, for botched communications and budget cuts that slashed basic fire-prevention inspections.

Determined that these "36 stars" not have died in vain, Dolan lays out a stark list of needed changes in local policy, fiscal priorities and communication systems. Woven through the dramatic scenes, Dolan charts her own journey through "the ongoing-ness of grief," which she likens to "navigating a maze blindfolded."

Her gripping book describes the struggle to bring herself out of that maze–"Each morning I begin again"–and the challenge of finding meaning in loss: "It wasn't their deaths that taught us a lesson, after all, but their brief, full, beautiful lives." Dolan has written a powerful story of love and determination that will hearten those on their own grief journey, and deserves the attention of parents, city officials, public safety advocates and all concerned citizens.

~ Nisha Zenoff, Ph.D., author of *The Unspeakable Loss: How Do You Live After a Child Dies?*

* * *

With a blend of wit and charm, Colleen Dolan is a modern-day Jane Austen. Magnificent!

~ Ben Reeding

* * *

Once every so often the world hears a new voice. Colleen Dolan is the person to whom that voice belongs.

~ Fellow Author

The Ghost Ship Fire

A Mother's Search for Answers

Colleen Dolan

*This book is dedicated to my two daughters, Chelsea Faith and Sabrina May,
and to the 36 Stars who died in the Ghost Ship Fire:*

Cash Askew
Em Bohlka
Jonathan Bernbaum
Barrett Clark
David Cline
Micah Danemayer
Billy Dixon
Chelsea "Cherushii" Dolan
Alex Ghassan
Nick Gomez-Hall
Michela Gregory
Sara Hoda
Travis Hough
Johnny Igaz
Ara Jo
Donna Kellogg
Amanda Allen Kershaw
Edmond Lapine

Griffin Madden
Joey "Casio" Matlock
Dravin McGill
Jason McCarty
Jennifer Mendiola
Jennifer Morris
Feral Pines
Vanessa Plotkin
Michele Sylvan
Hanna Ruax
Benjamin Runnels
Nicole Siegrist
Wolfgang Renner
Jennifer Kiyomi Tanouye
Alex Vega
Peter Wadsworth
Nicolas Walrath
Chase "Nex Iguolo" Wittenauer

Foreword

Death is the one journey none of us want to take. In fact, we are hard pressed to see it as a journey at all. What makes it a journey, we ask? Rather it is the end of everything. It is the final destination. It is the enemy and the thief that comes to strip away everything from us. It is the most powerful of dates and it the one we fear the most. Rightly so. Death is quite simply the end of life. At least it is the end of the physical world.

It is the Grim Reaper. The harvester of life.

It is such a flat word for the magnitude of the act. Death.

Thanatos, in ancient Greek religion and mythology, was the bringer of death. Thanatos was the son of Nyx, the goddess of night, and the brother of Hypnos, the god of sleep. He appeared to humans to carry them off to the underworld when the time allotted to them by the Fates had expired.

In various mythologies over time we believed that death had its own lands and immortal beings that ruled over it. In Hinduism, Yama, the lord of death, navigates souls to the afterlife. In Greek mythology, Hades is the god who rules the underworld with impartiality. Anubis, in Egyptian belief, guides souls onwards and through the afterlife's judgment. Norse mythology introduced Hel, the goddess of death who ruled the realm of the dead. These gods show us the different cultural perceptions of mortality, and give us a figure that holds that place real.

It feels good to think of the dead gathering in a place, doesn't it? But can we, with our modern minds, still hold those older beliefs?

I speak *a lot* about death. I have even written two books about it as I have had a very close and personal encounter to it. In fact, you could say that I've done my own deep research into experiencing death myself. My experience was through an extended near-death experience, so I was the lucky one as I came back. It was just that the research I did was unexpected, unwanted, and supremely badly timed. At the age of 36, I got flu. It feels ridiculously small a word to contain the devastation it caused in so many lives, so let's use its full name. Influenza. But even that does not convey the magnitude of the destruction it wreaked. Within 48 hours of getting a sore throat, I was in ICU and was put on life support. I was to stay in an induced coma for three weeks while my body was intubated and motionless on a bed as the virus moved from flu into an undiagnosed lung condition. What was happening to my body was one thing as it lay kept alive by a snake-like embrace of tubes and pipes and machines. A totally different thing was happening to my spirit or soul. During the entire process I had an extended NDE in which I gradually traveled further and further away from my body and into other realms and worlds.

I was lucky, and one of the very few who can claim that they came back from death.

So I write about it, and speak a lot about it, and the questions asked of me are often the same ones.

"What happens after we die?"

"What is really out there?"

This is the big question of our time and of almost every time before ours. It is the eternal question of the human condition. And yet death, that ever-silent stranger, withholds all the answers from us.

I live in Africa and we are lucky that in our indigenous communities we see our dead as part of our family still. The one cornerstone of African spirituality is the belief in ancestors. Ancestors are the departed members of the family and are believed to be intermediaries between the living and the Creator (or God). It also means that we speak to our dead, a tradition that gives a lot of comfort.

African tradition emphasises some core beliefs:

- Each human is made up not only of flesh, bones and blood, but also of spirit and soul.
- Although the human body dies, the soul or spirit does not perish.
- There is an understanding that human relations, especially within the family, do not die but go on forever.
- There is a unique relationship that exists between the Creator Spirit (which is God) and the human spirit.

The spirits of the departed play the vital role of intermediaries and are the link to the Creator.

That means that greeting death, in traditional African culture, does not mean the end–it simply means you are moving into the realm of an ancestor.

I know that none of these reasons or ideas can take away the pain of death. None of those old immortal gods, nor their reasons or bigness, can take away the pain of the loss. Death is simply unimaginable. Losing a child is so much more. It is unbearable.

And yet we do bear it, as humans. We do continue. We take our pain and our loss and we hold it in our arms and move forward.

The pain of such a huge loss as Colleen Dolan experienced is so great, that words fail. This book is remarkable as it manages to wrap words around the journey of such deep pain. It is a place that, for many of us, words fail. Colleen Dolan manages indeed to speak about the unspeakable, and she writes about it with such power and force.

She holds death in one hand and walks forward with the pain of it all. This story is a remarkable testimony to the human spirit.

Sarah Bullen is a multi-published author and literary agent. Her books include "The Other Side: Journeys into Mysticism, Magic and Near Death"; "Love and Above: A journey into shamanism, coma and joy."

PART ONE
The Fire

Chapter 1

The Call

Friday, December 2, 2016

My phone rang from the far corner of the bedroom, startling me awake. It continued to ring and then thankfully stopped. I tugged the comforter up to my chin. How long had I been asleep? Not long enough. I was exhausted from hiking that day. A few seconds later, a text note sounded. I debated whether to answer. Then the insistent ping sounded again. Reluctantly, I rolled out of bed and dragged myself across the room to the annoying phone. Who would be calling me now?

I grabbed the phone and looked at the time. 11:25 p.m. Had something happened to my mother? She'd just turned 90, and it wasn't out of the question.

Oddly, the call was from Chelsea's boyfriend, David Last. I listened to his breathless voicemail about a fire where Chelsea was playing music that night and that she hadn't emerged yet. The text message was also from David. It said, "Call me!" I called David back, and he told me he'd been trying to reach Chelsea, but she wasn't answering her phone. His voice cracked as he spoke about how worried he was.

His words rang false. Was he just being dramatic? My body tensed as he spoke, and I wanted to tell him he was wrong, but my heart began to pound, and my mouth went dry. What if it was true? I asked him to text me the address so I could put it in my GPS and tossed the phone on my bed. If it was true and my daughter was going to the hospital, I would ride in the ambulance with her.

My dirty hiking clothes from earlier that day lay on top of the laundry basket. I threw them on and grabbed a new pair of wooly socks from the drawer, leaned against the dresser, and stuffed my feet into them one at a time. Then I pulled on my dusty hiking shoes without bothering to tie the laces. This was taking much too long. I shoved my arms into my sweater coat, zipped it, and picked up my phone as I raced toward the bedroom door.

Another text ping sounded. I glanced at my phone. David had sent an address. Chelsea was in Oakland. Oakland! I was in San Rafael, at least a 45-minute drive away. It was 11:27 p.m.

Panic gripped my bones. Oakland. The East Bay freeways were a mess of loops, overpasses, and ambiguous exits. I didn't know any of the neighborhoods.

Disbelief and mother instinct swirled around my brain. There's a fire! Chelsea's not answering her phone. I can't drive alone. I don't know Oakland. What good is it if I go there? I hesitated for a fraction of a second at the bedroom door and told myself, 'Stay home. You know Chelsea. She'll be fine.'

But my body had no idea what my brain was saying. I lunged down the two flights of stairs to my garage and slammed my hand on the garage door opener by the door frame. The heavy door rumbled behind me as I jumped into the driver's seat. Panting, I clicked on the address David had texted. That little voice in my head nagged again, '*She's smart. She's fine. Wait for someone to call you.*' Anyone reasonable would have thought the same thing, but I was beyond reason. I had to go.

Chapter 2

The Drive

Friday, December 2, 2016

Google Maps said it was 31 miles to the 1300 block of 31st Avenue in Oakland. Something about those numbers lining up made me shiver. It didn't feel right. I forcefully shoved the gear shift into reverse, but in fearful overreaction, I backed the car out of my garage painfully slowly, afraid I'd run over a cat or crash before even starting out.

Carefully, I wound my way around the neighborhood streets. Three blocks of hyper-cautious driving clenched my muscles into knots. By the time I entered the freeway, my breath was coming in gulps, and sweat ran down my back. I cemented my hands to the wheel to keep them from shaking and pressed down hard on the gas pedal. That stupid little voice of doubt saying, 'Stay home,' bounced around my throbbing skull. I angrily rasped out loud, "Just stop." My head was exploding. The nagging voice got quiet, and the female voice on my phone GPS came through my car speakers, "Take exit 451B to 580 East and the Richmond Bridge."

I nearly flew over the 12-mile Richmond Bridge, sped down Highway 580, slicing over the three lanes toward Highway 80 and past the Bay Bridge exit that led to San Francisco. Then, I was faced with the surreal maze of overhead passes and a confusing array of forked exits toward Oakland. I panicked. Should I go left or right? Thank goodness for the female navigator voice on Google Maps: "Stay left! Get in the right two lanes." The freeways were dark and creepy. Only a few other cars were on the road with me. Truthfully, I shouldn't have been behind the wheel, frantically driving too fast without really knowing where I was going. David called a second time to check on my progress, which knocked out the GPS on my phone.

I fumbled, attempting to re-enter the address, but the roads were too foreign, and I couldn't read the small print on the screen. There was no place to pull over. I had no choice but to drop my phone on the passenger seat and gaze ahead, following the rising black pillar of smoke above Oakland. I continued driving in that direction but had already raced past one exit that seemed close to the fire. There was another up ahead. I veered off the freeway. The intense smell told me I was close. My car clock said it was 11:58 p.m. I hadn't looked at my speedometer once.

I wound up in a dowdy neighborhood close to the freeway. Cops and orange traffic cones lined the intersections, waving cars away from the source of the smoke. I lowered my window and yelled, "My daughter is in that fire!" A young, sympathetic cop nodded and waved me over to a side street where I could park my car. I hurriedly pulled off to the curb, grabbed my phone and the winter parka from the back seat, threw open my car door, and ran full speed toward the smoke. I heard a car door slam behind me. I turned around and saw a cop beside my car. I'd left the door wide open. I shook it off with a '*So what*' and ran ahead, leaving all things normal behind.

The fire as seen from the freeway on Friday night, December 2, 2016. This is the smoke plume I followed to find the Ghost Ship warehouse. Photo courtesy of Julianna Brown.

Chapter 3

The Fire

Saturday, December 3, 2016, Midnight-Early Morning

Half a block away, I could see fire trucks and ambulances surrounding a huge, white rectangular warehouse. Flames jumped out the windows, upstairs and down. Smoke rose, thick and putrid, straight up and then mushroomed out into the sky. Young people wrapped in blankets and sleeping bags crouched against the brick walls of a Wendy's hamburger joint across the street from the fire, shivering in the cold night air.

I crossed the street toward the warehouse to see if Chelsea had come out yet and yelled her name. I expected to see a small crowd of her friends standing in the street in front of the building. She wasn't there. Truthfully, I would have looked inside when I didn't see her on the sidewalk, but a slim female police officer with short, blunt-cut blondish hair ran up to me and blocked me with her body. She gently but firmly held my shoulders and told me, "Step back and stay in the Wendy's parking lot."

I could have shoved her out of my way; she was that slight, but her kind face stopped me short. Before she blocked me, I'd managed to get close enough to peer around the front of a fire truck and saw there were no partygoers gathered on the sidewalk in front of the building. I looked past the row of fire vehicles lined up in the street. No ambulances were being loaded with victims or rushing to the hospital. That was a relief.

Oddly, none of the firefighters appeared to be doing anything. They were propping up a ladder that got caught in the overhead electrical wires. Not one firefighter was climbing toward the second-story windows, aiming a fire hose, or going in. When I asked why no one was attempting to rescue any people who might be inside, the officer told me the fire battalion chief had declared the building unsafe, and firefighters were not permitted to enter. I gasped, "Unsafe?!" I'd never heard such a stupid statement. Wasn't that why they were issued breathing apparatus and heavy fireproof gear? Wasn't that their job?

This photo was used extensively by every news organization in the U.S. Original source of photo unknown.

9

A group of young people stood in the parking lot, staring at the burning warehouse without making a sound. No one was shouting or pointing or acting excited. Did they know everyone got out safely? I guessed they probably lost all their belongings in the fire, but they didn't act like anyone was hurt. Still, that didn't relieve the growing tension in my body. Chelsea was missing, and I wanted to find her.

My phone rang, and it was my younger daughter, Sabrina. David had called her, too. "Do you want me to come be with you?" Oh my God, yes! I shivered alone in the cold night air. I couldn't do this alone. Sabrina was my rock.

Sabrina lived half an hour away in the East Bay city of Vallejo. I couldn't just stand there waiting for her. The fire was raging, smoke pushing its way out the windows and roof, while firefighters milled about doing nothing. *What the Hell!* My body shook from the cold and a surge of adrenaline. I began pacing back and forth from one end of the parking lot to the other, cursing under my breath, hoping to get a better view of the sidewalk in front of the warehouse.

From this angle, firefighters and fire engines completely blocked my view. What if Chelsea and others were lying on the ground out of sight? I wanted to be with my daughter if she was injured and ride with her in the ambulance. Near the corner, an ambulance waited with its inside lights shining brightly, ready to take survivors to the hospital. Was Chelsea in there? I strode over to get a closer look in the windows. Again, a cop, this time an older man, blocked my way and told me, "Stay in the parking lot with the other people over there." He pointed to the huddled group sitting on the ground near the lighted windows of the hamburger joint.

The bright lights inside the restaurant were an insult to my fears. The normalcy of Wendy's overhead sign lit up with the image of a smiling, pigtailed little girl and some young kid standing behind a counter ready to fill fast food orders jarred my anxious brain. I walked around the perimeter of the hamburger restaurant, looking at each face, hoping to see a familiar smile. Maybe one of Chelsea's friends could tell me what happened. The rag-tag group of young people were mostly crouched on the ground close to the building for warmth. Someone had distributed blankets and sleeping bags, and these were draped around shoulders. A few people were crying, but most were just talking quietly.

One bearded guy stood near me, and I thought maybe it was Chelsea's friend, Joel, but when I walked over and looked closely at his face, I realized it wasn't him. I was desperate for news. None of the people I saw were part of Chelsea's crew from her various events and performances. She had a lot of friends who played electronic music with her and loved to dance as much as she did, but not one of them was there. How strange.

David, Chelsea's boyfriend, came over and stood near me. I told him I didn't see any of Chelsea's friends. He talked about the phone call he had received telling him about the fire. He mentioned the name of the person he spoke with, but it didn't register in my befuddled brain. David continued to talk, and although his words blended into a hum in my ears, the sound of his voice was reassuring. His face, his glasses, his dark sweatshirt, and his jacket looked perfectly normal, and the expression on his face was worried but hopeful.

Several times, David walked over to the people leaning on the Wendy's restaurant walls and windows to ask questions about missing friends. Then, he'd return with a shrug. Nothing new to report. At one point, his frustration turned to anger. "She didn't even want to be here!" He told me that she was doing a favor for a friend that night.

Joel, known as The Golden Donna, was performing in the

Bay Area and needed other musicians to help him fill in with music for the night. Both Chelsea and another musician named Johnny Igaz were on the same record label as Joel, 100% Silk. They were happy to support him in his Bay Area debut.

I stood numbly, staring at the flames and smoke, not fully comprehending my purpose in being there. It felt as though half my being was being pulled away. I'm an odd mix of extrovert and introvert. My two daughters split my personality in half and took off in opposite directions. Chelsea was my extrovert. She was known amongst her friends and family as a magical being. She was driven by music, color, and love. Every experience with or around her was high vibration. Even as a little girl, the "best day ever" and the "worst day ever" could happen within hours. She chose to move toward peak experiences in a conscious, decisive manner. Chelsea loved being on stage. Her daily life was filled with music composition and practice, but her love was the club dates, where she applied every cell in her body to the perfection of her performance.

Sabrina, my younger daughter, is Chelsea's polar opposite. She loves animals and nature. Her kindergarten teacher called her the calmest student she'd known in her 30 years of teaching. Even when she was born, Sabrina didn't cry. She looked around at the lights and people as if she'd just stepped into the room. Sabrina abhors attention, preferring instead to work quietly on her own, singing to herself, doodling, enjoying the moment from within. I could always count on her to settle my soul just by watching her play or work.

That night, I needed Sabrina's calm presence. Finally, around 12:30 a.m., she and her boyfriend, Joe, strode across the parking lot, a vision of reassuring sanity. Sabrina's blond hair peeked out from under her dark blue hoodie. She was already shivering in the cold despite her heavy parka layered over the sweatshirt. Sabrina looked fragile, barely 100 pounds, with a pretty face, pale white skin, and blue eyes, but she had the strength and stamina of a bull. I leaned into her stability and tried to make my face look hopeful for Sabrina's sake, but my lips were quivering, and I couldn't stop shaking. Joe, tall and lanky, tucked Sabrina under one arm and put the other arm around my shoulder. His dad was full Ojibwe, and Joe had inherited his resonating, indigenous calm, as well as his mother's Bavarian practicality. He and Sabrina were a perfect match. They even seemed to speak their own language, leaning into each other's sphere and whispering words only they could hear and understand. I trusted Sabrina and Joe to carry my fear with wise tenderness.

Sabrina was practical; she knew how to take care of what needed to be done. She told me in a matter-of-fact voice that urgent messages were going out in phone calls, texts, and social media looking for Chelsea and others. Quite a few people were missing, but one by one, some had started to mark themselves safe from the fire. She kept glancing down at her phone to see if Chelsea had checked in and typed messages with her thumbs. Joe did the same.

That vapid little voice in my head started up again, 'You know Chelsea. She's fine. It's too cold out here. You should go home.' But I knew what I had to do. I was Chelsea's mother, and I was going to be there if she needed me. There was no choice. I had to stay.

Sabrina, Joe, and I stood side by side, staring at the fire as it seemed to boil up to a frenzy and light the windows from within. David came in and out of our little huddle, reporting on the news he'd gleaned from the thinning crowd around the restaurant. He told us they were mostly residents who lived in the warehouse. One by one, they were getting picked up by friends who arrived and bundled them off in their cars. As that young crowd dispersed, concerned neighbors who had previously peered out from their windows now began to emerge from nearby homes wearing bathrobes and winter coats. They were the only other adults my age in the parking lot.

The mood was somber. Engine noise filled the air. I didn't know how to react or even how to feel. We didn't know if Chelsea was dead or alive. I was a coil of anxiety, waiting for someone to walk up to me and tell me she was safe. My muscles ached from the strain of trying to contain myself.

Then, a new crowd of rubber-neckers arrived by the car-full and stood in a growing clump in the parking lot to look at the fire as though it were a tourist attraction. A couple of teenage boys passed by me on bicycles, blaring rap music out of a boom box strapped to the back of one of the bikes. I took a few steps in their direction and asked them to please turn down the music. There were people missing, and this was not a party. One kid did, and as I said thank you to him, another yelled at me, "What are you deaf? We just turned it off!" Yeah, his friend turned it off because I'd asked him to. I turned my back on the snarky kid, shaking, and returned to Sabrina's side.

Another older man, bearded and scraggly looking, rode up on a child's bicycle. He got as close to the street in front of the warehouse as the cops would allow and screamed "Fuuuuuuuuuuck! All my stuff!" into the night. He continued to yell and moan. I didn't approach him. This guy must have lived in the warehouse, but he was clearly insane. It was possible people were trapped inside, but he was screaming about his stuff. I instinctively hated him for his stupid, material selfishness. Eventually, he rode off, and I was relieved to see him go. Nearly a year later, I would learn his name was Derick Almena.

Occasionally, I broke away from Sabrina to pace the parking lot, trying to use up my overflow of adrenaline and maybe get a peek into the brightly lit interior of the ambulance. Whenever I got too close, I was pushed back by firefighters or police. That seemed to be their only job.

Still no victims. And no other family members or friends showed up. I was the lone concerned parent in the parking lot. Sabrina was the only sibling. Reality hung suspended in a zone of quiet disbelief. No one was screaming for a rescue. No one was wailing for their dead. I wanted to scream out for Chelsea but instead held tightly onto the thin hope that she was safe somewhere other than this ugly parking lot. I paced until my legs shook. Returning to Sabrina's side felt like home in the cold night air. There was nothing else I could do.

Meanwhile, David came back from one of his information-seeking forays with the news that someone in the parking lot had seen one of the musicians, Johnny Igaz, driving away with a car full of people. Oh my God! Johnny was Chelsea's friend and record label mate. I didn't realize I'd been holding my breath, but at that moment, all the air locked in my lungs burst out in a long stream of relief. I smiled and then took in a deep breath of hope that felt like a celebration. Of course, she got a ride with Johnny!

Sabrina and I started up a rolling banter about Chelsea doing something that we would probably laugh about in the years to come. We ran through all the possible scenarios that would find Chelsea safe in the morning. We laughed that it was entirely possible Chelsea had left early and not even heard about the fire.

She could have gone to another club or driven off with Johnny Igaz and the others to someone's apartment. Maybe they'd held an impromptu party there, not knowing how severe the fire had become. Who would bother checking social media if they'd left before the fire had grown fierce or maybe even before it started? I wondered if Chelsea had driven home and didn't let David know. They had only recently gotten back together, and it occurred to me that maybe she just wanted to be alone, knowing David was out driving for Uber.

Sabrina and I both knew that if anyone could get out of a situation like this, it was Chelsea. She was magic. She was always at the center of events, and when Chelsea performed, she made sure her guests were having fun. Sabrina and I continued making up stories to account for Chelsea not telling the world she was okay. The more we talked, the better I felt. Like Sabrina, Chelsea was a thinker and a doer. She was the first to respond with action rather than words. I counted on her resilience to get her through this emergency, finally finding solace in that little voice in my head, 'She's fine. Chelsea knows what to do. She's safe.'

David strode quickly back to our side and said, "Travis Hough is missing, too." That dampened my spirits a little, but Sabrina and I continued our forced lightheartedness with that news. Travis and Chelsea were bandmates. She played keyboards, and he sang. Maybe they had taken off together! Maybe they were both with Johnny. Maybe, maybe, maybe ... I was manic with hope, but a pit of terror began to solidify in my stomach.

The sounds coming from the trucks, hoses, and firefighters yelling all blended into a roar of white noise. I felt like I was going deaf. Occasionally, the clanging of equipment, breaking glass, or a revving truck motor would pierce through the humming drone. Mostly, one sound was indistinguishable from the next.

Suddenly, the wind changed, and the thick, black, choking smoke poured over the parking lot where we stood helplessly waiting for a miracle. I wrapped my paisley woolen scarf around my face. A burly, dark-haired firefighter in full gear and a chaplain's white collar brought Sabrina a wet towel, instructing her to put it over her mouth and nose. Our eyes were watering from fear and toxic fumes. The chaplain pointed out a cherry-picker truck with the basket hovering above the warehouse and a fierce stream of water arcing down toward the roof. My focus on the flames was so intense, and the noise of all the engines so loud I hadn't even seen it arrive. He explained that firefighters couldn't go inside, but a hole had been cut in the roof, and the fire was being fought from above.

The fire after several hours, early Saturday morning, 12/3/16. (Photo courtesy of Julianna Brown.)

Gradually, a vision began to form in my imagination. It was like a dream. I pictured Chelsea being brought out to the ambulance on a stretcher, burnt and unconscious. I would tell her not to worry, that I would take care of her. I saw my living room outfitted with a hospital bed. After months of burn-unit hospitalization, Chelsea would be home with me, unable to move. She would be suffering, her smoked brain unable to think or create, her internal organs ruined. I would take care of her for the rest of her life. I convinced myself this would be our future. If she was truly inside that warehouse, the alternative was unfathomable.

Then I shivered as a new sensation washed over me; it felt like Chelsea was hovering in the sky, looking down on Sabrina and me in the bleak parking lot. She told me, "I see you and Sabrina, Mother, but I have to leave. I have work to do elsewhere," and whooshed off into the universe. I shook off the impossible feeling and turned my attention back to the burning building. If I concentrated on Chelsea being safe, maybe I could save her. I repeatedly whispered the mantra: 'Chelsea is alive. Chelsea is safe. Chelsea is alive. Chelsea is safe.'

Chapter 4

The Vigil

Saturday, December 3, 2016

All night, the flames kept re-igniting. Firefighters milled about. It looked like they were just bumping into each other, not doing anything but trying to appear busy. I saw one fire hose aimed ineffectively at a window. Cops lined the street like a blue fence, pushing back onlookers who wanted to get a better look at the newsworthy scene. The uniformed men infuriated me, and my yelling, "Is everyone okay?" at them, didn't do anything but get me pushed back another 10 feet. I needed to be close enough to look around every vehicle. There was a chance Chelsea was lying on the ground somewhere.

A few TV trucks showed up, and cameramen started pointing cameras at the fiery windows. Once they had all their horror show video footage, the TV crews began to circulate amongst the crowd gathering in the Wendy's parking lot. I walked out of the shot whenever I saw a camera approaching. Who wants to be seen crying on the morning news? It all felt so invasive. And what if Chelsea woke up in the morning and saw me on TV wailing for her? I had to let her know I had faith in her ingenuity. In this time-warped reality, it seemed like the right thing to do.

Reporters began interviewing the young people who had lived in the warehouse and lost their homes. While all this was happening in the parking lot, firefighters and police officers milled about the building. A cop with a clipboard in hand began walking through the parking lot, taking down the names and phone numbers of everyone standing there. I suppose he was looking for witnesses, but he wouldn't give a reason for compiling the list. A few clumps of young people scattered away from him and left the parking lot, not wanting to give up personal information. I gave the cop my name and said I was looking for my daughter, Chelsea Faith Dolan. Others also quietly complied. There were no other parents there for me to talk to, no one my age other than the neighbors. It didn't make sense. Was Chelsea the only person still missing? In my mind, I begged her to call me. I repeated my mantra: *Chelsea is alive. Chelsea is safe...*

The water continued to blast down on the building from above, and firefighters continued to mess about aimlessly, shouting to one another and carrying hoses to nowhere. After several hours, the fearful excitement was spent. I was still pretty sure Chelsea was okay. She had to be somewhere else, but I stayed just in case she returned to the warehouse. I wanted to see her before I would allow myself to go home.

Fire tourists came and went. Occasionally, a crescendo of "Oh!" would rise up from the onlookers as the diminishing fire would suddenly roar up again and flare out of one of the windows. Smoke continued mushrooming up into the night sky, though gradually becoming lighter and lighter gray.

I saw the Fire Chaplain standing near the ambulance and cut across the parking lot to his side. "Do you have any news about the people who were at the party? Did everyone get out?" He gently told me he didn't know. He asked if I was warm enough, and I said yes. He brought over a blanket for Sabrina and wrapped it around her shoulders. I continued to wander around the parking lot, avoiding the machinery and hoses but getting as close as I could to the action, or rather inaction, of the uniformed professionals on the scene. The discordant soundscape and visual chaos were the scene of an emergency but not yet a tragedy.

Around 3:00 a.m., the woman police officer who had originally pushed me away from the front door of the warehouse approached me. Her eyes softened. "You need to steel yourself for bad news." Despite her soothing tone, those words clanged against my hope that Chelsea was alive. I asked her if anyone was inside, and she whispered, "Yes." When I asked how many, she answered, "I can't say."

Up till that point, no police or firefighters would answer my questions about victims, but I could clearly see that no one had been taken to the hospital. The ambulance stood brightly lit and empty all night. Sabrina's arm and body pressed into my side, holding me upright. If anyone was still inside, that meant there were bodies, not living victims.

Where was Chelsea? Did she make it out? Was she trapped inside? I felt a small hot surge of anger build behind my eyes, not at the feeble firefight, but at my missing daughter. Why didn't she call me? If anyone could make it out of a situation like this, it was Chelsea. She had the strength and determination it would take to survive under any circumstances, but no one could survive the massive billows of smoke I'd seen pouring out the roof of the building. No one could have evaded the flames that spread throughout the building, spitting out of every window. Even so, knowing Chelsea's indomitable spirit, I was certain that if there was any way out, she would have escaped, and if she had, she would have called. So, dammit, where was she?

At 4:30 a.m., the ambulance and two fire trucks drove away, and there, right in front of the only exit, was Chelsea's silver Honda Civic. She loved that car. Sabrina and I looked at each other. Sabrina quietly said, "That's Chelsea's car."

It was her way of saying Chelsea was dead. That sad little car sitting alone in the street made me cry. Hope sank to the asphalt, extinguished. I stood rigid against the truth, unable to breathe, tears streaming down my face. Sabrina and I leaned against each other. The rumor about Johnny was untrue. Chelsea didn't make it out.

Chelsea's silver car sitting out front after the fire engines left. That's how we knew she was dead. (Photo courtesy of Carol Cidlik.)

The wait changed. For the rest of the night and into the morning, Sabrina, Joe, David, and I kept vigil, staring at the ugly warehouse, waiting for Chelsea's body to be carried out of the char. My beautiful daughter had been inside while I watched the flames. I wanted her to know I was there, that she was loved as she took her last breath. She must have been terrified. I longed to hold her body in my arms and cradle her one last time.

By 6:00 a.m., we were told that wouldn't happen. Several uniformed people came up to me and suggested I go home and wait for word. I stayed. As the sky lightened, the collected mass of firetrucks and official-looking cars and vans around the warehouse suddenly revved their engines at once and drove away. Men and women in uniforms disappeared. When I looked around, most of the people in the Wendy's parking lot were gone, too. The fire chaplain told me the bodies would be left in place until fire investigators could frame the scene and determine what caused the fire and the deaths. I watched as several police officers roped off the warehouse with caution tape and erected temporary barriers to traffic and tragedy tourists.

After the fire (Getty Images, US-Fire-California, photographer Josh Edelson)

The kind female police officer who had first pushed me back from the fire and then told me to steel myself now gave me directions to the Alameda County Sherifff's Office annex a few blocks away. It was being set up as a waystation for families who needed a place to wait for news of their missing loved ones. She gave me her card and told me to call if I needed anything. I looked at her dumbly and shook my head. I was dead inside. I needed Chelsea. She couldn't help me.

Chapter 5

The Family Center

Saturday, December 3, 2016, approximately 6:00 a.m.

S abrina, David, Joe, and I piled into David's car and headed over to the sheriff's office. We entered a lobby through glass double doors, passing clerks who stood behind a counter on the right. Beyond the counter, there were hallways leading in both directions, left and right. We continued straight ahead down a short hallway toward a wall of windows leading to a much larger room. The windows were covered with a colorful ribbon-like display of calligraphy of some sort. A large room with exercise equipment clumsily shoved to the walls served as a gathering place. Endless rows of picnic-length tables, beige metal folding chairs, and an ever-moving bevy of Red Cross volunteers filled the space. How many people did they expect in this place? How many victims were there? Parents who had just received an early morning phone call that their children were missing began to show up. Why weren't they notified sooner? I was grateful David had called me the night before. Crowds of young people in their 20s and 30s spilled into the room. I scanned each of the faces, looking for Chelsea.

As we entered the large room, a beautiful woman with long, dark hair told me to turn around and check the window separating the large room from the front lobby. Facing the colorful squiggles from the other side of the glass, I could make out the names of the missing, which had been written on the glass with erasable marker pens. The woman pointed to one name, Cash Askew, and said, "This is my child. They just called to say Cash was missing." I nodded in stunned sympathy, then looked at the window, not wanting to see Chelsea up there.

Each name was written in a different style and color, some printed in sedate blue, others written in flamboyant script of pink, orange, and purple. Pane after pane of glass was filled with a sad scroll of colorful names. The beautiful woman touched my arm as I pointed to Chelsea, who was listed on that window by her stage name, Cherushii, in neon pink. I printed her full name next to it in blue: Chelsea Faith Dolan (legal name.)

Other parents began arriving and crowded around the window, looking for their children. Some people left. Their children's names were not posted. I reeled with envy. Family members and friends of those people named on the window filed into the waiting room and sat on cold metal chairs in stunned silence.

After sitting numbly for a while, my phone started ringing. The news was out. I told Sabrina I couldn't talk to anyone and handed her my phone. She quietly called relatives to let them know Chelsea had been in the fire that was now on every morning newscast around the world. She told them we hadn't heard from her.

Sabrina, Joe, David, and Chelsea's closest childhood friend, Josey Duncan, sat with me in the ever-growing crowd of concerned families and friends. Josey cried quietly at first, then wiped her face and silently held my hand until I had to stand up and pace the room. Sabrina sat upright in stoic calm, occasionally answering calls from friends and relatives. Joe kept his arm protectively around her shoulder. We waited in morose expectation for some positive news to be announced in the huge, clattering, sterile-looking room in the Alameda County Sheriff's Department annex that was now called The Family Center. More and more families whose children were missing began to show up. The place was crowded with well over a hundred people by noon on Saturday, and every person in the room breathed in and out with the hope that there were survivors. If not, the work of gathering DNA samples and dental records, and then submitting information on official forms would begin here.

By the end of Saturday, the first day after the fire, my legs gave out. I pace when nervous, so I nearly cut a groove in the linoleum floor that day. Around 6:00 p.m., the Red Cross volunteers handed out vouchers for nearby hotels to anyone who would be returning the next day and didn't live in the area. Sabrina, Joe, and I went to the Waterfront Hotel at Jack London Square. My room was large and incongruously luxurious. I was waiting for word of whether my daughter had been burned alive, and I was given a room fit for visiting dignitaries or wealthy patrons of the arts. I had no change of clothes, but a new toothbrush, toothpaste, and comb provided by the hotel sat on the bathroom counter waiting for me. The thoughtfulness of those few items broke my heart. I stripped off my smoke-saturated clothes and sat on the tile floor of the shower, crying for what felt like hours. The streaming water melded with my tears in comforting warmth.

This was the one time in my life that I desperately needed a man to comfort me, to spoon up behind me in bed and just hold me, but there was no one. I shivered with an empty ache and stood up. The water wasn't good enough anymore. I wrapped my hair in a towel and pulled the soft, thick terry cloth robe around my wet, adrenaline-shaking body. Chelsea was gone, and I was alone. Sabrina and Joe had each other. I would lean on them in the morning, but tonight, I would sleep alone in my sorrow. I slipped between the pure white sheets and curled into a fetal position, feeling the feather-bed softness cleanse me of this lonely, exhausted ache. It had been 24 hours since I'd been jolted awake. Tomorrow, my world would be forever altered. Tonight, I would sleep the sleep of the dead.

Sunday, December 4, 2016

On Sunday morning, brilliant sun forced its way through the crack between the hotel drapes. I didn't want to see the morning. I wished it would rain, sad, drizzly, and cold to the bone. Instead, I pulled back the drapes and took in the glittering view of water, sailboats, and sunshine that forced its cheer on me like an insistent, overly enthusiastic friend. I wanted ugliness that equaled my pain. I dressed myself in the sad smell and prepared to face another day of bureaucratic chaos at The Family Center.

News crews and vans with satellite structures on their roofs surrounded the drab county government building. Only family members were allowed into The Family Center to ensure our privacy. This was the sheriff's office, so a bunch of reporters hovered in the lobby, trying to look like citizens who had business at the front desk. That's where the bathrooms were located. Reporters had been banned from coming inside the building but hoped they looked like sympathetic neighbors asking innocent questions. Then, they would reach into a pocket or purse and pull out small notebooks that felt like weapons. I was fooled once by a kindly, frumpy, middle-aged woman who gave off a motherly vibe. I wanted kindness, and she offered it. I said a few words about what had happened, and then she asked the telling question: "How did you feel when you found out." She pulled out the notebook. I turned and ran toward the bathroom, knowing I'd been betrayed by a smile and gentle eyes.

Outside the front doors, television and radio reporters stood with microphones at the ready, straining to catch every drop of worry and fear from vulnerable people hurrying past them. We had no choice. David and Joe had to move Chelsea's car away from the front of the Ghost Ship warehouse before it was towed. They also had to retrieve Chelsea's hairbrush and toothbrush from her apartment for DNA samples. Meanwhile, I filled out forms that were handed to me by Red Cross volunteers. Each form asked for the same information over and over. Then, there was a question about cars.

Sabrina and I needed to get registration information from the glove compartment of Chelsea's car, which was now parked a block away from the sheriff's office. David and Joe were juggling cars and left it where it would be easy to move again when we found a permanent place for it. As Sabrina and I left the building, reporters shouted their unintelligible questions at us, hoping for the shot or the soundbite that would make good television. The Guardian newspaper from the UK published a picture of Sabrina and me from behind as we walked away from their photographer. That picture was used extensively in the days that followed.

*Sabrina and I walking away from reporters at the
Alameda County Sheriff's Annex, which was set up as a
gathering place for families of the deceased.*

Soon, the disjointed bureaucracy of the various city and county government agencies became obvious. Over and over, we were asked to print out the same painful information on an endless series of forms, some for the City of Oakland, others for Alameda County, and others for the Red Cross and other relief agencies. While family and friends sat anxiously in The Family Center, government officials came to speak with us.

Oakland Mayor Libby Schaaf showed up in what looked like some weird firefighter's jacket to pat herself on the back, saying, "I'm a friend of the homeless," and told us that she would not close down other unofficial warehouse homes. What? For some reason, she thought that would resonate with us, who were waiting to hear if our loved ones were dead or alive. My anger at those words blurred out her image. Instead, all I could see were the images of young people clinging to each other in the fire. Friend of the homeless? In a room full of families waiting for news of our dead children, this was her response?

Microphone in hand, Mayor Schaaf brushed her dark hair

back from her face and read the following statement to us before repeating it later to camera crews:

"Last night's fire was an immense tragedy. I am grateful to our first responders for their efforts to deal with this deadly fire. Our focus right now is on the victims and their families and ensuring that we have a full accounting for everyone who was impacted by this tragedy. We are fully committed to sharing as much information as we can as quickly as possible. The most critical information to share at this time is the phone number where victims' families can get information, which is (510) 382-3000 at the Alameda County Coroner's Bureau."

The Oakland Fire Chief, Teresa Deloach Reed, a serious-looking African American woman with short, black hair and heavy, dark glasses, showed up in full uniform. She stepped in front of the mic and said she had no information, but she wanted us to know they were investigating and this would take days to complete. Other uniformed firefighters, sheriffs, and police officers stood there in a row on either side of the speakers, looking supportive, not of the families, but smiling up at the mayor, fire chief, and other agency leaders who came to let us know they were busy doing their jobs.

The families and friends in attendance gathered in a disheveled horseshoe ring around the speakers and shouted out angry questions. We had been sitting for two days, some of us in the same clothes we'd worn the day before, waiting for answers, tired and emotionally fragile, but when the officials finally showed up, we learned nothing.

Families who had possibly lost a child or sibling began arriving from out of town. Some parents who had just been informed that their children were missing late Saturday or Sunday morning screamed out, "How many people died?" and "When can we identify the bodies?" I stood at the back of the crowd and watched the doors, hoping to see Chelsea. If she

31

showed up, I could leave this angry place. More voices shook the room. "Why was no one rescued? Did you even try?" Someone else yelled, "How could this happen? My son is missing." Most of us were crying.

A group of young people, some of whom had lost their warehouse home, arrived with their friends. They pushed to the front of the crowd and shouted out their loud accusations. "Affordable housing is already being shut down, forcing people onto the street. What are you going to do to stop it?"

Affordable housing versus the death of our children. The disparity in our immediate concerns caused an ugly shouting competition between the two groups.

Mayor Schaff nodded and stepped up to the microphone again to remind us that she was a friend of the homeless and would not move people out of their unauthorized housing. She said absolutely nothing to help those of us waiting to find out if our children were alive or dead.

I am usually easy-going, but with tensions rising in the room, even I got into a shouting match with a woman who was a friend of one of the victims. Each family had staked out a specific area where we gathered each day at The Family Center. Our family sat together in a tight ring of folding chairs. Others sat at lunchroom-style tables. Next to me was a group of about 10 young people sitting in a large circle of chairs. They were laughing and joking and generally having a good time, making the occasion of multiple deaths their excuse for a fun-loving, raucous get-together. My heart was clenched shut with grief while they made jokes about telling the difference between one genre of electronic music from another.

The party atmosphere was an insult to my sorrow. Heat rose in my chest, then traveled out to my throbbing fists. My fingernails dug into the palms of my hands. Blood was pounding in my ears with each round of laughter. Sabrina saw my discomfort and walked over to the group. She quietly asked, "Could you maybe keep it down? Other people in the room are upset." The revelers lowered their voices, and I felt relief for a few seconds.

Sabrina returned to sit beside me, and I thanked her for saying something. Then, one stocky girl, red in the face, stormed over and shouted at Sabrina, "Who do you think you are telling other people what to do? Everyone grieves differently!"

Okay, I had one daughter dead, and another was being verbally attacked. Mama-bear kicked in, and I shouted, "This is not a celebration! Take your party somewhere else."

The girl screamed something unintelligible at me, and a young man at a nearby table stood up to defend me, saying, "Walk away." His face was calm but stern. His dark hair shook down into his face as he glared at the girl. She skulked off. I later found out he was Cyrus Hoda, and his sister, Sara, had died in the fire. He sat beside his mother, Farzaneh, that day, who sat quietly crying and shaking her head. I saw in her restrained sorrow a reflection of my own loss. Cyrus was a good son, just as Sabrina was a good daughter. The protective presence of these two brave siblings calmed my distress, even though my whole body was trembling. I couldn't stop shaking, and nausea washed up the back of my throat. Suffice it to say, tension was high in The Family Center. All day Sunday, my veins thrummed with a relentless electrical buzz.

Joe and Sabrina drove me home and stayed with me that night. My condo felt plastic. It was too cute and coy. The Wendy's parking lot was real. The contentious Sheriff's Office was real. The home I'd barely managed to purchase ten years earlier was supposed to keep us safe. I thought nothing bad could happen here, but I was wrong.

I lay down in the same bed I'd rolled out of two days before when David pinged a message on my phone. That seemed like years ago. It irritated me to be in the same bed with its pretentious black comforter and burgundy silk pillows. I tossed constantly, listening for the phone to ring. Maybe Chelsea would call. Sleep never came.

Monday, December 5, 2016

On Monday morning, I stood limp in a steaming shower. After drying myself, I put on clean clothes, but the soft sweater and pants felt like a betrayal. They didn't smell of smoke. If Chelsea was drenched in smoke, I should be too. It wasn't right.

When we arrived at The Family Center, a Red Cross volunteer pointed to a list on a far wall with the names of about twenty people who had been found safe overnight. I crossed the room and saw Chelsea's name! It was crossed out and then re-entered. My blood started pumping again. She was alive! Then, a woman came over and crossed out her name a second time. She told me the phone caller had second-hand information. I stumbled back to my metal folding chair and put my head between my knees. Waves of nausea rose from my toes to my head. I choked back vomit.

Sometime that morning, the mayor, fire chief, and other county officials returned and stood in front of the microphone placed at the front of the room. I joined the other family members and friends who formed a semi-circle around them. The officials didn't seem to be talking to each other. We listened uncomfortably as Oakland Fire officials told us they were handling the investigation. Alameda County officials contradicted them by saying the Federal Bureau of Alcohol, Tobacco, Firearms and Explosives, ATF, was handling the investigation.

Oakland Fire Chief Teresa Deloach Reed stepped up and

spoke again. She told us matter-of-factly that there were nine known fatalities. She said an assessment was still being made of any additional victims associated with this incident.

Since there were more than nine people missing, everyone in the room dreaded the news that there would be more dead.

Deloach Reed took the microphone, her calm voice filling the room, and tried to clarify who was in charge. She told us the Alameda County Arson Task Force and other federal "partners" were working on an investigation into the cause of the fire. She told us that due to structural damage from the fire, the ongoing investigation efforts and search for additional victims would be methodical and were anticipated to take some time. She said public information officers would provide media updates throughout the day, on the hour, and news conferences would be scheduled daily.

The official briefings and the constant buzz of rumors and speculation about the cause of the fire and the lack of a rescue were unnerving. Some young people thought the fire was deliberately set to close down all illegal housing in Oakland. Others said the Oakland firefighters purposely didn't try to rescue the victims, fearing for their own safety.

By Monday afternoon, I was numb. None of this was real. Against all evidence, I fully believed Chelsea would walk through the door and hug us all. She would laugh and ask me to take her out to dinner, as she always did. We would leave all the arguing and trauma behind. My eyes strained for the first sight of her as I constantly peered in the direction of the glass double doors.

Everyone in the room stumbled about in circles or sat in stunned silence. The air we breathed was thick with sorrow. The interminable wait bore down on our shoulders. I choked on a bite of doughnut that had been offered to me by a Red Cross volunteer and swore I would never eat again until

Chelsea came home. All I could do was sit and cry or stare at my feet as I paced between the table of deli food and doughnuts near the back of the room and my metal chair toward the front. While fire investigators sifted through rubble looking for bodies, the hours in The Family Center were filled with nothing and nothing and nothing.

It was almost a relief when the coroner began calling us, one by one, into private offices to confirm identifying marks that would help identify our loved ones. Did they have tattoos? Piercings? Broken bones? Implants? Chelsea had none.

At one point, Sabrina and I were called into a room with several gray metal desks. We sat in front of one and were asked to give DNA samples. My fingers shook as I held the long, hard, wooden stem of a medical Q-tip and swabbed it around my dry mouth. My lips were cracked. I'd cried out all the fluid from my body and didn't want to eat or drink for fear of vomiting it right back up. The person sitting behind the large desk could have been a man or woman, young or old. Nothing registered in my brain anymore. Without knowing how I'd gotten there, I was back in The Family Center, sitting on my usual folding metal chair.

We hoped we could leave this glaring confusion of The Family Center behind, but our turn didn't come that day or most of the next. Bodies were being identified, but not Chelsea. We sat, cold and numb, through Monday.

That night, Sabrina and Joe drove me back home to Marin and stayed with me again. I crawled into the same bed that had betrayed me on Friday night. This time, I was too exhausted to stay awake. When sleep finally came, I dreamed I was in Chelsea's body. I could see through her eyes as she desperately looked for a way out of burning hallways that led nowhere. I opened strange-looking doors and panicked as flames jumped out at me. Slamming one door and searching for another, I was totally lost. Flames were getting closer. Smoke filled my lungs. I choked and coughed and started screaming for help. Then I woke up, my pillow wet, my blankets a mess around me. Chelsea was dead.

I lay in bed, breathless. This wasn't real. It couldn't be. I curled up on my side and jumped a little each time I started to fall asleep. I didn't want my sweet girl to die again.

Chapter 6

Chelsea is Found in the Rubble

Tuesday, December 6, 2016

On Tuesday morning, Sabrina, Joe, and I rode together in my car for the hour-long traffic jam from Marin back to Oakland. Joe drove. Then we sat in the interminable nothingness of The Family Center. My body ached with longing. Finally, late Tuesday afternoon, the coroner called the three of us into a quiet room and asked us to sit around a large wooden desk. Joe offered to take notes because I was in a fog. Someone handed me a bottle of water. I took it with two shaking hands. I waited for them to tell me Chelsea's body hadn't been found, that she was still alive somewhere.

In the end, it was Chelsea's flamboyant wardrobe that confirmed her death.

Sabrina is usually quiet and reserved, but at that moment, she was the strongest person in the room. In a clear voice, she described Chelsea's usual outfits: A colorful mini skirt or dress. Chelsea rarely wore pants. She would wear hot pink or harlequin tights, always big boots, and she would have worn

gold cat. It was the perfect size to be an urn. She'd always used it as a lucky charm, even taking it with her to classical piano competitions when she was in high school. From the age of 13, when she first bought it with birthday money, her gold Maneki-Neko held a place of honor, sitting on a shelf in every bedroom in which she slept.

That night, when Sabrina, Joe, and I arrived at my home from the funeral parlor, I said goodnight, went straight up to my room, and sat down on my reading chair in the corner. The spongy tan chair hugged my body. I plunked my laptop down on a pillow on my thighs and began typing a message on Facebook for Chelsea's friends, family, and other interested people. I included the professional bio that was written on her own webpage for my friends who had never met her, but it wasn't enough.

"This evening, Chelsea Faith was identified as one of the victims of the Oakland Warehouse Fire. Here is Chelsea's bio, but she was so much more than that. Chelsea Faith Dolan has always been an extraordinary person, full of exuberant joy. Her personality, intelligence, clothes, music, and kindness were legendary. She discovered at the age of three that she could pick up any musical instrument and play a tune she had heard or the well-composed song she'd just written in her head. At age 13, she picked up a Japanese music magazine and acquired 78 pen-pals, handwriting personal letters to each of them. Some of those friendships endure to this day. It was on a solo trip to Japan at age 15 that she picked up her adopted name, Cherushii. It was easier to pronounce than Chelsea. Her high school experience says so much about her. She didn't want the typical cookie-cutter experience, so she put together a plan to attend an alternative home-study program while attending the local community college music program and taking the bus to the San Francisco Music Conservatory to study classical piano.

She turned to electronic music when she realized it allowed her to play the complex and haunting melodies she heard in her head. What she wanted to produce was more orchestral than one instrument could provide. Composition was her specialty. Performing Live PA was her love.

Her favorite city outside of San Francisco was Berlin, and she traveled there as often as possible to perform. She has made close friends around the world and the US while on tour. Because she loved music so much, Chelsea had a radio program as DJ Cherushii at the UC Berkeley radio station, KALX. She loved doing special shows that told the history of electronic music. She had an encyclopedic knowledge of the electronic genres, as well as classical piano works.

Nothing Chelsea Faith did was ordinary. She was an adventurer; she was stellar in every way, and she will always be the star of our hearts. Chelsea was just about to release a new Cherushii CD. I hope one of her friends will make sure that happens."

Chelsea lived a full life, more so than most. As Sabrina quietly whispered after Chelsea's body was identified, "She did everything she ever wanted to do." Chelsea's motto was "Do it." She followed her heart. She lived.

From Chelsea's photo collection.

Chapter 7

The Funeral Home and Crematorium

Friday, December 9, 2016

So, here's what shocked me: Chelsea looked beautiful in death. Even though it had taken three days for her body to be removed from the burnt-out shell of the building that took her life. Even though it was several more days before she was removed to the coroner's office for an autopsy and a full week before her body was moved to the funeral home. She was in an early state of decomposition, but still, she looked beautiful.

Lying in a plain cardboard cremation box on a white cotton sheet, Chelsea wore the colorful clothes Sabrina and I had chosen from her closet. Most of her skin was dark and taut, and her blond hair was now soot-brown. Her eyes were lowered in peace, partially closed. Her mouth was open, exposing her teeth, but that was to be expected since the fire would have dehydrated her lips and the moist skin around her mouth. The flaked skin of her hands, which rested by her sides, was golden. Her arms were orange and marbled with dark veins, like some Michelangelo statue.

The well-lit room where she lay was decorated like a small, white chapel with candles and a few chairs off to one side. Chelsea's coffin was placed on a high table, so I could easily spend the evening talking with her and kissing her as I told her how much I loved her. The fact of her death still wasn't real, so I took pictures of her. In the future I would look at those photos often to remind myself that she was really gone. I knew I would need that proof.

After a long time, I'm not really sure how long, I reluctantly stepped out of the viewing room to give Chelsea's dad, Dan, some private time with her. I knew Sabrina had filled Dan in on our arrangements with the funeral home, but my muscles still tensed when I saw him. It had been 15 years. His dark hair had turned white since the last time we'd been together, but he was still handsome and fit. His presence added to the shock and leaden weight of my sorrow.

Dan had refused to marry me for 17 years, and although he was the only father Chelsea had ever known, he refused to pay child support for her because she was not his biological daughter. Now, he acted like he cared. I knew he must have felt her loss; she was the magnificent glue that held our world together, but aside from occasionally taking Chelsea and Sabrina out to dinner, he'd gone missing. Sabrina, Joe, and I sat in silence, staring at the grandmotherly furniture in the waiting area, while Dan walked into the private room to see our sweet girl. I avoided his sad eyes when he emerged again.

When Dan reentered the waiting room, Sabrina hugged me, and then she and Joe slipped in to see Chelsea. I sat stiff and awkward in a frumpy chair across from Dan, purposely pointing my gaze anywhere but in his direction. Neither he nor our acrimonious split were important anymore. Instead, I closed my eyes and pictured a younger Chelsea playing and laughing. Abruptly, those memories were crowded out with the image of Chelsea in that sad cardboard box, and I started crying. Dan said something, but I didn't look up. Painful history lay on the floor between us.

Sabrina and Joe emerged with heads bowed, and it was my turn again. As I entered the chapel, I was overwhelmed by the smell of smoke that arose from Chelsea's body. I hadn't noticed it the first time I saw her, but now I recognized it as Chelsea's smell. The closer I got to her, the stronger the smell. It was something I would always associate with her sweet, lifeless body. Smoke.

Saturday, December 10, 2016

The next day, we drove in a caravan to the crematorium in Napa. First, the hearse with Chelsea's body, then Dan and his girlfriend, and finally Sabrina, Joe, and me in my car. Dan's girlfriend waited in the car for him while he went inside with us. We were led to an unlit chapel where Chelsea lay in her coffin until we were ready to say goodbye. The room was darkly gothic. Red velvet curtains were draped in an alcove at the back of the room, where tall red candles burned on either side of Chelsea's coffin. Her cardboard cremation coffin was still draped in clean, white sheets, just as it had been at the funeral parlor. The effect was that of some ancient altar with Chelsea lying in the center as if in a trance, her eyes half closed.

The funeral director told us in a kindly voice to take our time and let him know when we were ready. We could take as long as we liked. The four of us walked past rows of ominous-looking wooden chairs covered in stiff red velvet that had been set up for some kind of service. The empty chairs looked like dead people to me. Sabrina and Joe sat down in the front row. Dan stood off to one side at the foot of Chelsea's coffin.

Although they were in the dark room with me, I felt alone.

My firstborn was lying there, burnt and silent. I knew this would be the last time I ever saw her in person. She lay there with half-closed eyes as if resting, deep in thought. I wanted to shake her awake. A power surged inside me and told me I could change all this. I could bring her back. And I believed it!

Frantically, I whispered in Chelsea's ear to come back. "Transfer yourself into my body. I've lived long enough. You come back, and I'll go where you are!" I quietly cried to God, the little gods, powers of the Universe, and myself, trying to bargain her back to life. "Take me instead!" My voice grew louder as I begged her to please come back and let me take her place. I touched her and kissed her and waited for the change to happen. I was ready to go.

My actions must have alarmed Sabrina and Joe, who leaped up to comfort me. Dan held up both hands, palms out, and stepped back in horror. Sabrina moved closer beside me and her sister's body and motioned to Joe that he could sit down again. She calmly told me the story of a mother monkey she and Joe had seen on their vacation in Costa Rica. She gently told me, "We saw a mother monkey carrying her little baby's body. She was desperately jumping from tree limb to tree limb, chattering excitedly to all the other monkeys around her, trying to find help." Sabrina nodded to Joe, who nodded back. "The mother monkey was crying like you are, trying to bring her baby back to life. Your reaction is perfectly normal." She stood beside me for a moment, then sat back down with Joe in the front row of ghastly chairs and said nothing more. Her story sunk into my bones.

Standing beside Chelsea's lifeless body in the dim candlelight, I desperately sought help from God or magic to bring Chelsea back to me. I would give away my future to go back in time and relive our years together. Like the mother monkey in Sabrina's story, I tried to convince myself she was still there in that sweet, burnt, beloved shell.

Unbearable anguish closed off my throat and welded my swollen eyes shut. How could I let her go? I would never be able to see her again. This body was all I had. I fought back the need to keep her imprisoned forever in that gloomy chapel with the candles and red velvet drapes, rows of wooden chairs, and dark carpet. I looked up from my daughter's body, turned around, and saw Sabrina, Joe, and Dan sitting stoically in the front row of chairs. Reluctantly, I whispered, "Okay."

Chelsea's coffin was transferred to a gurney, and several men wheeled it into a cavernous, gray, industrial-looking room. We followed. Metal pipes looped and covered the gray walls and ceiling. A large metal box the size of a van stood directly in front of us as we entered the room. This was the furnace. A low sound rumbled within. The men lifted the cardboard coffin holding Chelsea as she lay inside and gently placed it on a platform with metal rollers that led up to the furnace. The doors to the furnace opened, exposing a fire roaring within.

As she was about to enter the fire, I leaned over and kissed Chelsea goodbye one last time, and told her, "Don't be afraid. I will always be with you. We all love you and will always be with you." Then I nodded, sobbing.

The funeral director asked me if I wanted to push the button to send her into the furnace. He pointed to a flat, circular knob about five inches across placed ominously in the upper right corner on the front of the furnace. I hadn't noticed it previously, but now it looked evil and foreboding. At that moment, it became the instrument of Chelsea's destruction. My body shook, and my stomach curled into a black knot. How was this even a thing? How could I push that hand-sized button that would send her into the flames? Horrified, I rasped out, "No."

Then, a vision-memory filled my brain. I saw myself telling my obstetrician that I refused to cut the cord when baby Chelsea was born. Such severing! How does one let go of a child? I couldn't be the one to send her into the flames, just as I couldn't cut the cord that once bound our bodies together.

I touched Chelsea's hand one last time and kissed her on the forehead. Dan reluctantly agreed to be the one. He looked me in the eye with a sad expression on his face, then pressed the large button on the front of the furnace. The rolling board took Chelsea into the roaring flames. The heavy metal door slowly slid shut, and she was gone.

PART TWO

BEFORE THE FIRE AND SAYING GOODBYE

Chapter 8

What is Time?

Thursday, December 15, 2016

For weeks after Chelsea's cremation, I lay on my bedroom floor sobbing. The weight of mourning was impossible to bear. Each day, I cried out for Chelsea to come home. Each night, I dissolved into nothingness and nightmares.

It was dark. I pushed against a turquoise door and found myself moving through a winding hallway. From somewhere above, a lamp without a shade fell on my head. I dodged more debris on the floor. Smoke swirled around my head, stinging my eyes. I turned to the right. A room littered with junk. No exit. No windows. I ran down another hallway lined with doors. Pounding on each one, none of them opened. Panting. Yelling, "Help me!" I turned down another hallway, smacking into a dead end of wooden studs and plywood wall. "Help me!" Spinning in circles. Flames filled the hallway. Trapped! No way out!

I woke up on the floor, panting, my heart pounding. My elbow hurt from the fall. The dream, in endless variations, came every night. I would be deep in a black sleep when suddenly I was Chelsea trying to find her way out of the warehouse. I felt her frantic panic. She and I clawed at the wooden beams, trying to escape the fire. No matter which way I turned, death was inevitable.

It was no use trying to go back to sleep. The nightmare left me limp with grief every morning. I tried to meditate. That was a joke.

A few weeks later, the nightmare returned as usual, but this time, I was determined to roll over and go back to sleep. Almost miraculously, the morning sun woke me from a dreamless sleep and a child's voice joyfully singing in my head, "I'm gonna let it shine, this little light of mine. I'm gonna let it shine..." A memory vision came to me.

When Chelsea was a small child, just three years old, she walked up to me and asked me a question. I was sitting at the dining room table, perhaps drinking tea, perhaps not. I was pregnant with Sabrina. Chelsea approached me with a curious look on her face, so innocent, so knowing. She looked into my eyes and asked, "Mama, do you remember our old house?" Now, we had just moved from the hills of Mill Valley to a slightly larger house in the flats. I had read about young children needing a gentle transition from an old situation to a new one, so I responded with the knowledge of a mother who wanted to help her child accept changes in her life.

I asked Chelsea, "Would you like to go visit our old house? We can drive by and say goodbye again." She shook her head at me as though I were a pitiful, ignorant being. And, in truth, I was.

"No, Mama, not THAT house, our OLD house. You know, the Big White One that burned up in the fire!"

I was taken aback. Chelsea was precocious. She was wise. Was she asking me about a past life? I asked her to describe the big white house. I asked her what she remembered about it and what her life was like there, but she had already lost interest. If I didn't know what house she meant, she wasn't going to pursue it. Chelsea turned away and went back to her bedroom to play with her toys. I was left wondering what terrible dream she must have had to bring on this horrible vision.

Immediately, I called my friend Patsy and told her about Chelsea's question. We both wondered how a three-year-old could have even heard about house fires, let alone understood the terror of one's own home burning down. It was beyond my ken. Chelsea never brought it up again, and eventually. I forgot about it...until now.

That morning, as I heard Chelsea's sweet, high voice singing about her little light, I was reminded of my toddler Chelsea asking me about our "big white house that burned up in the fire." I had always pictured in my mind a large, white, plantation-style home with pillars in front and green acres all around. I thought Chelsea may have had a past life as a Southern belle. She certainly had the attitude of a young woman who knew wealth and property in spite of our meager means. Chelsea always expected good things. She was relentlessly optimistic.

After the fire. (Photo courtesy of Carol Cidlik.)

But now...I don't think little Chelsea was describing a dream or a past life. I think she saw her future. Never throughout the years did I imagine she was describing a huge, old, white, run-down warehouse in Oakland, California. I now believe she saw her own death and wanted to ask me about it. And I didn't understand.

I felt woefully inadequate at the time, and still do today. I often felt that way with Chelsea. She was beyond us. She couldn't understand inequality or injustice. She couldn't understand bullying or intolerance. Chelsea truly believed that one day we would all come to know love and kindness as a given. She thought life should be fun Her little light shone from within.

Two days before the fire, I went to the theater alone and watched *Arrival,* a movie about the fluidity of time. The subplot of the story concerns a mother who is shown a future in which her yet unconceived daughter dies of a terminal illness. She has the choice to accept or reject that life. Of course, she chooses to marry, give birth to her daughter, and then watch her die. How much better to have given that little girl eight years of love than to lose out on knowing her. I needed to have that movie under my belt to process my unfathomable loss. Yes, I would have mothered Chelsea again, even knowing she would die a violent, terrifying death. She lived an incredibly full life. Chelsea brought light to the lives of everyone she touched, including her own.

Chapter 9

Thanksgiving 2016

November 24, 2016

The last time I saw Chelsea Faith alive, she was mad at me. Chelsea had broken up with her new boyfriend, David, nearly six months earlier, so I was surprised when she called and said she wanted to bring him to our family Thanksgiving dinner at my sister Leslie's house in Foster City. Chelsea tended to overshare with me about her personal life, and I'd heard all about their volatile relationship. When she asked about Thanksgiving, I gave her my best motherly advice: "Remember, you broke up for a reason. If you don't resolve those issues, you're headed for the same problems."

Chelsea wasn't used to me criticizing her decisions, so she sulked a bit. "Okay, Mother, but if he doesn't come, I'm not coming." I told her he was welcome, of course, and nothing would be the same without her. I said she was a big girl who could make her own decisions. She brought David to our family gathering, and I assumed they'd worked out their difficulties.

She was still somewhat sullen, which, for her, looked like a slight smile. Her blond hair shone softly, with hot pink and turquoise tips on either side. She wore her turquoise "going to a wedding" dress, a turquoise and pink scarf around her neck, her shiny triangle-shaped necklace and earrings, harlequin tights, and a sparkly black cardigan sweater. On most occasions, Chelsea would enter a room and get everyone laughing. This holiday was different; she wasn't as ebullient as usual. Rather than dancing from room to room, fetching drinks, and sparking conversation in her usual fashion, Chelsea spent most of the afternoon sitting on the tailored, white sofa next to David with her black and white legs pressed together and chunky black boots crossed at the ankles. Of course, Chelsea wasn't one to hold a grudge. I knew she'd forgive me for being outspoken, and truthfully, she'd probably taken my advice.

I felt a little sad that she was miffed at me, but I was sure we would be okay the next time we met. It wouldn't be long before she would call me and pretend to be crying, saying in a baby voice, "Boo-hoo-hoo, I just want to talk to my mommy." She always made me laugh. Either that or she would burst in my front door unannounced, singing out, "Mother! I brought my laundry!" Then, she'd lug her big turquoise laundry basket upstairs to my washer and begin stuffing in clothes... not sorting the colors because she had too many colors! Her wardrobe was a veritable rainbow of glitter, neon, sparkles, and patterns. Once the washer was loaded, she would plop down on the sofa in my living room and laugh, "Let's talk!" And talk, she did. I learned about every dream, hope, new boyfriend, old boyfriend, performance, friendship, you name it. Chelsea loved to talk. I looked forward to her next visit.

At dinner that evening, we sat around the long table; my brother-in-law Neal sat at one end with Leslie at the other. Their son Dan, his girlfriend Aubrey, plus Joe and Sabrina sat on one side, Chelsea, David, and I on the other side. My sister,

Leslie, loves preparing a huge feast of turkey and all the usual side dishes for Thanksgiving each year, and because special dinners were usually just the three of us, my girls and I loved having an extended family tradition.

Ever since she was little, Chelsea loved the idea of a day set aside just for being grateful. There were no obligations, no presents, and only one expectation. Chelsea insisted each of us take turns saying what we were thankful for that year. Thanksgiving was her favorite holiday, and she was enthusiastic about this part of the meal. That year, we all moaned in our usual good-humored, agreed-upon complaint. "Oh, come on. Do we have to?" Then we took turns expressing our gratitude for family, Sabrina and Joe's engagement, special trips, work going well, and that sort of thing. Chelsea softened after that.

Thankfully, after dinner, as we said our goodbyes, Chelsea and I hugged and said, "I love you." Then she and David left for the long drive from Foster City over to the KALX studios at UC Berkeley for her usual Thursday midnight radio gig as DJ Cherushii. I would have been devastated if we hadn't said, "I love you." Had I known it was our last time together, I would have done more to make sure we were at peace.

Sabrina, Mother, and Chelsea on Thanksgiving Day, 2016.
The last time we were together. One week later, she was
dead.

Chapter 10

Pizza and a Quiet Evening at Home

December 2, 2016

Two nights before the fire, Chelsea performed at Public Works, a nightclub close to her home in San Francisco. It was her favorite performance space. Her set went well, but she was tired. She complained to David the night of the party that she was exhausted and confided, "I'm kind of sorry I told Joel I'd DJ for an hour at his show, but I guess I have to go."

Chelsea had heard Joel Shanahan play on her last road trip through the Midwest. She told him, "You're so talented; you really ought to take your music more seriously." When he told her he was playing in the Bay Area, she naturally agreed to perform with him that night but said she wouldn't have the energy to perform live. Instead, she'd play a DJ set using a thumb drive with all her favorite "end of the night" music. It would be an easy gig. She was scheduled to go on stage at 6:00 a.m. Chances were, the party would be over by then, and she could go home early.

David understood how tired she was and told Chelsea she

didn't have to go. He was also tired. He'd been driving for Uber and would have liked a night off. That night, they ate pizza for dinner and discussed staying home and spending a quiet evening together.

Chelsea had spoken with her dear friend, Josey, earlier that day. They had a running joke, "She's my oldest friend, not in age, but I've known her the longest. Ha ha." Chelsea told Josey that she didn't feel like going out that night. She was still considering staying home with David when the time came to leave, but the memory of being the one who talked Joel into taking his music more seriously haunted her.

Travis Hough, her EasyStreet bandmate, texted her around 7:00 p.m. and asked if she was playing in Oakland that night. He'd heard that one of their mutual friends, Johnny Igaz, was playing, and if Chelsea was also playing, he had twice the reason to go. The two of them had been sharing music files for their new album, *Into the Stars*, and Travis wanted to talk with Chelsea about it. They needed to discuss their form-breaking acoustic ballad.

Chelsea wrote the music, and Travis wrote the lyrics to *Places I Will Never Go* after visiting Chelsea in her favorite city, Berlin. He was miserable there and just as miserable when he returned to San Francisco. She'd told him, "This is my best motherly advice: You have to be happy within before you're happy anywhere else." Travis took that advice. He played in several other bands with their mutual friends and loved the new direction his music was taking. He wanted to include Chelsea in his transition.

Chelsea and Travis were both classically trained musicians, and he was tired of the Italo-disco schtick they'd been doing in San Francisco clubs for several years as the duo EasyStreet. Chelsea once said, "It's silly how popular we are. We both want to play our own music, but this is what people want to dance to." They still had to work out the details of some of their new songs and think about a recording studio that would suit their needs, one that housed a grand piano for Chelsea's accompaniment to Travis' vocals.

Despite her misgivings about playing that night, Chelsea decided to visit with Travis and her other friends. Chelsea hadn't seen her good friend, Amanda Allen, for months. She would be there taking pictures; it would be fun to hang out. Johnny Igaz, her record labelmate and Amanda's new boyfriend, was playing, and, of course, Joel was the headliner. Griffin Madden would be there, too. He worked at the UC Berkeley radio station KALX with Chelsea. She had seen him perform recently and decided to showcase him in her upcoming Monday club night, Run the Length of Your Wildness. Other friends were sure to show up. They always did. She would wait for Joel to finish his headliner set, and then she could go home and eat her leftover pizza for breakfast. Yum. Chelsea told David she was going to the party and got dressed for the night. She left her home in San Francisco around 8:00 p.m.

Once the stage was set up, Chelsea wandered around the funky Oakland warehouse and texted David, "I just want to be home eating pizza with you." She also described the place as "... a labyrinth with a wall of organs, not the intestinal kind but the musical kind. Ha ha. If I weren't so jaded, I'd be impressed." The funny thing was, Chelsea was probably the least jaded person in San Francisco. She was curious about everyone and maintained a childlike sense of wonder. The fact that she was unimpressed with this culturally appropriated attempt at interior decorating said more about the place than about her. It was dusty and cluttered with junk. She didn't like dirt.

Joel Shanahan nodded at Chelsea and Travis on his way outside to smoke a cigarette. They were sitting together on a sofa upstairs and talking in their usual animated fashion. Johnny Igaz had just started playing his set. The party was underway. Joel wound down the rickety staircase to the first floor and out a side door to the "smoking area," which was nothing more than a cluttered, fenced-in side lot. He was outside finishing his cigarette when the fire started.

Chelsea and Travis Hough in the studio (from Chelsea's photo collection).

Chelsea and Joel Shanahan (from Chelsea's photo collection).

Chapter 11

I Won't Die

December 7, 2016

After the fire, my sweet Sabrina and calm, capable Joe moved in with me for a month. They took over the guest room and bath in my condo and settled into their own routine. Sabrina still worked steadily as a dog walker, and Joe managed several non-profit outdoor education camps for children. I was grateful for their steady presence, although I secretly felt it was probably a suicide watch. They didn't have to worry. I craved Chelsea's presence, but I didn't want to die. I just wanted her to live.

I took a leave of absence from my work as a learning specialist at Marin Country Day School for the rest of the school year. The Oakland Warriors and other private groups set up funds for the families of the fire victims. I used that money to stay home and try to recover from the shock of Chelsea's death. I also gave the parents of my private after-school students the names of several tutors who were willing to take my place. I was too anxious and sad to teach. It was hard for me to leave the house without breaking down in tears. The teachers at my school arranged a food train of meals for the three of us. They left food in a cooler on my front porch each day, sometimes adding flowers, chocolates, or a bottle of wine. I didn't have to cook for a month. All I had to do was breathe, go for long walks, eat, and sleep. Sometimes, even that felt like too much.

At first, I thought I was doing okay, but a sharp kernel of anxiety began to grow whenever I wasn't sitting next to Sabrina. My fear didn't come into sharp focus until one rainy night shortly after the cremation. Sabrina had to drive to her home in Vallejo to pick up a few things. Her home was about 40 miles away. It was getting dark, and rain was pouring down, turning low points in the road into lakes. I remember telling her in a shaky voice, "You don't have to go. You should stay here with me. It'll be okay."

Of course, Sabrina had her own life. She was incredibly calm, as always. She looked at me with a steady gaze and said, "It's okay, I won't die." And that, of course, was the crux of the matter. I was afraid to let her leave my sight because I was afraid she, too, would die.

Somehow, I would have to learn how to let Sabrina live as full a life as Chelsea had experienced.

* * *

WRITING CHELSEA'S EULOGY

December 10, 2016

A week or so after Chelsea Faith died, I sat down alone in bed with my sorrow and wrote her Eulogy. Diffused evening sunlight shone through the sheer curtains on my bedroom windows, warming my face. Sabrina and Joe were both out, and I was glad to be alone with my thoughts. So many memories swirled and flooded my brain that day, some long forgotten, all muscling their way to the surface, fighting for my attention. How could I say goodbye to my beautiful, beloved daughter? Four words kept repeating in my brain, "Unbearable sorrow. Unbearable joy."

UNBEARABLE SORROW, UNBEARABLE JOY CHELSEA FAITH DOLAN, CHERUSHII, MY BELOVED DAUGHTER

Thank you all for bringing your love here today. My Chelsea had too much enthusiasm for life—to keep her life celebration small and quiet.

Chelsea's exuberance could not be contained. She burst out in colors, showing us how to live a Beautiful and Interesting Life.

She didn't have a backup plan; Chelsea had ONE TRUE PLAN, and she followed it faithfully: Do that thing that makes you happy to get out of bed each morning. Do it morally and ethically, and share what you learn.
And when she met someone in pain, my sweet Chelsea embraced them with love, letting them know they were perfect just the way they were. She never gave up and never compromised who she was.

Chelsea inspired her friends to tap into their natural talents and use their creativity for good—for themselves and for others. She offered kindness to everyone who was open to it—BUT that girl was FIERCE in her opposition to those who would use or abuse others.

I often shook my head in awe after learning a lesson in strength, humility, or forgiveness from my courageous daughter.

Chelsea Faith was a force of nature: innocent as air, lyrical as water, grounded by humility, and eternalized by fire.

I will never be the same without her, but I made a promise to my beloved daughter that I will be true to her unique spirit, and I encourage all of you to live your lives fully in love with each day given to you.

Be yourself, bursting with pride. Follow your wildest dreams despite all that well-meaning advice to be ordinary. For you are beautiful just the way you are. You are extraordinary. You are loved.

As my wise and gentle Sabrina says: "You are braver than you think you are."

I love you all.

* * *

Here is what Sabrina wrote about her sister:

"Everyone who met Chelsea knew there was something special about her. She was an open book; she was unapologetic about who she was and chased her dreams like most people don't have the courage to do. She was incredibly independent but also deeply valued and leaned on the people around her. She found joy in the silly things; she loved to laugh and laughed loudly. She was incredibly kind and accepting of others, no matter who you were.

The word that keeps coming up for the many who knew her is 'magical.' She was always dressed in colorful clothes. Glitter, sparkles, neon, iridescent, stripes and patterns. She was still a child in many ways; she never lost that. She wanted everyone to have fun and be happy, and when she was in your presence, you were usually smiling. I was always jealous of her social skills, the way she was able to put everyone at ease around her. I was also jealous of her intelligence, as she was smarter than most but was also so modest. Modest about her talent as a musician. Modest about her schooling. Modest about her effect on the community.

As I write all this, none of it seems to do her justice. Words can't describe her. You just had to experience her. I am so grateful she was my sister. We got to grow up together, and what a crazy and unique life we both had side by side for those years. She was one of a kind, truly, and the world will never be the same.

The photo is one of my favorites. Chelsea dressed up as, what she insisted then, a 'queen Japanese butterfly'."

Colleen Dolan

Chapter 12

The Memorials

December 3-17, 2016

The days and weeks that followed the fire were filled with public tributes, private family funerals, and individual memorials. I didn't have the strength or will to attend the massive public gatherings at Lake Merritt in Oakland that were organized immediately after the fire. After Chelsea's body was identified, I couldn't remember how to breathe, let alone plan or participate in memorials. How could I when I didn't believe Chelsea was gone?

Some of the Ghost Ship families did attend. A part of me wanted to be there with them, but it was all too much. Reporters, cameras, mourning friends, and concerned strangers gathered by the thousands to wail into microphones and sing together.

I remained curled up on my bedroom floor. I knew that radio and TV stations played the artists' music and featured the life stories of each of the 36 victims every night for weeks. I couldn't listen. There were other Celebrations of Life held throughout the Bay Area that included orchestral music and poetry recitations, but I sat on my sofa, paralyzed with grief, unable to walk through my front door. Churches in Oakland and each of the victims' hometowns held services that were covered in the media. Newspaper articles about the fire dominated the headlines. None of this attention helped. I couldn't bear to see or hear it.

Night after night, I had the dream that I was in Chelsea's body, seeing through her eyes, frantically searching for a way out of the burning maze of a building. The continual public memorials kept the horror going.

Though a large community lost their loved ones, my pain felt singular and deeply personal. I knew Chelsea deserved a proper send-off, but I couldn't do it. That's when Chelsea's best friend, Josey Duncan, stepped up just as she always had. Josey took on the event with a vigor that was equaled only by her and Chelsea's love for each other. They had walked through life side by side from the age of eight, pulling silly pranks together, taking on massive school projects, filling each day with imaginative plans, and holding each other in support throughout all the usual childhood setbacks, teenage loves, and adult relationships. Josey arranged everything. Chelsea's Memorial was planned for December 17, 2016, just two weeks after the fire. I sent another message to Facebook once I realized this event was bigger than my personal grief. Chelsea was part of a massive community of family, friends, and admirers. This is what I wrote:

"I would like to invite my family and friends to a memorial for my beloved daughter, Chelsea Faith Dolan, on Saturday, December 17th, from 1:00-5:00 p.m. The Celebration of Chelsea's Life will be held at Public Works in San Francisco, a music venue where she is known and loved. Because of Chelsea's open heart and inclusive spirit, I open this invitation to the public. Anyone who would like to say goodbye is a friend. Please know this is a celebration of the entirety of my fun-loving, beautiful daughter's life; she was a seeker and a teacher from her earliest days.

I want to honor her childhood days with our fortunate family, as well as her achievements as a musician. Her music will be celebrated forever; her legendary kindness will live on in the hearts of everyone she has ever touched. Chelsea's message: Be who you are with pride. Follow your dreams despite all that well-meaning advice to be ordinary. Oh, and wear clothes that make you feel happy. Chelsea would be appalled if everyone wore black! She spread color, joy, and love wherever she went. No doubt, her new home is sparkling with rainbow glitter. I love you.

Colleen, aka Mother"

December 17, 2016

Chelsea's memorial was a disco party! A stage was set up, and Chelsea's friends played sets that included much of her music. A giant screen flashed a slideshow with hundreds of pictures from her life. Public Works was the last club Chelsea had played two nights before the fire. They opened their doors to us with love and generosity.

The main room featured a large disco ball, which lit up the darkened spirits and helped keep the atmosphere loving and joyful. Hundreds of people showed up, many of whom I had never seen before, and others who were my life anchors. Even some of my friends from high school, Frank Poyer, Michael Lownie, and Lynn Leslie, who had also moved from Buffalo, New York, to the West Coast, came to offer their support and love.

Chelsea's memorial. (Photo courtesy of Nazar Vojtovich.)

Chelsea was inspirational to many and a beloved figure in the San Francisco music scene.

Chelsea and her best friend, Josey Duncan, made a video of Sherlock Holmes being interviewed by a news reporter. Little brother, Hardie Duncan, was Dr. Watson. The memorial included a slide deck of hundreds of photos projected on the wall behind the stage.

People danced and laughed at memories of their times with Chelsea. They also cried on each other's shoulders. I wore a gold lamé dress and gold sparkle shoes. I read my eulogy, and David and Josey also spoke. Josey wrote a poem for the occasion. There was an open mic for others to come up and share their stories and love. The room shone with colors, glitter, music, and Chelsea's favorite flowers, red Gerbera daisies. Chelsea would have approved. I approved.

Chelsea's memorial. (Photo courtesy of Nazar Vojtovich.)

Sound Warrior's tribute to Cherushii.

Chapter 13

Game of Thrones

December 21, 2016

Once the memorial was over, my grief had nowhere to go. Overwhelming tension grew inside every cell of my body. I tried morning yoga and long walks, but nothing released the tightening pain in my soul. Each time I brushed my hair or took a shower, huge clumps of hair would fall into my hands or swirl the drain. My muscles went limp. My stomach ached constantly. I found myself making up soothing stories: *'Chelsea is away in Berlin again. Maybe I'll have a little German grandchild one day.'* or *'Chelsea might come by with her laundry next week. It's been a while.'* I kept the stories running silently in my head from morning to evening. From the outside, I must have looked semi-normal. On the inside, I was living a fictional chaos.

Every night since leaving Chelsea behind in the crematorium, I had nightmares that left me gasping at the desperation she and the others must have felt. I craved a way to lessen their pain, to make it bearable. I couldn't let that nightmare image be the worst thing that could happen. Something had to be worse.

That's when I stumbled onto *Game of Thrones* on TV. It was worse. Humans torturing humans. Children being taught to hate and kill. Bloodshed in the name of power. It all gave me a feeling of proportion, the knowledge that my daughter's death was not as horrific as this evil recitation of treachery, bloody body parts, and scalded murder. I didn't stop watching until the last episode available at the time was finished. Even then, I wanted more. It had to be worse than watching fire and smoke come to choke and consume you, knowing your life would be over within minutes.

Sabrina and Joe were still living with me when I started watching the series. Joe took on the task of helping me sort out the stacks of insurance forms, bank accounts, car registration, rental agreements, and other paperwork that must be completed when someone dies. All require death certificates. Sabrina tiptoed carefully around my feelings and took over household chores. She avoided talking about Chelsea, but once, when I asked her how she was doing, she said, "It sucks not having a sister." They might have been different, but they each complemented the other. Now, Sabrina was an only child and had to take on the full burden of my grief while still dealing with her own.

One evening, Sabrina stood beside me and touched my shoulder as I sat, stretched out on the sofa, watching a man being tied up and castrated. She whispered, "Are you sure this is okay?" I nodded. She repeated, "I just want to be sure you're okay." I nodded again. I would never be okay, but this television show made me feel that my pain was somehow manageable. I couldn't prevent Chelsea's death, but I could place it in a category that did not include evil perpetrated for the sake of a throne. She died as a result of stupidity, neglect, and incompetence. Looking back, those paltry reasons seem even worse. But in the first days after Chelsea's death, I needed something to be more monstrous than the fire that took 36 lives, more monstrous than the nightmares that continued to haunt me every night.

Chapter 14

Losing My Words

Christmas Day, December 25, 2016

During the first week after Chelsea's death, I used Facebook as a vehicle for my grief. Each day, I wrote a story from her life. She was an extraordinary little kid and a magnificent young adult. Her story ended too soon, but it soothed my soul to talk about her with my online friends. The loving responses eased my pain. Then something odd happened.

On Christmas morning, 2016, Sabrina and Joe were still sleeping. I was grateful to have them upstairs; their presence filled my home with warmth. We didn't have much planned for the day other than waffles in the morning and dinner in the evening. Sabrina and I split the meal prep that day. She baked a lovely dinner of chicken with mushrooms, potatoes, and green beans while I arranged shrimp, cheese, and vegetables on a platter. It was all I could do. I placed some of Chelsea's favorite gifts, a guitar, mandolin, and a little white, plunky, wooden toy piano, under a tiny, living tree that Sabrina had thoughtfully brought home and decorated with a few of their childhood ornaments. We didn't have the emotional wherewithal to buy presents for one another. Cheerful sweaters and stockings just seemed wrong, somehow. We would keep it a quiet day.

After dinner, I climbed up to my bedroom and sat down in the comfy tan chair in the corner of my bedroom. I found my abandoned journal tucked beside the armrest. My small room looked just as it did that awful night. Years ago, I had painted the walls a terra cotta color, hoping to soften the cold whiteness of my newly built condo. I was grateful for the womb-like warmth as I sat there but frowned looking at my bed. The black embroidered comforter and the irritatingly pretentious pile of burgundy and black decorative pillows mocked my once-smug overconfidence. Who did I think I was? Well, now I knew; I was a broken woman whose daughter had died.

The streetlights below shown through the sheer off-white window curtains onto the wall hung with black-framed photos of my friends and family. Christmas music and colored lights filled the night sky with an empty holiday glow. I picked up the pen stuck within the pages of my notebook, intending to write, but no words came out. What could I possibly say? Words made no sense. Chelsea was gone. I didn't have a cogent thought in my head... just jagged feelings ricocheting aimlessly around my body.

I picked up my laptop and tried looking through all the newspaper articles about the Ghost Ship fire that I had set aside. For some reason, I couldn't make sense of what was right in front of me. With each word, an image of that awful fire screaming out the warehouse windows would distract me from the next sentence. Words were empty clumps of letters. I had lost the ability to read.

The irony was that I had been a reading teacher for nearly 30 years. One thing I knew was that children are best able to read their own words, so I began my reading rehab in early January 2017 by returning to Facebook and writing one short passage about Chelsea each week. It took me days to piece together each simple paragraph. After four weeks of concentrated focus, I began writing a "Chelsea Story" on the 2nd of each month in remembrance of December 2, 2016. I kept that practice going for five years.

January–March, 2017

I wrote about Chelsea's preschool penchant for rescuing leaves and "pretty" garbage from their tragic trashcan fate. I included the time she watched a Carmen Miranda movie on TV at age six and decided that's the colorful character she wanted to be for Halloween.

Chelsea and Sabrina on Halloween.

I tried to transcribe some of the intricate lyrics from songs she recorded at ages 15 and 16, though the sound on those old four-track tapes was muddled. Even so, the chord changes and melodies she recorded on piano, bass, and guitar were haunting.

I wrote about Chelsea's facile acquisition of languages, always making sure she could communicate effectively no matter where in the world she traveled. And I wrote about her love of music and color, the foundations of her being.

Others joined in. It seemed everyone who met her had a Chelsea Story. Each anecdote was filled with love and laughter. I wrote slowly but with growing appreciation for the fullness of her desire to stride out into the world with open arms.

Chapter 15

Therapy and an Understanding Friend

March 2017

I patted myself on the back for easing back into reading, but my inability to focus and constant anxiety that something terrible was going to happen to Sabrina were disorienting. The recurring nightmares had already exhausted what little stability I had left. The physical manifestation of that fear was my hair falling out. I needed help, and I also wanted a safe place to open the large box of Chelsea's clothes that had been shipped to me from the coroner. I needed to touch the clothes she wore that night but didn't trust myself not to fall apart. It was pretty evident; I needed a grief therapist. Margie Schwartz, the child psychologist at my school, was also a friend, so I asked her for a recommendation. That was perhaps one of the wisest things I did in those few months.

Debbie Duggan became my grief counselor. She welcomed me into her softly lit, peaceful office. The colors were subdued blue, gray, and beige. I sat on a comfortably upholstered chair on one side of the room. Debbie sat across from me in an identical chair. Beside her was a narrow wooden table on which she kept a notebook and pen. She had long, silvery blond hair, a gentle, understanding face, and dressed in pastels. Debbie appeared almost angelic in the dappled sunlight that shone through floor-to-ceiling windows on the far end of the room and opened onto a lush, green garden. In her soft voice, Debbie encouraged me to keep writing about Chelsea, saying it didn't matter that it was slow or tedious. She could see that it helped me. Debbie understood when I told her there were times when I inexplicably found myself standing in front of the fire or watching Chelsea enter the furnace at the crematorium. She heard my anxiety and gave me a practice of noticing what I saw, touched, heard, and smelled to keep me connected to the present.

I saw Debbie twice a week. During one of our first sessions, I felt ready and lugged the heavy box of Chelsea's clothes into her office. I knelt on the floor next to the box and took three cleansing breaths. Debbie nodded. I'd learned that lesson pretty well. Then I took the scissors she handed me and cut through the taped cardboard. The smell of smoke poured into the room. Within the box was a plastic bag sealed with a metal tag that read 36/36 and some other numbers. I said, "Chelsea must have been the 36th of 36." Then I pried off the tag and opened the bag. I had to sit back on the floor. The smell of Chelsea's sweat and perfume, Black Orchid, mixed with the overwhelming waft of smoke rising from the box. Debbie asked, "Do you want to take a break?" I'd come this far. I had to do it then or never.

The item on top was Chelsea's blue, faux leather jacket. It was singed black on the shoulder and sleeves but was still intact. Next, I pulled out her black and blue checkered winter scarf. The fringe on one side had melted. Underneath, her black mini-skirt and see-through black rhinestone-encrusted blouse were neatly folded. Within the sooty folds were her black bra, a black lace-trimmed teddy, her black and gray striped underpants, and her zebra-striped tights. At the bottom of the box were her silver iridescent cross-body purse and the black mid-calf boots with buttons up the side that I'd given her for her birthday in September. Everything was intact. Nothing was destroyed by the fire. I was confused and turned to Debbie frantically, "Why wasn't she rescued? If she wasn't burned, why is she dead?"

Debbie reminded me that I could take a break or stop whenever I needed to. I stubbornly shook my head at her and kept going. Inside the purse, I found the soot-covered metal case with her silver glitter custom earplugs tucked inside. Her brown leather wallet was warped, and the contents, her driver's license, business cards, and $38 dollars, were blackened on the edges. I remembered Chelsea in the funeral home. Her hair was thick with soot and ash. It got into everything, even her purse. In the silky lining at the bottom of her purse were two tampons and the thumb drive with her "end of the evening" music she would have used to DJ that night. Both were covered in black smudge. Her phone was missing.

Tears wet my hands and arms, but I didn't realize I was crying until Debbie offered me a box of tissues. She asked me if I would like to talk about Chelsea. I couldn't and rasped out the word, "No." Chelsea was right there in the room with me. These were the clothes she wore when she died. Her death was immediate and concrete. Her DNA was in the smell, the soot, and the cloth. I looked at her clothes again, now spread out on Debbie's office floor. So much black! Where was her joyful rainbow? What was her mood when she got dressed that night? For Chelsea, the outfit was almost funereal. Then I remembered: She didn't want to go that night. What kind of premonition led her to dress in black and blue? I think if she owned a black jacket, she would have worn that, too.

Debbie waited patiently for me to sit with Chelsea and, one by one, put the items back in the box. I folded the top shut and climbed back up onto the chair across from Debbie. My breathing was ragged. She could see I was still inside the warehouse with Chelsea, so she led me through an exercise to bring me back into the moment. Reluctantly, I acknowledged five things I could see and four things I could touch. I listened for three things I heard and two things I smelled. That was easy. Smoke and Chelsea smells filled the room.

Debbie told me about several grief groups I could join. Hospice by the Bay in Larkspur held Tuesday and Wednesday morning groups for all grievers. A private therapist held a small Friday afternoon group just for mothers. The Compassionate Friends meetings for bereaved parents were held on the third Monday of every month. After that day, I drove to every grief meeting in the county, searching for the company of others who understood my loss.

Of course, my friends were well-meaning, but they didn't get it. Often, they would say, "I can't imagine what you're going through," and that was the most accurate thing they could have said. I needed to be around people who understood.

The Hospice by the Bay grief groups mostly included middle-aged adults who lost their aged parents and grandparents. Those sessions left me feeling irritated. Their loved ones had lived long and full lives. They got to say goodbye. One group even included adults who lost their pets. I just couldn't listen to that. I know grief is grief, but I needed a group exclusively for bereaved parents.

I attended my first Compassionate Friends meeting on the third Monday in March 2017, and it was there I found my people. I was weepy and lonely at first. A beautiful woman with shiny blond hair and a soft expression sat down next to me. She looked kind. We began talking, and I learned that her only son had died in January, just one month after Chelsea. We shared the shocking stories of our children's sudden deaths and then began to talk about their lives. I remember thinking how easy it was to talk with Sioux. She was gentle, open, and a quiet crier. I had learned to avoid people who wailed loudly in public. Highly charged displays of grief left me shaking and breathless. I later found out that Sioux was an actress. She dressed herself in composure though her sorrow was great. I had much to learn by standing in her presence.

Sioux and I looked for each other at the monthly meetings and eventually started to get together weekly for lunch and a long walk. Twice, she asked me to accompany her to her son's gravesite. I felt honored.

Colleen and Sioux.

Little by little, through therapy, grief groups, and friendship with Sioux, I acquired the ability to navigate the crunchy, broken glass of my reality. Rather than sinking under the weight of unbearable sorrow, I found that talking, writing, and reading about Chelsea unlocked a well of joyful memories. Tensions began to diffuse. My sorrow remained, but so too did my love for that incredibly precocious little person who became an extraordinary young woman. Remembering my two daughters' childhood buoyed my soul. I was here for a reason if only to bring these two incredible people into the world. Debbie reminded me I was here to experience my own life, as well. I leaned hard on therapy, grief groups, and writing down my memories. Gradually, my hair began to grow back just in time for Sabrina and Joe's wedding in June.

Chapter 16

The Gift

April 2017

It was shortly after I opened the coroner's box with Chelsea's clothes that I had a vivid dream about her. She was a young girl, about five or six years old, wearing her favorite white lace party dress, kneeling on the floor of a small, white, empty room. In front of her was a big box about two feet cubed wrapped in shiny, red foil wrapping paper. On top was a red velvet bow as big as the box. True to form, Chelsea started wildly ripping through the wrapping paper just as she did on every birthday and Christmas.

If you know Chelsea, you know she loved unwrapping presents; it was always so exciting! Some people carefully unwrap presents and fold the paper for another occasion. Not Chelsea! The paper never survived. As she pulled the top off the box and peered in, Chelsea stopped moving, sat back on her heels, and exclaimed, "Oh! My! God!" I was standing in a doorway behind Chelsea, off to one side, and she turned back to me, looking up over her shoulder, and flashed a jubilant grin.

"This is the BEST PRESENT EVER!" Then she turned back, raised herself back up on her knees, reached inside the box to touch her gift, and proclaimed, "I get to live my life exactly the way I want...and I get to DIE exactly the way I want!"

Chelsea looked back at me over her shoulder again with a soft smile, and my heart sank. Sadly, I had to agree with her, "Yes, Sweetheart, that is the best present ever." The gift was not from me; it was a gift from God, or the Universe, or whatever you want to call it. I was as surprised by the gift as she was. Chelsea continued smiling, and I woke up...melancholy but smiling in concert with her. So, did Chelsea push her way into my dreams to reassure me, or did I dream of a way to make her death transcendent rather than final? Was this her gift to me?

The Gift of Celwick

Chelsea Faith was immensely proud of me for providing her with a sister. She called Sabrina "my baby." Sabrina is and was the perfect sister for Chelsea—a gift to all of us—lovingly tolerant, gracefully strong-willed.

I was only about a month pregnant when Chelsea matter-of-factly told me I was going to have her baby, whose name was Celwick. I was stunned. First, how did she know I was pregnant? I had only just discovered that myself. And HER baby, Celwick? Selwick? Where did that come from? When I asked how she had thought of that name, she bestowed a benevolent smile upon me and shook her head gently at my pitiful ignorance. "Oh, Mama, I didn't name her that. Our baby is ALREADY called Celwick." When Sabrina was born, I carefully explained that new babies needed a new name. Chelsea was sad, but after a few minutes, announced, "We can name her Flower." Another talk ensued. There were a few early years when Chelsea called Sabrina Celwick, but little by little, the nickname was left behind.

The last time Sabrina and Chelsea were together, on November 27, 2016, Chelsea hugged Sabrina goodbye as they parted and said, "Goodbye, Celwick."

The last time they were together, Chelsea said, "Goodbye, Celwick."

Chapter 17

Sabrina and Joe's Wedding

June 3, 2017

C helsea had wanted to help Sabrina with her wedding. It was scheduled to take place in June 2017, six months after the fire. Sabrina and Joe considered postponing, but Chelsea loved weddings and parties and enthusiastically looked forward to participating. She'd been the Maid of Honor in quite a few, and as she said, "I know how these things work!" She, the effervescent party girl, would want the wedding to go on; this we knew for a fact. Joe and Sabrina still debated whether to postpone the date, but Joe's dad was gravely ill with pancreatic cancer, and they wanted to make sure he would be there to give his blessing and share in the joy.

Sabrina and Joe loved camping near rivers, and they especially loved camping in Yosemite National Park. They'd had to make the reservation for the wedding next to the Merced River a year in advance. Finally, it was decided: the wedding would go on, and it would usher in a new day.

The wedding ceremony took place amidst the trees of

Cathedral Cove beside the flowing Merced River. Sabrina wore an ivory vintage lace dress and flowers in her platinum hair. She looked like an enchanted princess from some old European fairy tale. During the ceremony, I was surprised to learn that she wore white moccasins. Joe's father, a blues musician known as Cool Fox, was from the White Earth Ojibwe tribe in Minnesota, and a cousin brought the moccasins for her to wear as a sign that she was now part of the Ojibwe family. Joe's mother, Katrina, is a musician and dance instructor from Bavaria. I think Joe's parents have a lot to do with his calm yet strong demeanor and his love of music. He stands nearly a foot taller than Sabrina, thin and handsome with dark hair and eyes and a black goatee. He wore a black suit but stood tall with his bare feet touching the earth. Together, they looked mythically beautiful.

I brought a picnic of Greek food to the park area a few feet from their wedding site. We sat on blankets on the ground and sang and ate in peace. The crowd was small and local, about 30 people, all dear friends and family who lived in the Western US...all but my brother, who came from Buffalo, New York. He'd invited himself on a recent visit to California, and Sabrina couldn't refuse. It turns out he came for a specific purpose. He came for me.

Later that evening, there was a formal dinner reception at the famous Ahwahnee Hotel, and all went well. Pictures were taken, and there was plenty of music and laughter. Young friends mingled and talked. Joe's dad, who performed under the name Cool Fox, played the guitar for a while. Dan was there with his girlfriend, Shanna. I liked her.

Sabrina and Joe cut the cake, which was topped with felt figures of bride and groom foxes. Their last name was Fox. When Chelsea first learned that Sabrina was marrying Joe, she said, "I don't usually like it when women take their husband's name. After all, Mother didn't, and she gave us her last name. But the name Sabrina Fox is too good to pass up. I think you should take Joe's last name." Sabrina, ever her own person, nodded and said she was planning to all along.

The memory made me smile. Then, I felt it creeping up on me. I sat at the table with my sister Leslie and brother Jim, unable to move. A dense blackness started in my toes and worked up to my knees; then, my legs shook violently. Rumbles churned in my stomach, and my chest tightened. My throat closed. My head swelled into a throbbing universe of pain. A terrible internal storm was coming, and I had to get outside.

"I'll be right back." My voice echoed, high-pitched and clear, over the hum of conversation in the room. Someone else could have said it; I didn't feel my mouth move, but it was me. The door lay ahead past some tables to the right. If I could just get there, Sabrina would be safe. She couldn't see this, not on her wedding day.

The Ahwahnee Hotel at Yosemite is rustically luxurious. The heavy wood beams, stone, and manicured wilderness surrounding it exude peace. Darkness had settled in the valley, bringing a cool respite from the heat of the day.

"I need a drink!" I think I might have yelled too loudly at the outdoor bartender. He poured me a glass of champagne, and I grabbed it desperately. I felt anything but peaceful. I stumbled a few paces down a flagstone path toward a stretch of lawn that led to the forest beyond. If I could just get to the trees, I thought, I would be okay. I never made it. My knees hit the pavers, and I crumpled with my face to the stone.

"Come back, Chelsea! I just want you to come back!" My champagne spilled out onto the pavement in front of me. "No God would take you instead of me." I swept the flute with my hand, and it turned into sparkling shards amidst the tiny, dark leaves and delicate white flowers bordering the path. A tiny sliver of glass embedded itself into my palm. "You should be here, Chelsea," I scolded. "You should be here with Sabrina. Use my body. Come take my place, please, please, please come back! I'll go instead of you!" Nothing. I knelt with my face to the cold stone and muttered, "There is no God."

Gulping sobs enveloped me in blackness. Feet came and went in front of me, and voices sounded above my head. I couldn't stop. My body convulsed in sorrow. This was my beloved daughter Sabrina's wedding in the perfect natural setting, and I was eons away in another part of the universe, begging God to take me in exchange for Chelsea. He didn't, and I will never forgive him for that. I looked up and spit out, "I hate you. You don't exist."

My brother, Jim, was standing there when I gave up. "I'm here for you, Col." Did he think I meant him? I couldn't bother to ask. Too much effort.

"I can't get up."

"I know. You don't have to." Then Jim sat down on the stone path with me. We said nothing.

I played with the tiny flake of glass in the palm of my hand. The pain verified that I was still alive. Jim started talking, and though I'm not sure what he said, his voice was soothing. We sat side by side, my head resting on his shoulder. After an endless muddle, he asked, "Do you think you can go back inside?" I nodded. We stood up, he handed me a wet towel from the bar, and I wiped off my face.

We walked slowly back to the reception arm-in-arm. I needed his support to walk through the bubbling crowd. Somehow, Jim had managed to pick up another glass of champagne for me on the way back to our table. Joe's dad, Cool Fox, who was sitting at the table across from me, nodded with a kind smile. I nodded back. He knew. He, too, was having his own dark night of the soul. He was dying, and this wedding was a bittersweet reminder of the cyclical nature of love, life, and death. Sabrina and Joe were radiantly in love, walking from table to table in animated conversation, beaming with joy. I fondled the bloody speck of glass in my palm, "Chelsea should be here."

Sabrina and Joe's Wedding.

Chapter 18

Charges Filed & The Summer of Memories

June, July, and August of 2017

On July 1, 2017, just a month after Sabrina and Joe got married, I sat alone in my living room and watched the local TV evening news. A reporter stood in front of the Alameda County courthouse and announced that the District Attorney's office in Alameda County had filed criminal charges of Involuntary Manslaughter against two men, Derick Almena, the master tenant of the Ghost Ship warehouse, and Max Harris, his event manager.

Just when the incessant pain of Chelsea's loss started to soften, the news report brought back the sharp stab of reality. What had these two men done to cause the fire? Could it have been prevented? I waited for an explanation, but it never came. All I learned was that the preliminary hearings would begin in January 2018 at the Alameda County Courthouse. That was six months away.

That first, long summer without Chelsea was excruciating. I went to bed when it was still daylight because the night terrors returned with exhausting regularity at 3:00 a.m. I had trouble going back to sleep after traversing the burning hallways with Chelsea in panicked desperation. During those long waking hours until daylight, I reread my Facebook postings about Chelsea as a child, precocious and curious about the world. Memories filled my days as I sorted through hundreds of childhood photos, and of course, I kept writing.

As a toddler, Chelsea told me, "I want to know everything!" And she set out to do so. She was always full of questions. She used her pre-teen and teenage years to bravely step out into the larger world. I was constantly amazed and bewildered by her audacious confidence.

Chelsea drew people to her with a light that shone from within. Once, when she was five, we visited my hometown of Buffalo, New York. She rode on her uncle's shoulders at an outdoor jazz show, beaming a big smile and waving to people. A woman came up to me and asked, "Who is that little girl? Is she on TV?" I smiled and said she undoubtedly would be one day. Throughout her life, no matter what the occasion or event, Chelsea managed to be the one chosen to be the master of ceremonies, or the star dancer, or the lead actress. She always put on a good show.

KidStar Radio - 1996

I don't even know how it happened, but when she was 12, Chelsea was hired as an on-the-scene reporter for KidStar Radio, KDFC-AM in San Francisco. If you knew her then, you know she was in love with the Smashing Pumpkins. Imagine her thrill when she was chosen to interview celebrities at the 1996 Tibetan Freedom Concert in Golden Gate Park in San Francisco. Oh, sure, all those Hollywood actors and headlining musicians like Bjork, Beck, Beastie Boys, and others made for fun, fascinating conversation, but "Billy Corgan and James Iha?! Oh my God! Oh my God! Oh my God!"

She shivered at the prospect. Wearing her ever-present silver choker with a heart-shaped charm engraved "Billy C," she entered their backstage tent. She was at the end of a long line of adult TV, print, and radio reporters brought in one by one. As Chelsea stepped up for her interview, the first words of her report were: "Billy, you're a lot taller than I expected you to be!"

Chelsea, the KidStar Radio roving reporter.

Chelsea said Billy stood up, looked down at the top of her head, and laughed. It had to be odd being interviewed by a little kid with a microphone. "And you're a lot shorter than I expected YOU to be." During their talk, he kicked lightly at her yellow Converse sneakers and said, "I'll bet those were made in China." Chelsea held onto that shoe for years because Billy had touched it with his foot.

78 Pen Pals - 1997

When Sabrina was 10 years old, she discovered Sailor Moon, the star of Japanese manga and a television cartoon series. Sabrina looked a lot like Sailor Moon with a pretty face, long blond pigtails, and big, round blue eyes. Sailor Moon was a Japanese schoolgirl who performed magic feats by holding up a compact and shouting, "Make UP!" The cartoons were sanitized for American TV, and Sabrina was completely enamored. She heard about the Kinokuniya Book Store in Japantown, San Francisco, and asked if we could go there to buy authentic Japanese manga.

Sabrina had struggled with reading, so I was enthused with her desire to read more books. It didn't matter that they opened from back to front, and the pictures and text were placed from right to left. Some of the books were translations, so anytime Sabrina wanted to read words, I was all in.

Chelsea, always interested in an outing, came along for the adventure. While Sabrina was looking at Sailor Moon books, and I was busy censoring out the ones with explicit sex stories, Chelsea wandered off to the magazine racks. All the magazines were in Japanese, but that didn't deter Chelsea. She paged through them until one magazine with a picture of the Smashing Pumpkins on the cover caught her eye. She looked at the pictures in the feature article and then turned to the last page. There, in English, was a three-line ad for pen pals. "Please write to this address if you would like a Japanese pen pal," followed by the address.

Of course, Chelsea wrote a letter, which was published in the next magazine issue, along with her newly acquired Post Office Box address. She received 78 requests to be an American pen pal. We went to the Kinokuniya Stationary Store across from the bookstore on our next visit, where she bought all the "kawaii" or cute stationery she could afford. When we got home, she began writing. I screened the letters she received and only removed four; proposals of marriage from four adult men. The rest were sweet attempts at English by Japanese schoolgirls and boys.

Chelsea kept up correspondence with most of them, making sure she used "kawaii" stationery, and answered questions that were specific and individual. I suggested she write one letter and make copies, but she shook her head and answered, "Oh, Motherrrrrr." She loved writing each one of those letters and looked in her Post Office mailbox every day for the usual stack of colorful envelopes. Her Japanese pen-pals (and a few from Hong Kong and Malaysia) were prolific letter-writers. Obviously, so was Chelsea.

Pen pal letters.

Keeping pen pal mail organized.

Her Own Private High School - 1998-2001

Chelsea wanted to attend a private high school, and she applied to many in the Bay Area. She was accepted at several, but she especially wanted to attend Dominican High School, an all-girls school that had a strong music program. Unfortunately, I couldn't afford the tuition, and she was not given a scholarship.

Chelsea withdrew into her bedroom for a few days after I told her the cost was more than I could bear. She emerged one evening with a paper in hand. Chelsea had written out her plan for her own private high school. She would attend Tamiscal High School, an alternative home-study program for students who had ambitions in sports, dance, acting, modeling, and other full-time professional careers.

Chelsea showed me how she could attend the local Community College for advanced music classes that were not available at Redwood High School—music theory, cello, and composition. Twice a week, she would take the bus into San Francisco and attend classes and private piano lessons at the San Francisco Music Academy. I was afraid she would miss being part of a high school community, but Chelsea didn't want the typical cookie-cutter experience. How could I say no?

An Indigent American Abroad - 1999

Chelsea Faith has been called many things, but this title, Indigent American Abroad, spoke to a mother's panic. Chelsea's pen-pal friendships evolved over the first year. Some of her pen pals came to the States with student tours over the summer. Chelsea asked me to take her to Seattle, San Francisco, and Santa Clara to greet large groups of Japanese girls in person. The tour guides would often have to translate their conversations, and that was when Chelsea decided to study Japanese at the College of Marin. The following year, we welcomed her new and dear friend, Erika Seito, into our home for a visit. When Chelsea was just 15 years old and felt she knew enough of the language to get by, she accepted Erika's invitation to visit Japan on her own. I couldn't afford to go with her. Sabrina and I stayed home.

Chelsea with her friends in Gunma, Japan.

It was on that first trip to see Erika that she discovered her passport was missing—on the day before she was to return home! She had budgeted her money so frugally that she only had enough funds for snacks on the flight home.

On the day she was supposed to leave, Chelsea and Erika took the Bullet Train from Gunma Prefecture into Tokyo. Two young girls on their own in that immense city—can you imagine? They found their way to the American Embassy, where Chelsea was declared an Indigent American Abroad.

Chelsea's Japanese passport photo - "No smiling, please!"

Back in Fairfax, California, I was on the phone with the State Department in Washington, DC, for three days in a row. Dozens of calls. Money sent by wire. Verification of her ID. My personal information was investigated and cleared. Their main fear seemed to be that I might be in the business of selling passports. Finally, Chelsea was issued a new passport in Tokyo. As you can well imagine, every flight she took for years after that brought second looks, pat-downs, and stern questioning from airline boarding agents. An American passport issued in Tokyo??? Wonders never cease with this girl.

First Job - 2000

Chelsea's first job was in the Classical Room at Marin Tower Records. Often, customers would come in looking for suggestions, take one look at the baby-faced, 17-year-old Chelsea, and ask her to get the manager. She would patiently ask a few questions, then pull a few CDs, and the customer would wind up buying exactly what she suggested. This girl had classical chops.

From Raves to International Clubs - 2001-2016

Chelsea's early music gigs were self-created. She and her boyfriend, Sean O'Shea, would rent a recreation hall or some other big room, set up music equipment, invite other musicians to play, and put up posters advertising a party. They called themselves DEF SF. I attended several of these parties. The music was loud, and the crowds were eclectic, ranging from young high schoolers (no alcohol was served) to women my age who were "trance dancing" on the floor by themselves. My guess is they were former hippies or New Agers who needed a dance venue. Much of the music was dreamy and ethereal, with a deep bass beat.

Chelsea performing.

It took a long time before Chelsea felt ready to start performing. Although she wrote and recorded a lot of music on her own, she didn't want to be on stage until she felt she was "really good." Is that a Virgo trait? I don't know. At all the early shows, she provided the food for a vegan feast table and charged a small donation for the snacks. That was her contribution. She learned how to run a party from start to finish and took in the lessons on setting up electronics tables.

By the time Chelsea was finally ready to start performing, she had practiced hours each day for several years and written a large repertoire of music she memorized so she could perform live. Electronic Music suited Chelsea's desire to control all aspects of the production. Her style of performance is called Live PA. This meant she would produce the music using her own pre-recorded voice, keyboard, and bass riffs, plus other sounds and samples, all mixed in the moment. In that way, she could turn up the bass if she saw the dancers needed it or slow things down if the night was ending. She blended each composition's beginning and end so there was no gap in the music. Chelsea loved the sense of control she felt

Chelsea performing.

writing and performing electronic music. Although a pianist at heart, electronic music incorporated her intricate melodies into full orchestral production.

The Electronic Music world also suited her neon, iridescent, mixed-pattern, and rainbow-hued clothes. Always a colorful character, the rave culture provided this sparkly girl a home. Chelsea said music and emotions could be seen in colors. Certain notes and emotions could be composed in rainbow hues, glitter, lights, and patterns. She wore her music and her emotions on her sleeve...quite literally.

Throughout her 20s, Chelsea moved from Rec Rooms to performing in high-end clubs and music festivals in San Francisco, Los Angeles, New York, Las Vegas, Berlin, and other smaller cities on the road throughout the West and Midwest. Like a little kid, she was always amazed to see her name on the posters and signs.

Chelsea performing.

Can You Sing?

Chelsea also loved words. She asked for a huge dictionary for Christmas when she was 13 years old and used to study it for fun! She liked to write intricate lyrics taken from her experience but didn't trust her own voice. She used to say, "I whistle better than I sing."

For a while, I encouraged her to sing "...like Diana Krall, who started as a pianist and then started to sing along..." Chelsea shivered in revulsion, even though I thought she had a sweet, whispery, on-key voice. She sang in musical productions at school, but for her, that wasn't good enough. She strove for perfection.

It irked Chelsea that "Club owners don't ask dudes to sing along, only women! I'll sing when I'm accepted as a musician." She liked to work with vocalists who would sing her lyrics. Maria Juur, known as Maria Minerva, and Kara Marie were her favorites. She appreciated their talent because "the voice is an instrument." Maria and Chelsea drove through the Midwest in Chelsea's first car, a big, old, blue Buick that she called "The Living Room" because the blue velour seats were so soft and cushy, like a sofa. They played all sorts of venues in little towns and had a great time! Chelsea made everything fun.

My Fluffy Head - July 11, 2016

The summer before Chelsea died in July 2016, I visited my hometown, Buffalo, New York, to celebrate my mother's 90th birthday. Chelsea was flying from San Francisco to gigs in Chicago and New York City that week. She was a featured performer and workshop leader at the Daphne Festival, a celebration of women in electronic music held at Smart Bar in Chicago the weekend of July 7-10th. The following weekend, she would be performing at the Bossa Nova Civic Club in Brooklyn, New York. The timing was perfect for her to make a stop in Buffalo and celebrate her grammie's birthday.

I picked her up at the Buffalo airport that Sunday in a rental car, and we headed straight downtown to Grammie's birthday party at the Buffalo Club. On the way there, Chelsea showed me several copies of the Chicago's *Reader* magazine with her picture on the cover. She excitedly bubbled, "Mother, I got off the plane in O'Hare and saw my fluffy head on every newsstand!" She said she picked up a few copies for herself, me, and her grandmother. When we arrived at the ornate, red brick building, Chelsea decided to leave the magazine in the car. She said, "Today is Grammie's day. I'll save it for tomorrow," and thoughtfully tucked the magazine away.

We arrived at The Buffalo Club, which was built in the mid-1800s and still had a men's smoking club vibe. Grammie's party was held in the staid, wood-paneled club room on the second floor. The room was lined on either side with floor-to-ceiling bookshelves. A massive fireplace took up most of the far wall. Pictures of Presidents Millard Filmore, Grover Cleveland, and then Vice President Theodore Roosevelt, who were members, were hung between the stacks of books. The men in those portraits looked old and fusty compared to Grammie, who looked vibrant, standing at the top of the stairs, nodding her sassy, platinum pageboy haircut at each of us as we climbed the elegant staircase. In her dressy, cornflower blue pantsuit, Grammie looked much younger than her 90 years. Chelsea said, "Grammie, you look great!" Then she flitted from person to person, reconnecting with her Buffalo cousins, aunts, and uncles.

On Tuesday, we drove to Grammie's apartment for a visit. Chelsea held the Chicago *Reader* magazine in her lap and said, "Maybe now Grammie will understand what I do."

My mother had hopes of Chelsea playing classical piano or maybe becoming a lounge singer, but that wasn't in Chelsea's nature. Grammie was mystified by her choice of a career in electronic music. We walked into the apartment, and Chelsea beamed as she strode over and proudly handed Grammie the magazine with a picture of her head surrounded by clouds on the front cover. My mother glanced at the picture as she led us to her guest bedroom. She said, "I want to give you some of my clothes, Chelsea. They're in the guest room closet." Then she folded the magazine in half and casually tossed it on the bed, saying, "It doesn't look anything like you." I looked over at Chelsea and could see her face drop. She'd hoped to impress her grandmother and instead felt the weight of rejection. My mother didn't mention the magazine again during our visit.

My mother opened the closet doors and brought out some of her more dramatic outfits. There were velvet hats with feathers, a fur coat, several black net "fascinators," which are nets that cover the face, and a long, white leather coat. Chelsea was tall, like my mother, and she was particularly taken with a floor-length, heavy, red wool cape my mother had splurged on in her younger days. When Chelsea tried it on, she twirled around in front of her Grammie and said, "Oooooh, it's me! I LOVE IT!" She looked absolutely stunning in her tall black boots and the cape. It came with a tall red woolen pillbox hat that had curly black lambswool on the top, like a red Teutonic crown.

I could picture her wearing the outfit to a winter performance in Berlin or New York and then taking it off to show her sequined, rainbow self onstage. Of course, that never happened. After Sabrina brought all the items from Chelsea's apartment back to my house, I placed the red cape and hat in my closet. Now, they quietly wait for someone else's dramatic entrance. The only two people I know who could carry it off were my mother and Chelsea.

I think flamboyance may be a heritable trait, but I'm from the skipped generation. My earth-toned monochromatic clothes choices made Chelsea giggle. My look is simple and subdued in sharp contrast to her sequin sparkle. Chelsea may have laughed at my browns and greens, but she also respected the fact that I dressed for myself and no one else.

The one thing we have in common when it comes to clothes is our love of scarves. Now that Chelsea's scarves have been added to my collection, I have hundreds. She picked up the scarf-habit from me, and I wear them every day in honor of her. It's my silent daily nod to her memory. She is always with me.

Chelsea on her way to Berlin...again.

As we sat in the Buffalo airport a few days after Grammie's birthday, Chelsea on her way to New York City and me traveling back to San Francisco, Chelsea told me she was sad Grammie hadn't acknowledged her magazine cover but said, "I still have that cover and interview. It might be my first, but I won't let it be my last." She was making a living playing her own music, and she was getting a lot of positive attention. A friend of hers in Los Angeles, Lulu Danger, was a professional make-up artist, and her husband, Jeremy Danger, was a photographer. They took professional pictures of Chelsea that landed her even more gigs than she already had lined up. At the time of her death, Chelsea knew from the growing number of requests for interviews and future bookings she received that she was ascendant.

After the fire, my mother was interviewed by several major New York television news stations. Months later, as I watched the recorded interviews, I saw, there on the table beside her, the picture of Chelsea on the front of *Reader* magazine. A crease ran right across Chelsea's face. At first that crease made me sad, but then I realized my mother finally had opened that cover, read the article, and understood the respect Chelsea held in the music world. She might not be a lounge singer or classical pianist, but she was well-loved for her electronic music prowess. I wish Chelsea could have seen Grammie showing off that magazine cover on national TV. Chelsea wanted her grandmother's approval, and she finally got it.

Chelsea's first and last magazine cover - the Chicago
"Reader."

I'll Pay You Back - August 2016

One evening, while Chelsea's laundry was churning away in my washer and dryer, she and I sat in my living room sipping champagne. I asked Chelsea why she hadn't asked me for rent money for a long time. It takes a while for a musician to get established, and during Chelsea's early years, she relied on my help to pay the rent on her San Francisco flat. I wondered aloud with a hint of hope in my voice, "You don't need help anymore?"

Chelsea laughed, "How much do you earn per hour?" I make a pretty good living. When I told her, she laughed again, "Mother, I earn ten times that!"

I scoffed, "Yeah, but I work more hours."

"Not for long! I'm going to buy you a house to pay you back for all the times you paid my rent."

Now it was my turn to laugh, "I already have a house! Why don't you buy Sabrina a house; she needs it more than I do." It all felt like a joke, but I was truly relieved that she was on sound financial footing with her music career. I knew she was working often and at ever-increasingly large clubs and music venues. It felt good to know Chelsea was doing well.

With a solemn face, Chelsea stated, "I will pay off your mortgage, and I will buy Sabrina a house. I mean it." Then, Chelsea turned her attention to the champagne and asked, "Is there any orange juice in the refrigerator? I want to make a mimosa." As a matter of fact, there was orange juice, and Chelsea topped off the champagne in our glasses. Mimosas were her favorite drink. "Cheers!" We clinked glasses and never spoke of money again. Five months later, she was dead.

Throughout the summer days of 2017, I continued sifting through old photos of my girls and wrote Chelsea stories for Facebook. Every night, I breathlessly fought my way through a maze of hallways, looking for an exit as flames crackled closer and louder. I could see my hands, Chelsea's hands, pressing on walls and pushing debris out of the way, crying for help and not finding an escape. And in the early morning hours, I would wake up sobbing and panicked, not knowing where I was until reality punched me in the gut. Chelsea was dead. Again. I looked for five things I could see, four I could touch, three I could hear, two I could smell. Blankets, my own hands, the windows, and...sometimes I heard screaming and smelled smoke and felt the heat of flames surrounding me. I couldn't count. I couldn't breathe. I just fell back on the wet pillow and cried.

As those summer days wore on, daydreams and nightmares spilled together, pulling me ever closer to the opening of a new school year. My leave of absence would be over soon. I had to return to work in September 2017. It felt wrong for the rest of the world to go on when Chelsea was dead. Didn't they know? How could bills and responsibilities make sense when my world had stopped? It wasn't fair.

Could I do this? When people say, "You're so strong," I don't think they realize strength isn't the issue. There is no choice. We do what we must do. Period.

Chapter 19

Back to Normal

Wildfires - September and October 2017

California broke out in wildfires across the state. I had just resumed teaching after having left in December 2016 for the duration of that school year. The break, therapy, and nearly daily grief groups had helped me learn some strategies on how to cope with my deep grief and recurring nightmares. Night visions of seeing the burning horror through Chelsea's eyes continued.

Anchoring sensory techniques, noting what I saw, felt, heard, and smelled, would bring me back from the flames shooting from warehouse windows and roaring flames in a crematorium furnace by day. Those visions could be countered well enough for me to return to work. I was able to cope.

Then fire swept through Sonoma County, edging closer, destroying whole towns. The destruction felt personal, as though the element of fire was following me, burning up my sanity wherever I turned. I became highly wary of fireplaces in homes and restaurants, of birthday and decorative candles, and even the gas stovetop in my own kitchen. I purchased a small electric toaster oven so I wouldn't hear the whoosh of flames start up in my gas oven that sounded just like the fiery crematorium. Fire knew where I was and was ready to pounce. I could feel it sneaking up on me just behind my right shoulder.

In the classrooms, I put on a smile and pretended to be normal, unaffected by the fire in my brain. I managed to continue my work as a literacy specialist for the kindergartners in our school who needed a little extra help learning their letters and sounds. The children knew nothing of my loss, and that helped.

It was the concern of some adults around me that made me feel uncomfortable. I sent out an email to the faculty and staff saying that I did not want hugs or even to talk about the tragedy. Most listened to my plea and gave me a nod or smile. That helped. I avoided the adults who walked up to me with arms outstretched, head tilted, and a sad look on their faces. It was the exuding of sympathy and extra "kindness" that caused me to break down in sobs.

A few other incidents also broke through my calculated calm. The annual faculty CPR training included a roomful of Resuscitation-Annie practice dummies laid out on the cafeteria tables, looking exactly like 36 dead bodies. I gasped in horror and ran from the room.

Another time, I walked into a classroom and looked down at a picture one kindergartner had drawn of a house on fire. His stick characters had their arms waving up in the air and their mouths the shape of shocked circles as they watched their home succumb to the flames. I stumbled backward away from the little boy's side. Because wildfires had broken out in Northern California, not far from our homes and school, it was only natural for the little ones to draw what they feared and what they saw on the TV news. Just the same, seeing that drawing was enough to send me running out of the room so I could cry in my office. Reminders of the horror were everywhere.

As the fires north of us grew, the smoke moved south toward our school. Children were kept indoors during recess because the air quality was so poor. I stayed indoors because the air smelled like Chelsea's body. In my mind, the air became Chelsea's body. I missed her viscerally, and every breath smelled of her. While the fires up north raged, I stayed at home, crying. It took over a week for the smoke to clear out of Marin County, and I hid from the smell of tragedy until it had dissipated. When I ventured back outside, Chelsea was gone from the air. In a way, I missed breathing her in. I missed her everyday presence in my body.

BBQ

After another few months of isolation, a friend suggested I join her for dinner at a local restaurant. She was trying to get me out of the house for something other than work, therapy, or grief groups. I reluctantly said, "Okay." As soon as I walked through the door of the restaurant, I knew something was wrong, but I couldn't quite put my finger on it. Sorrow welled up inside of me. Why?

Then the smell of a wood fire and cooked meat hit me full force. The restaurant was filled with the smell of Chelsea's body. People were eating barbecued meat all around me, and the idea was nauseating. I tried to sit there being friendly, smiling stupidly, talking about nothing, but after a few minutes of that charade, I made my excuses, saying I felt sick, and ran out of the restaurant. All the memories of the funeral home and crematorium swam through my brain on the drive home.

They say smell is a key connection to memory. This is true.

To this day, I cannot eat BBQ ribs or chicken. When someone else eats it, I look away. Chelsea was a vegan from childhood because the idea of eating animal flesh made her gag. She was probably watching me and laughing at the cosmic nature of this joke. I am not vegan nor even vegetarian, but my attitude toward charred meat changed because of the smell, the smell of Chelsea in a funeral home.

Chelsea outside the Vegan House restaurant.

Part Three

Before the Trial

Chapter 20

Ghost Ship Trial in the News

November 2017

TV news reports surrounding the upcoming criminal trial started heating up in the Fall of 2017. For unknown reasons, the warehouse Derick Almena rented was called Ghost Ship. The name was fitting because the deadly fire left the place gutted. I began to wonder who Max Harris was and how he was involved. Who were these two men, and why were they the only two people charged? And who were the people the newscasters kept referring to as the "Chorings" or "Ings?" What were the facts behind the fire? I couldn't see the big picture.

Derick Almena didn't do himself any favors by making himself the center of the growing media firestorm. I watched old videos of his interviews, first with *Good Morning America* and later from his jail cell. The man acted like he was somehow justified in operating outside the law because of his devotion to Art. To me, he looked more like a pirate than an artist, buying up wooden artifacts and furniture on the cheap from artisans in

Bali, India, Thailand, and Nepal and selling them for a profit back home in the States. He filled up an empty warehouse with his collected junk, then put an ad on Craigslist to attract renters, who would help finance his storage unit, calling the warehouse a "hybrid museum, sunken pirate ship, shingled funhouse, and guerrilla gallery." He seemed more of an empty vessel than his Ghost Ship.

On the evening of November 17, 2017, I sat in my living room and turned on the TV news to see a report on the Ghost Ship investigation, including footage of an older woman as she walked through a parking lot, shielding her face from the cameras with a piece of paper. Her name was printed at the bottom of the screen: Chor Ng. That was the name I'd heard mentioned in previous reports about the Ghost Ship fire investigation, so I paid attention. I was stunned to learn that Chor Ng, named as the owner of the warehouse, had just received a $3.1 million payout from her insurance company. What gall! She was profiting off the death of 36 people. The report shifted to an interview with Curtis Briggs, who was the attorney defending Max Harris. He said Chor Ng owned several buildings in the Bay Area and, "She essentially created this fire trap by being a slumlord. She didn't see human life; she saw dollar signs." That statement gave me chills.

I naturally wondered, "If she was the owner, why wasn't she charged?" This woman received more than $3 million less than a year after the warehouse was destroyed by fire. Why had she taken out such a large insurance policy on an old building in a poor neighborhood that could only be described as a "tear down?" Could she have had something to do with the fire? The money seemed to point in that direction.

I had a lot more questions after that news report, so I sat down at my dining room table, opened my laptop, and typed "Ghost Ship Fire" into my Google Search.

I clicked on a link about Ghost Ship from the National Fire Protection Association: "...we saw 36 people perish in the Oakland Ghost Ship fire, a former warehouse being used as living and entertainment space. The fire raised questions about appropriate permitting for its use, code enforcement, lack of fire alarms, and the role of occupants in understanding the impact of their surroundings on their own personal safety." *NFPA TODAY* "Connecting the Dots on Today's Fire Problem" by James Pauley - June 21, 2017.

That was my first glimpse into the plodding litany of information about permits, inspections, and codes that would later fill the trial. Those facts were certainly important, but they weren't giving me insight into the events of that terrible night.

Every day that I wasn't working, I got out of bed early, took my laptop into the living room, and stretched out on the sofa, sitting sideways with my legs extended. I propped pillows up behind me, placed my laptop on a flat pillow on my thighs, got comfortable, and spent hours each day looking up the news articles I had been unable to digest immediately after the fire. The first anniversary of the fire was approaching, and I began to feel a shift from not wanting to acknowledge my daughter's death to desperately craving a means to close the circle of birth and death. I brought her into this world and needed to be with her when she left. I had to find out how and why she died.

I mostly studied the Bay Area Newsgroup articles that had been written in the weeks leading up to Harris and Almena's arrest. *The East Bay Times* won a Pulitzer Prize for its thorough coverage of the fire. Its articles were descriptive and helped me get some perspective on what led up to the fire, but one article that laid out a timeline for the firefight stunned me.

The article described the growing concern of friends looking for Chelsea and others who were missing on the night of the fire. I wasn't looking at social media that night, so I could understand how I might have missed that. But when I read about the residents of the building screaming at firefighters to go upstairs and rescue the victims, I was incredulous. The article described people climbing on cars and a ladder, breaking windows, pulling down the fence surrounding the side yard, and calling out to the people inside, trying to help them escape.

When I arrived on the scene, I didn't see any of that. At first, I thought these stories of desperation and chaos must be lies. The young people I saw that night were crowded around the windows of Wendy's, silent and morose. My impression when I arrived was that there were no victims, mainly because there was no outcry. I was the only adult my age in the parking lot, aside from fire and police officers, and I had begun to think my presence was an overreaction. With no ambulances rushing to the hospital and no injured or burned victims in the parking lot, it looked to me like everyone who was there got out safely, including my Chelsea.

What I didn't know was that on arriving half an hour after the fire had begun, I walked into a cloud of depression. Energy spent; the young people sat in stunned silence. Now, while reading the article, I learned that only one of the victims was a resident at the warehouse. All those people I had seen sitting and talking quietly amongst themselves in the Wendy's parking lot were people who lived at the warehouse and had escaped. Their possessions were burned, but all but one of the people they loved were safe. Their huddled exhaustion was not a reflection of the terrible reality; thirty-six people were left behind in the fire.

I buried my face in my hands and cried guilty tears when it hit me that I hadn't screamed at the firefighters to save my daughter. Yes, I was furious when they just seemed to be milling around the building, but it looked like there were no casualties, let alone deaths. I arrived after all the commotion. I was too late. Chelsea and her friends were already dead.

No one in that parking lot who had been in the burning warehouse came up to me and told me what happened. Not one. The hushed, insular stillness of the survivors led me to believe Chelsea was alive, not that they had given up. On reading the account of that night, I felt betrayed by the survivors, the police, and the firefighters, allowing me to desperately hope from midnight until dawn that my daughter was alive. I had to read about what they knew a year later in a newspaper.

Fortunately, most of the articles I read after that account were tributes to the fire victims: 9 at first, then 24, then 36. I drew some comfort from the respectful tone of the stories. Eventually, I found investigative articles and interviews that described the conditions in the warehouse prior to the fire, including drawings of the confusing building layout. A graphic in *The New York Times* showed the exit path from the second-story dance floor to the front door. It was marked with arrows, depicting a stairway and ramp, then a winding maze around pianos, chairs, and other obstacles that kept the victims from finding the door that led outside. I shivered when I pictured Chelsea and her friends clawing their way around a labyrinth that led nowhere.

There were accounts describing Derick Almena as a rogue character who flaunted the laws regarding safety. Neighbors had frequently complained to police of noisy parties and garbage strewn in front of the building and in a large side lot. They worried about fire and rats. Max Harris was said to be the event director who managed the party that night. Then, they were both arrested.

Two parallel strains of concern filled my brain: What was the sequence of events on the night of December 2, 2016, and what circumstances led up to such a massive and deadly fire?

Perhaps the answer could be found in pictures of the Ghost Ship warehouse taken before the fire. A simple Google search showed me what I was looking for. The place was an appalling maze of desiccated wooden junk and debris. People lived in several full-sized RVs and travel trailers parked inside the warehouse, along with loft-like room structures built from logs, doors, countless old pianos, organs, wooden pallets, and other miscellaneous collected garbage. It looked like tapestries were also draped for privacy. Was there gasoline in the RV fuel lines? The vehicles must have been driven inside. I also saw propane tanks next to a sink. What was that about? Hot water? Cooking? Then it occurred to me: everything in that warehouse was flammable. That place was a death trap.

The place was huge, 10,000 square feet. I read that there were 25 people living downstairs, while Almena, his wife, and three children lived upstairs. The upstairs space was also where events were held. Almena had separate bedrooms for the children and another for himself and his wife, as well as a kitchen area. These living quarters were off-limits to guests. A wall divided this home unit in the front of the second floor from the event space in the center and rear of the building.

The event space consisted of an old sofa, chairs, a smattering of small tables, and a large, wooden, canopied "Bali bed." The center of the room was covered in an expansive, faded, oriental-style rug. The floor, walls, and wooden rafters were strewn with broken wheels, toys, lamps, salvaged paintings, tapestries, and dumpster tchotchkes of every kind. No windows were visible since they were behind the flimsy walls of Almena's private family space.

I was beginning to understand why Chelsea felt "jaded" about this place. It was supposed to be an "art house," but it was just a cluttered, dirty, dark mess. This was the room where 36 radiant young people died. I tried to shake off the gloom as it descended upon me once again. I snapped my laptop shut, letting it rest, hot and damning on my thighs, and sank back into the pillows on my sofa. I lay there until the heaviness in my bones subsided enough for me to climb the stairs to bed.

That night, nightmares gripped me again, but this time, I saw myself surrounded by the debris I'd seen in the pictures. Wooden wheels, lamps, dolls, fabric, and other junk fell on top of me as I ran down pointless hallways, looking for an escape. I woke up fighting off the sheet that covered my head, batting at it as though it were on fire, sobbing in confusion. Then came the devastating realization flooding me all over again. Chelsea was dead.

Everyone grieves differently. Sabrina and many of the parents and siblings of the victims felt it necessary to turn away from the horror and focus on a positive future. I was different. For me to begin healing, I needed the truth rather than the chaotic, imagined terror that filled my brain. I continued my study of the news reports and investigative articles for another six months. The cause of the fire was still unknown. What was the spark? Why did so many people die that night? It felt inexplicable. News reports and online searches left me with more questions. Then, there was the question of who Derick Almena and Max Harris were. Perhaps a trial would uncover those answers. That was my hope. Then, right after Sabrina and Joe's first wedding anniversary in June 2018 came the bad news. There would be no trial.

Chapter 21

Plea Bargain and The Families' Objections

June 29, 2018

I opened my laptop on the dining room table to read my emails that late June morning and was taken aback by a short message from Stephanie Lynch, my Victims and Witnesses court liaison, saying a plea bargain had been reached in the case. What? Without consulting the families of the victims, Nancy O'Malley, the Alameda County District Attorney, had decided to settle the trial of Derick Almena and Max Harris with a plea deal. My face burned with anger. She betrayed us. She was the professional who was supposed to lead the charge toward truth. Instead, she turned and walked away. Could it be that she didn't want to spend the money on a lengthy trial? Could it be as simple as that? Or was there something else she wanted to avoid? The plea bargain felt like a punch in the gut. My head was throbbing, and my stomach churned as I immediately responded to Stephanie, letting her know this decision was unacceptable.

A few days later, Stephanie replied that the assistant

district attorneys, David Lim and Autrey James, had agreed to hold a meeting in the District Attorney's office in the Alameda Courthouse with any members of the victims' families who wanted an explanation of the plea deal. Although none of us had spoken to each other, ten family members decided independently to show up to protest the DA's unilateral decision. We gathered in the office lobby until a young woman directed us to take a seat and wait for the two assistant DAs in one of the smaller conference rooms.

I took a seat in one of the stiff metal chairs near the head of a large wooden table. There were two young men sitting across from me. One was a friend of some of the victims, and the other was a brother of a girl who had died. Several couples sat at the far end of the table, and a few other women were clustered together near the center. I assumed at first they were all mothers, but two of the women said they were aunts. We introduced ourselves as we waited for Assistant District Attorneys David Lim and Autrey James to arrive. I wanted to remember the names of the people sitting with me; I had a notebook in front of me, but in my nervousness, I forgot to pick up a pen.

Autrey James, a large, heavy-set African American man who would have looked in place on a football field, filled the doorway as he entered the room. He pulled up a chair at the head of the table and sat comfortably, nodding at the people gathered around the table with a warm smile on his face. I immediately liked him and wondered if he agreed or disagreed with his boss's decision to give the trial away. I wanted him to be on our side. I wanted him to fight for a trial. He looked like a guy who could win any fight.

David Lim strode into the room dressed in a well-tailored suit. He looked precise to me, a man with answers. Why wasn't his meticulous judgment being used to lead a trial? Then I shook my head. Perhaps I was jumping to conclusions too soon. What could clothes tell me?

David Lim was a handsome Asian American man who held himself upright in a tall, confident stance at the head of the table while he explained the terms of the deal. He nodded at the rest of us in a no-nonsense manner, then said, "This is the deal: Almena and Harris will plead no contest to manslaughter. Derick Almena will get nine years, and Max Harris will get six years in the local county jail. With time off for good behavior and time spent in jail awaiting trial, this amounts to three and a half years for Almena and two years for Harris."

The young man who lost his sister half-jumped up from his seat and shouted, "That's outrageous! It's not even a slap on the wrist!"

One woman let out a sob, and her sister held her hand. Were they twins? They looked alike with similar faces and had long hair. Both wore soft dresses. I wished at that moment I had brought someone with me. My anger was boiling over, and I needed someone to keep me calm.

The couple I'd seen interviewed on television immediately after the fire spoke up. The neatly dressed young dad with a shaved bald head and black glasses said, "This is justice? We need a trial! Why weren't we consulted on this plea deal?"

His gentle-looking wife turned hard with anger. "My daughter is dead, and these two men spend a few years in jail? This isn't right!" Her husband put his hand on her shoulder and nodded in agreement.

Angry shouts popcorned around the table. I asked, "Is this just about money? Is a trial too expensive?"

Another mother joined in with my questions, "Is it money or just about putting this case in some virtual 'win' column?"

One couple had driven in from out of town, and I had the impression they were frazzled. She had long, gray hair falling to her shoulders and a deeply sad expression. The man was bearded and sat in silent accord with her. She asked, "What can we do to turn this around?"

Both attorneys shook their heads. They seemed rattled by our negative response. Autrey James said, "You were consulted about..."

Everyone shouted at once.

"We were not consulted!"

"We got an email after the fact!"

"No one called me for my opinion. We found out in the worst possible way. We got an email, and then we heard it on the news!"

"How can we fight this and get a trial?"

I was astounded that these two intelligent men would think we'd be pleased with a plea bargain, and a bad one, at that. I looked intently at both attorneys. David Lim had a surprised look on his face, and Autrey James looked impassive, just nodding and taking in our enraged shouts. Almost simultaneously, they both said, "The decision is final."

David Lim said something about the DA's decision being written in stone, and all we could do was write an impact statement to get our opinions into the official court record. "You can state how the loss of your loved one affects the living."

Autrey James agreed, "It's a done deal. Plea bargains are never rescinded."

Someone said, "Thirty-six people died, and this is the district attorney's response?"

A short, dark-haired woman asked, "Can we use our impact statements to affect the sentencing?"

Again, both attorneys said "No" at the same time.

A man and a woman stood up together and argued that we should write letters and speak out publicly against this injustice. "Our children died because of criminal negligence, and we need to speak up."

I didn't really know any of these people, but suddenly, I felt a warm camaraderie with them. I also felt a little guilty for not listening to their names when we were introduced. I was too embarrassed to ask again that day but vowed to listen more carefully the next time we met, convinced there would be a next time.

I agreed with the others that we needed to stick together in our common cause. We walked out of that meeting together, talking about ways to get our message out to the public. At the foot of the Alameda Courthouse steps, we stopped and worked out a plan. As much as each of us dreaded it, we all agreed to talk with the newspaper and TV reporters who continually asked for interviews, stating why we felt a trial was necessary.

Once home, we spread the word via Facebook and private messages. Many of the families of the 36 victims who lived out of town and could not attend that meeting also agreed to speak out. Most of us wanted the trial reinstated. A few did not because they wanted the reminders of their loss to end. Everyone I spoke with felt the sentence was too lenient. Our desire for justice was drowned out by the district attorney's unilateral decision. We'd already been told that nothing we could write or say would make a difference in the outcome, but at least we could be heard.

I drove home that afternoon feeling slightly energized. I wasn't just crying; I was doing something. I belonged to a circle of grieving families, but we were more than a grief group; we had made the decision to act. Since writing is my thing, as soon as I arrived home, I sat down with a tall glass of cold water at my dining room table and wrote an article for the *Marin IJ*.

My Article—*Marin Independent Journal*—July 1, 2018, Editorial by Colleen Dolan

I am the mother of Chelsea Faith Dolan, "Cherushii," one of the 36 young people who died in the Ghost Ship fire in Oakland. If you're a fan of the Fairfax Scoop, you probably saw her there. Chelsea was larger than life in many ways, and her "Scoop Disco Night" was a local legend. Chelsea loved growing up in Marin, and she loved performing her music around the world. She was one of the kindest, most colorful human beings on the planet. How can she be gone?

Recently, the Oakland District Attorney accepted a plea bargain in the Ghost Ship criminal trial without the input from the families of the victims. The two men directly responsible for the fire hazards and the death of those 36 beautiful young souls will be sentenced on August 9th and 10th. Of course, there were other people guilty of greed, neglect, and apathy surrounding Ghost Ship, but they were not brought up on criminal charges. While these two pathetic men are guilty of inviting 36 people to their deaths for a mere $10 apiece, even more culpable are the owners, agencies, and utilities who saw the dangerous conditions in their official capacities and did nothing.

Supposedly, the plea bargain spared families from being exposed to "...graphic photos of the victims...and having to relive the night of December 2nd." Oh, really? We relive that night over and over, imagining the horror, or in my case, remembering what it felt like

to stand outside in the cold, breathing in the toxic
smoke and watching the fire consume the building,
desperately hoping my extraordinary daughter wasn't
trapped inside. I saw my daughter's blackened hair and
face and kissed her goodbye. What photo could be
worse than that?

No defense or plea bargain could erase the guilt of
these two stupid men and the other people who knew
about the deadly conditions at that decrepit warehouse
but allowed people to live there and invite
unsuspecting guests. The deaths of all those beautiful
people, who didn't know about the frequent fires or the
blocked exits, were completely preventable. A plea
bargain simply keeps the bureaucratic mistakes and
apathy from being exposed. That is as traumatic and
insulting as any graphic photograph of my daughter
and the other victims. I am traumatized by my
daughter's death, but I am determined to say my piece
now, then follow in Chelsea's life path of forgiveness,
love, and exuberant joy."

It was the first time I had gathered my thoughts in some kind of
logical sequence. By the time I finished typing, I felt a sad little
quiver at the corners of my lips, almost like smiling.

After I finished the article, I returned the call of a reporter
from the Channel 2 news team and invited the 3-person crew
to come to my home and talk about what had happened. Two
days later, they were in my living room filming as I spoke about
the neglect of the two men arrested and the incompetence of
the local agencies who had seen the dangers of the warehouse
and walked away. Over the next few days, I sat back on my sofa
and watched other men and women from our group of

bereaved family members interviewed on the various TV stations around the Bay Area. It felt good, like I was part of a movement, a cause larger than my own grief.

Reporters from local newspapers wrote articles and editorials on our behalf. At least three of us wrote letters to District Attorney Nancy O'Malley stating why we felt the owners and neglectful government agents should be included in the criminal charges and that there should be a trial. We never received a response. After several weeks, I was satisfied we had done what we could to let the world know a plea bargain was not justice. Only a trial would expose the truth.

After the brief flurry of interviews and articles, TV News broadcasts stopped mentioning the Ghost Ship trial. My writing and interviews were finished. I felt let down, and a simmering depression boiled over into bleak helplessness. Then, something else caught my attention on the news. Each evening at 6:00, I sat transfixed on my living room sofa, waiting for the TV news to cycle through all the events of the day. A human-interest story mesmerized me. My whole being merged with scenes of a mother orca whale pushing her dead baby's body through the waves for two weeks. Day after day, she tried to reintegrate her dead calf into the pod. They traveled the Pacific coast of Canada and the Northwest United States. I watched her progress as she continually nudged her baby to the surface, trying to keep her alive through sheer momentum and will. I held my breath through the evening news each night, waiting for the brief Whale Update, hoping somehow the baby would suddenly start swimming on her own. Through my writing, my Facebook posts, and my hopes for a trial, I was that mother whale, blowing life into Chelsea's lungs.

Judge Nixon was one of five judges assigned to the Ghost Ship trial. L-R: David Lim, Autrey James, Kendra Miller, Derick Almena, Jeffrey Krasnoff, Judge Nixon

Chapter 22

Sentencing, Impact Statements, a Trial

August 17, 2018

When the morning of the sentencing hearing arrived, I was wrung out. The nightmare came, as usual, about 3:00 a.m. I didn't dare go back to sleep for fear of reigniting the terrifying dreams. I got dressed, though I cannot recall what clothes I pulled on that day. A dress, I supposed, out of respect for the court. Sorrow ran down my cheeks as I drove to the Oakland courthouse. Dense, black weariness weighed down on my shoulders. I listened to the GPS voice tell me what lane I should be in and when to get off at the Jackson Street exit. I obeyed dutifully. The car and my body felt sluggish. What was the use of this empty exercise?

I parked my car in the Oakland Museum parking lot and crossed the street to the Alameda Courthouse. I pulled out my phone, hoping for a message from Sabrina, and saw she had left a voicemail for me. She was on her way from her job as a dog walker but might be a little late. I called her back and told her,

"I'll meet you upstairs. The courtroom is on the 5th floor. I'll save you a seat." Then, I walked into the courthouse alone.

I held my tote bag up to my chest protectively. In it, my impact statement felt fragile. Was it good enough? I headed toward the elevators, but they were packed with people, so I trudged up the stairs, feeling bewildered. Where was I going? The DA's office was on the second floor of the huge building. Were we meeting in the same conference room where we had met to talk about the plea bargain last month? About 40 or 50 friends and family members of the victims gathered in the echoing vestibule in front of the elevators, all wearing neatly pressed slacks or dresses, all grim-faced. None of them looked familiar. Where were my nameless comrades?

A distracted, middle-aged woman with short, straight brown hair led us in a clump down a short hallway away from the DA's office and through glass double doors to a large, windowless meeting room on the second floor. The two prosecuting attorneys and other court personnel stood in the front of the room. Family and friends who would make their statements in the courtroom that day sat in metal folding chairs at long metal folding tables. The only other furniture was a portable whiteboard in the front of the room. The nondescript room felt cold. I felt miserable and oddly alone. Sabrina wasn't with me.

District Attorney Nancy O'Malley finally met with us for only the second time, the first time being at The Family Center in the Alameda County Sheriff's building immediately after the fire in December 2016. She was shorter than I remembered. Her messy blond hair and wrinkled suit gave me the impression that she was addressing people who meant little to her. As she stood in the front of the room, people angrily called out how upset we were over the plea bargain. Not only had we not had a say in her decision, but the delivery could not have been more impersonal. Someone shouted out, "Email. We found out by email!"

A man's voice called out, "Will charges be brought against the owner of the building?" The DA's answer was a string of words about doing everything she could in a professional manner, but she never answered the question.

Then DA Nancy O'Malley dropped the bomb that Judge Morris Jacobson, who had arranged the terms of the plea deal, had taken a leave of absence. She wouldn't say why he had to leave but said another judge, Judge James Cramer, was going to preside over the sentencing.

One of the mothers in our group asked, "Is he even familiar with the case?"

DA O'Malley mumbled something like, "Of course," and hurriedly left the room. When she was gone, we were reminded once again by Autrey James and David Lim, the assistant DAs, that although we didn't like the decision, it was a "done deal." A judge never reverses a plea bargain. I dropped my head; our protest articles and interviews were useless. We had acted and failed. I sank back into stagnant despair.

I had written my impact statement as a direct address to the defendants, but at the last moment, Judge Cramer sent a message through our attorneys telling us to address him and not the defendants, Almena and Harris. I sat at one of the tables in the barren room, making last-minute edits, but my message remained the same: This was not justice. We all picked up our papers and headed out to the elevators that would take us to the courtroom in Department 11. Where was Sabrina? I needed her, but she hadn't arrived yet. What if she didn't make it before the courtroom doors closed? Tension balled my neck and shoulders into knots. I tried to take three cleansing breaths, but the air that should have entered my lungs got stuck in my throat.

Stephanie Lynch from the Victims and Witness office greeted us at the elevators, led us to the courtroom, and directed us to our seats on the left side of the gallery. The more I spoke with Stephanie, the more I liked her. She was a tall woman with a warm demeanor. Stephanie always greeted me with a smile, and during the pre-trial hearings, she made sure I knew about courtroom procedures and etiquette. Looking around for Sabrina, Stephanie understood my anxiety and kept the seat next to me empty for my younger daughter. I turned around and took in the sad faces of the victims' family members and friends packed into the courtroom. We sat quietly, waiting for the proceedings to begin. I recognized a few of the people from our meeting in the district attorney's office, and we nodded sadly at one another. Sorrow hung in the air. My spirit lifted slightly as Sabrina tiptoed through the double doors at the back of the courtroom, wearing her brown flannel shirt and corduroy pants from work. She quietly slipped into the seat I'd saved for her. I could breathe again.

The two defendants entered the courtroom through the door nearest the bailiff. Max Harris entered looking emaciated and hunched over with his head hung low. Under his orange jumpsuit, he wore a pastel, tie-dyed t-shirt. His hair was pulled into a bun, showcasing his face and neck tattoos. He stopped at the door for a moment and said something to the bailiff, then was led by his attorney, Curtis Briggs, to the table facing the judge; his back was to the visitors in the gallery. I was angry that he wasn't facing us, the bereaved.

Derick Almena entered next. This was the first I'd seen him in person, though I had watched his long-winded television interviews. He was led into the courtroom by the bailiff and stood at a long podium for a few minutes, whispering and looking at a paper. Then, he was escorted by his attorney, Tony Serra, to the closest defense table.

Like Harris, Almena wore an orange jumpsuit. That was the first thing I noticed. It was rumpled in most places but stretched tight around his belly. The man's long dark hair was pulled taut away from his face in a bun, stretching his eyes slightly. His dark brown goatee couldn't hide the pudginess of his cheeks and neck. His visage, once gaunt, devilish, and threatening, had transformed into a slovenly mask of self-pity.

Almena sat at the table with his head down, seemingly absorbed with the sight of his pasty-white hands folded in front of him. His eyes were half-closed. His mouth was set in a sullen line. No expression crossed his face.

The new judge, James Cramer, quietly entered the courtroom in his black robes and sat still for a moment on the judge's dais. He was slightly gray at the temples with a gray goatee. His eyes shone kindly out toward the people in the gallery. When the courtroom was silent, his first words were an announcement that he would allow every member of the victims' families and their friends unlimited time to speak on the record. Heads nodded in agreement. This is what we, representing our loved ones, had hoped. If there wasn't going to be a trial, at least we would have our say in the official court records. One by one, we would face the judge and stand up for our dead.

The first name called was Sara Hoda. A handsome, dark-haired young man named Cyrus and his lovely, slender mother, Farzaneh left their seats and walked up through the center aisle to a podium. Both wore black. Cyrus adjusted the microphone. I recognized him as the young man who stood up for Sabrina and me at the sheriff's office when a young woman screamed at Sabrina, and I shouted back. Then and now, he had an air of quiet strength. His mother, looking sad and exhausted, stood beside him. She cried silently, and her body shook slightly. I listened carefully, trying to assess my own words beside theirs.

Cyrus' voice was warm at first and then furious, as his words turned from love for his sister and her accomplishments to rage at the two men he called "culture vultures" and the bumbling bureaucracies that failed our loved ones. His words echoed in some far-away place, and I knew in that moment that I was among my people. No one else could know the horror we felt for our beloved children's last moments. No one else could understand the shock of sudden death by fire. I was surrounded by my new family. I was not alone.

Linda and Rich Regan describe Amanda's love of family. (Courtesy of Vicki Ellen Behringer)

Linda Regan spoke next. Her daughter, Amanda, was one of Chelsea's close friends, but we had never met. She and her son, Chris, had traveled from Boston to recount Amanda's loving relationship with her siblings, including her twin brother and a large, extended family. They proudly praised her talent as a sought-after photographer. Amanda had focused her lens on the San Francisco music scene; that's how she and Chelsea met. I stared at Linda, admiring her strong voice and envying her large family, thinking it must be a blessing at a time like this.

As the first few family members spoke, I became increasingly nervous about reading my own statement. The families were called up to speak in some order I didn't understand. The names were not called alphabetically, and because we didn't know the order, a startling frisson of fear ran through each speaker before walking up to the podium. The shock of hearing our children's names read aloud caught each one of us off-guard.

*David and Kim Gregory talk about their effervescent
daughter, Michela Gregory. L-R: Derick Almena, Tony
Serra, Tyler Smith, Max Harris, Family of Michela Gregory.
(Courtesy of Vicki Ellen Behringer)*

Chelsea was number 16. I had expected her name to be called last since she was one of the last, if not the very last, body to be identified. Sabrina and I edged our way from our seats when we heard her name called, "Chelsea Faith Dolan," practically climbing over others' knees to the aisle between the rows of seats. It reminded me of a wedding, families of the victims on the left, families of the defendants on the right. My knees wobbled as I walked forward. Sabrina folded my arm in hers. The papers in my hand shook. Once I began reading, my hand steadied somewhat, perhaps because Sabrina held onto one side of each paper as I read and took each page as I finished reading it and moved on to the next page. Without Sabrina by my side, I could not have read my statement without sobbing. She was and is my rock.

I talked about what I had learned through the media—the ineptitude of the fire department, police, building inspectors, and Child Protective Services, all of whom had entered the building but decided not to write up reports about the unsafe conditions there. I mentioned the owner, who also owned many other properties in Oakland, and wondered if that had anything to do with the fact that she was not brought up on criminal charges. Public utilities were also at fault; PG&E installers had recently added a new Smart Box but did not mention the faulty electrical connections nor the outsized electrical usage for a storage facility. The neglect by all those who touched the warehouse in some official capacity was criminal, in my opinion. I held up a glamorous picture of Chelsea, then a photo of her soot-blackened face to show Almena what he had wrought, which the judge asked me to put down. Then, in a haze, Sabrina and I returned to our seats.

One by one, the 36 victims' names were called. Some of the families told meaningful anecdotes or a history of their loved ones' lives and accomplishments. One mother read her daughter's doctoral thesis out loud because her daughter would never get to read it to her professors. Others read poetry and shared examples of their loved one's artwork. We learned of dreams and ambitions, as well as fresh starts and enduring love. We heard stories of community activism and devoted family loyalty.

Thirty-six young community activists, poets, farmers, artists, musicians, lawyers, dancers, scientists, scholars, teachers, photographers, filmmakers, and psychologists died because people failed to do their jobs and then lied to cover up their incompetence. This group of young people who had gathered for a night of fun were exceptional human beings. They did not deserve to have their lives snatched away suddenly and without reason. Nearly every statement concluded by imploring, "Please reconsider this plea deal and reinstate the trial."

I cringed when Max Harris took to the stand and apologized for all he did and did not do to cause the fire that night. A gangly, thin man, he didn't look threatening, but he did give off an in-your-face counter-culture vibe. I had read in the newspaper about how he had cleaned up before the fire, moving furniture in front of a hitherto unknown back staircase. Only residents of the warehouse would have known it was there. Why would he do that? Now he was apologizing with downcast eyes and a slumped demeanor. The future of 36 young people his age ended that night. He lived on in a shroud of guilt. I didn't hate him, but I didn't feel sorry for him, either.

L-R: Max Harris, Judge Cramer (*Courtesy of Vicki Ellen Behringer*)

Derick Almena took the stand and apologized for not knowing the warehouse was dangerous. He was not a child, but his claim of innocence because "nobody told me" screeched in my head. He went on and on about his plan to have the names of all the victims tattooed on his body, which made the families of the victims nauseous. Then, he outdid himself.

Derick Almena's 14-year-old daughter had just testified about how much she loved and respected her father. She sat in the courtroom beside her mother as Derick told the families of the victims: "I would give my life; I would give my children's lives to get your families back." That did it. The family members in the gallery struggled to keep our mouths shut so we would not be removed from the courtroom, but it was difficult to not jump up and scream at this maniac. We strained in our seats, writhing at the insult. This megalomaniac thought his pseudo-magnanimous statement would please us! He thought we would be grateful to see his willingness to sacrifice his own children for our revenge. What he couldn't see is that we were grieving, not vengeful. We wanted justice, not the wish for more death. I shook my head. What was wrong with this man?

L-R: Derick Almena, Judge Cramer. (Courtesy of Vicki Ellen Behringer)

Judge Cramer listened intently to every statement read aloud. After Max and Almena spoke, he quietly stepped down from the bench and disappeared into his chamber to deliberate. A hush fell over the gallery, and a recess was called. I joined the other families as we filed out of the courtroom. The feeling of resignation hung heavy in the air. We had barely made the short trek down to the DA's office when Stephanie Lynch stopped us and said the judge was ready to finalize the sentence. We returned to the elevator and rode to the 5th floor in silence. It was done.

Judge Cramer walked slowly from his chamber door up to the dais. He sat down, faced out into the waiting crowd, and said, "I have reviewed hundreds of pages of files in the case." He explained that the files included a 23-page letter Almena wrote to a probation officer in which he blamed everyone but himself for the tragedy and described himself as a victim. The judge did not feel Almena had shown remorse.

The judge then shocked us all. It was unprecedented, but he was throwing out the plea bargain. Judge Cramer looked down at the defendants, then shifted his gaze back out to the gallery. "I believe Max Harris is repentant, but because the defendants' cases are tied, both men will be held for trial." Voices broke out in reaction. I turned to Sabrina on my right, who opened her eyes in surprise, and then we both looked back at the people behind us. They were open-mouthed and smiling. A few looked stunned. Like a ripple, the reaction of the victims' families spread out. We turned to one another and hugged, making quiet, celebratory sounds that eventually encircled us. A deep moan rose from the defense side of the gallery. Judge Cramer and the bailiff asked for quiet, and then he repeated, "There will be a trial."

Judge Cramer, Derick Almena, Max Harris. (Courtesy of Vicki Ellen Behringer)

Chapter 23

New York Times Sunday Magazine

December 12, 2018

Feature Story: "Max Harris. He Helped Build an Artists' Utopia. Now He Faces Trial for 36 Deaths There."

I was livid. Just as I had begun to feel a softening of the agony of Ghost Ship and was taking steps to heal with the help of many grief professionals and fellow bereaved parents, I sat on the sofa in my living room and opened the Magazine section of the Sunday *New York Times*. Max Harris' picture was on the cover in lush, Rafael-like splendor. The article was slanted to show off the injustice done to poor Max. The December timing alone was despicable so near the fire anniversary, but the effort to sway a potential jury pool was obvious and sickening. No jury had yet been called, but the probability that potential jurors in Oakland would have read the story in a major, national Sunday Magazine format was inescapable.

Timed to coincide with the second anniversary of the December Ghost Ship fire, the feature story was a long puff piece by a talented staff writer, Elizabeth Weil, portraying Max Harris as a sweet, innocent soul who literally would not hurt a bug. It read like a hagiography. Max was canonized for being vegan, not unlike most of the victims. He was spiritual, not unlike most of the victims. He'd overcome a difficult childhood, not unlike many of the victims. But the victims were not mentioned. This was all about holy Max. Any sympathy I felt for him dissolved with this "poor Max" narrative.

I never felt Max Harris was the evil villain in the story of the Ghost Ship warehouse fire in Oakland, California. He was the lieutenant who recognized the dangers inherent in a firetrap of a building and nervously moved away once but then returned to carry out his boss' orders anyway. I couldn't excuse his mistakes as "just obeying orders" when those mistakes caused the deaths of 36 young people. The fact that he was surprised he would be held responsible for booking the music event in a fire trap, blocking the second exit, and collecting money at the door speaks to his warped view of himself as a gentle, appeasing soul. Max Harris was alive. My daughter, a talented musician, and 35 of her dear friends were dead.

I felt sick reading about Mr. Harris as though he were a waif. He was a young adult, the same age as those who died. The difference is he must have known about the code violations: the web of electrical extension cords, the frayed wiring, the barred windows, the old wooden paraphernalia, propane tanks, dirt, clutter, the worn carpets, the makeshift wooden stairway, and the lack of sprinklers, smoke detectors, or a clear path to the ONLY known exit. Mr. Harris knew all of this, but rather than work to make his "Artists' Utopia" safe, he instead invited paying guests to help him cover his warehouse rent.

Those musicians and partygoers did not know about popped fuses, power outages, and frequent small fires that had taken place previously. They didn't know they were in danger. Mr. Harris did. No, Mr. Harris did not cause the code violations, nor did he own the dangerous building, nor work for a government agency or public utility that should have closed the building. Mr. Harris disregarded his own misgivings about the site despite those qualms.

No amount of "finding God" in jail, caring for his mother, being a vegan, or naming and saving the lives of countless insects in his jail yard absolves him of guilt. Of all the parties responsible, I would say he was the least responsible, but he played his part in the tragedy. Most of the victims were also vegan, and they were talented, open-hearted young people who loved life. It would be nice to see a lush, romantic photo of these young artists on the cover of the *New York Times* Magazine, but they weren't alive to pose for it.

That night, my panicked nightmare was threaded through with anger. I pushed my way past the pianos, knocked over a wooden statue, and shoved chairs and tables out of my way. Where was the exit? Who put all this junk in my way? Flames grew closer and larger. Smoke swirled around my head. I couldn't see. I woke up yelling, "Where is the door?" 3:00 a.m. My pillow was soaked with tears.

Chapter 24

Pre-Trial Hearings

January, February, March 2019

January, February, and March of 2019 were filled with Pre-Trial hearings that would outline the calendar for jury selection and allow lawyers for both sides to enter any motions that might affect the procedures or outcomes of the trial.

After the winter break at school, I cut my teaching schedule back to three days a week so I could attend any pre-trial hearings that landed on Wednesday or Friday. When I couldn't attend, I followed news reports on TV.

The first hearing was held on January 2, 2019, a Wednesday. I could go. The drive from Marin County to the courthouse in Oakland put me on edge. For over an hour, I had to nose into bumper-to-bumper traffic that seemed determined to keep me out. Getting over to a far-left lane for the switch from the San Francisco to the Oakland commute made my hands clammy. I wasn't used to this kind of driving pressure.

By the time I parked at the Oakland Museum and sat down

in the courtroom, I was frazzled and late. Other family members were already seated, and the chairs on both sides of the center aisle were full, but Stephanie Lynch knew I was coming and saved a seat for me. I smiled at her in gratitude as the new judge assigned to the case, Judge Trina Thompson, entered from the chamber door. She calmly entered the courtroom, almost gliding, and sat regally behind the judge's bench. Judge Thompson looked out into the courtroom, and it felt as though she was speaking directly to me when she said in warm tones, "This trial could last from a few weeks to six months." The air left my lungs. I was taking a leave of absence to attend the trial from April 26th through the end of the school year, but I couldn't extend it into the fall! I had to teach. My hope hung on the words "several weeks."

The term "Trombetta motion" came up several times, but it meant nothing to me. There was some confusing talk about the investigation that began immediately after the fire. I listened as carefully as possible, but no one was talking about the fire, and no one mentioned the 36 victims. The prosecuting attorney, Autrey James, argued that 12,000 pages of documents and many hours of video and audio tape precluded filing charges against anyone but Almena and Harris. I wondered why he was bringing that up now. Were other people going to be charged with a crime? And, if so, who? Judge Thompson listened to the men take turns arguing, then said she would read the documents handed to her by the court clerk and would rule on these motions at a later date. What was that all about? I had so much to learn about legal terms and procedures.

After the hearing, I slipped into the crowd of spectators who filed out of the courtroom, hoping to duck past the bevy of TV news cameras. Since I had given several interviews before the trial, I became a likely target for more. I stepped aside and listened as Curtis Briggs, one of the attorneys for Max Harris, spoke into the field of microphones about the district attorney, Nancy O'Malley, calling her actions corrupt. He made a fair point, saying she had only brought charges against the two men who didn't have the means to defend themselves. He and the other defense team members were working pro bono. He said the owners, the Ng family, had hired an expensive San Francisco public relations firm that was known to effectively "make charges go away." He was indignant that no charges were filed against police, fire, and government agents who entered the warehouse, saw the dangers, and did nothing.

Then Tony Serra stepped up to the bank of microphones, ran his hand over his shoulder-length, unruly gray hair, and spoke, saying he was delighted that Judge Trina Thompson was presiding over the case because of her background as a public defender and a private criminal defense attorney. He was in a good mood. I must admit, that made me a little suspicious. Would she lean too heavily toward the defense?

I had some homework to do that night, researching Judge Thompson and looking up the word "Trombetta." The first thing I did after climbing the stairs from my garage to the kitchen was pop a leftover chicken casserole into my little toaster oven. Then I propped my laptop up on the dining room table, put my head down, and cried. This trial was going to be hell.

The casserole was awful. The dried-up chicken fit right into my mood. I decided my first step was to read up about Judge Thompson after Tony Serra's gleeful little speech. A quick Google search told me she was the first African American woman elected to the Alameda County Superior Court. She was also appointed by Barack Obama to serve on the Coordinating Council on Juvenile Justice and Delinquency Prevention. Not bad. This trial wasn't focused on juvenile matters, but many of the residents and the deceased were young adults. I thought she might be more understanding of the situation because of her background. She addressed the attorneys clearly and thoughtfully. I liked that.

Then, I typed the term "Trombetta motion" into my search bar. I learned it meant the defense asked to have the case thrown out because crucial evidence was destroyed or lost. The whole case thrown out? No trial? This was getting absurd. An irritating little thought in the back of my mind said both sides were trying to suppress the truth. The prosecution didn't want to mention the city and county mistakes. The defense didn't want their clients held responsible. Neither side wanted a trial. Why not?

On January 18th, three weeks later, I slipped into the uncomfortable wooden courtroom seats for another hearing. This time, the defense lawyers had the opportunity to present their motions for dismissal. Before the hearing began, attorneys from both sides sniped at each other in a manner that seemed especially churlish and disrespectful.

Judge Thompson, Brian Goetz, Derick Almena, etc.
(Courtesy of Vicki Ellen Behringer)

Judge Thompson finally intervened and, in a curt voice, told the lawyers, "Work out your squabbles outside the courtroom. I am here to oversee the trial, not your petty differences."

I smiled and thought, *Well done.*

The rest of the hearing was a repetition of the previous one, but as the day ended, Autrey James noted that by speaking to the press, the defense was trying the case in public. Since no one from the district attorney's office was addressing the cameras every day, it was one-sided and prejudicial, especially before the jurors were chosen. At this, Judge Thompson declared a gag order for all court personnel and witnesses until the jury was seated.

As we were leaving the courtroom, David Lim took me aside and told me that because I was present the night of the fire, I was a possible witness and not allowed to speak out in public about the trial. As far as I knew, I was the only family member of the victims to be silenced. Even though I was uncomfortable with the gag order and with David's original statement that a plea bargain would "spare the families," I trusted him and kept my mouth shut.

In between the scattered pre-trial hearings, I still had to work. Most days, I managed the lessons and reports and attended various meetings without incident. I'd been teaching phonemic awareness and pre-reading skills to students with learning differences for nearly 30 years, so this kind of teaching came easily to me. I liked working with small groups of two or three students at a time. The cozy, well-lighted reading room in the school library where I worked felt like home.

One day, I sat on the floor with four little kindergartners extolling the virtue of vowels when a vision of the fire overtook me. Flames licked out of the warehouse windows. Smoke billowed up over my head, and I panicked. Why now? My palms were sweaty. My temples throbbed. Above the fiery warehouse, I heard lilting voices: "A for apple, ah, ah apple. E for elephant, eh, eh elephant..." My little ones were singing a song, and I was shaking.

I jumped up. "Let's dance while we sing the song!" The distraction was enough for me to keep going for the rest of the hour, but I went home early that day, citing a flu bug. The hearings were bringing up terrifying memories, and the trial hadn't even begun yet.

Chapter 25

Putting the Pieces Together

March 1, 2019

After another fruitless and acrimonious hearing, I dragged my heavy feet out of the courtroom. My quest for learning the whole story felt moot. The men arguing the case seemed more interested in bickering than in finding the cause of the massive tragedy. I ached for more information and decided to do something on my own to get a few answers. As I stepped into the elevator to leave, it occurred to me that if I saw the photographs taken by the fire investigators and the coroner, some of the circumstances of the fire might become obvious.

I was going to go straight home that day, but with a shaking hand, I impulsively pressed the elevator button #2 for the district attorney's office on the second floor. Was I doing the right thing? David Lim stood alone next to the office doorway, shuffling some papers as he was about to leave. My stomach churned as I approached him and said, "I need to know where my daughter was in the building, who she was with, and what caused her death." David looked a little stunned at first, then gazed down at me with pity in his eyes. I knew that look, and it made me cringe, but it could also work in my favor. David nodded his head and told me I could come to his office near the Oakland airport the following Friday. He would show me what I wanted to see.

That week, my friend Sioux and I had lunch at the Dipsea Cafe in Mill Valley. Over steaming cups of tea, she volunteered to drive me to David Lim's office. I said yes, knowing it was going to be an emotional day.

When we arrived at the nondescript office, a young woman led us to a conference room. A large wooden table took up most of the room. David Lim was seated in the center on the far side of the table. He stood when Sioux and I entered the room and pointed to the seats directly across from him.

Seated on David's right was a small woman about 40 years old with light brown shoulder-length hair who was a representative from the Alameda County Victims and Witnesses Department. There were several other official-looking people in suits to whom I was introduced sitting around the table, but David's voice buzzed as he told me their names. I didn't remember or even see any of them. David walked over to a chart stand at one end of the table. On it was a large piece of chart paper with a drawing of a building floor plan covered with yellow post-it notes.

He stood next to the easel, pointed to the drawing with one finger, and said in a clear voice, "This represents the second floor of the Ghost Ship warehouse." He then described the front wall, the opening where the winding staircase led up to the second floor, and a large area that was the upstairs dance floor. David pointed out a single file of sticky tabs with names written on them in pencil leading to the stairs. "This is where we found a single file of bodies leading to the staircase. They were standing in line to go downstairs." He said these victims were found on a portion of the second floor that did not collapse. I shivered.

A man sitting on the same side of the table as me called out that I wasn't allowed to take pictures or notes, even though I hadn't pulled out my phone or notebook. Sioux held her closed purse in her lap. Why was this a concern? David seemed to read my thoughts and mentioned that my impressions could be used against the prosecution's case. I nodded and said, "I understand."

I wanted to be reassured that Chelsea was with her dear friends when she died, so I cleared my throat, trying to sound confident, and asked. "Where was Chelsea found? Was she in that line? Were Travis and Amanda nearby?"

David turned back to the chart and pointed to the two sticky notes where Travis and Amanda were found, saying, "This is Amanda, and this is Travis." Then he pointed to the center of the drawing and looked back at me with soft eyes. "And this is where Chelsea was found." I focused on a yellow square of paper with Chelsea's name on it in the center of the chart, some distance from the other two. That was my daughter. The two friends I knew best were not with her, and that broke my heart, but she was not alone. David paused while I stared. David then pointed to the cluster of sticky notes in the center of the chart near her name.

"Chelsea was in a rug that hung between floors. Eight bodies were recovered together here. They were suspended as if in a hammock." He stood completely still with his finger pointing at the center of the chart, turned toward me, and looked deeply into my eyes, waiting for my reaction. I calmed my face, not wanting to cry or show emotion that might stop David from continuing, and nodded silently. His voice grew quieter, and he said, "The bodies were stacked within the rug.

It had been on the second floor but fell with the victims when the second floor collapsed."

So, Chelsea had been upstairs with a cluster of friends. This was not what I had imagined in my nightmares. I'd always pictured her searching desperately for a way out of the labyrinth, alone and lost. Now I knew she was with seven friends who had gathered in the center of the room. Perhaps they had even pulled the rug around them as protection from the flames.

Then, I asked, "May I see the pictures?" David tread softly toward his seat in the middle of the table, hesitating a moment before sitting down across from me. My eyes focused on the manilla folder on the table in front of him. David placed his open hand on it, palm down protectively, and paused again. I lifted my head slowly when he didn't move and saw him staring at me with clear eyes. The pictures were right there under his palm, but David wanted to reassure himself that I could handle what he was about to say and show me.

David's kind eyes held my gaze. "I've chosen pictures that are the least graphic and left out the ones that include other victims. Let me know if anything is too much or you want to stop at any time."

I bit my lip, pointed to the folder, and said, "I'd like to see them." Sioux leaned into my shoulder and placed her hand on mine reassuringly. I took a deep breath.

David looked hard into my face. I crossed my arms. I wanted to know more and waited in silence. His voice cracked slightly as he said, "Chelsea was in the middle. Three bodies were found beneath her and four on top." This took my breath away. I could feel the weight of four people falling on top of me. How could she bear it? "We removed the bodies from the top first and then moved down one by one. Do you want to see the picture of Chelsea when we found her on the scene?"

"Yes." Sioux glanced over at me to gauge my emotional state. I did my best to appear serene, but everything inside my body was churning. I took my cue from her and steadied my gaze.

David opened the folder with the pictures placed one on top of the other face down. He turned over the top photo and slid it toward me. I recognized Chelsea instantly, even from behind. The picture was dark, all black, gray, and ashy white. She was found face down. Her knees were drawn up to her chest protectively but spread out like a frog. Her arms were bent akimbo, palms down, as though bracing for a fall. That photo told me she knew she was falling. She was alive when the floor collapsed! Images of her falling flashed through my mind. I gulped in her terror, trying to stifle sobs that wanted to escape from my throat. My baby was terrified. Chelsea knew she was about to die.

The next photos were taken from different angles as her body was uncovered and removed. I saw a glimpse of the bodies beneath her. What an awful way to die!

Then David asked, "Do you want to see the coroner's autopsy photos?" He waited. I pointed to the few pictures that had not yet been turned over and knew I couldn't leave the room without seeing them. When he saw me nod, David said, "I chose only the pictures that did not show the coroner's work. I would never show you or any victim's parents a picture like that." I understood and silently nodded again.

The last two pictures were of Chelsea's back as she lay face down on the metal table and on her side from behind. David explained he couldn't show me the front. When he turned over the two photos, my mind raced in confusion, and I pulled them closer. She didn't appear to be burnt or have any broken bones or bruises, which I thought I would see because of the fall. My face felt hot as I pondered my daughter's death. How did she die? I supposed the others below her probably softened the blow. "Did she have any internal damage?" I asked because I remembered seeing blood in her underwear when I had gone through her clothes from that night. I hoped it wasn't from crushed organs.

David shrugged. "I don't know that." He handed me a page from the coroner's report, but it only had some numbers that meant nothing to me, something about carbon monoxide and soot in her mouth, throat, and nose. The words ran together. The conclusion was she had died of smoke inhalation. After seeing her unburnt, unbruised, and unbroken body, that made sense. Suddenly, the other nameless, faceless people who had been sitting silently at the table with me started speaking at once.

"That means she wasn't conscious when she died."

"She wouldn't have suffered."

"She didn't feel any pain."

The rush of voices was supposed to reassure me but had the opposite effect. I saw her body braced for a fall. I understood the panic and pain of the intense heat and the weight of bodies falling on top of her. She suffered.

The room quieted. I could feel David's gentle eyes on me, Sioux's hand on mine. David's voice had that kindness others take on in the face of another's grief. "Do you have any questions?" I could only shake my head. I found out what I had come to learn. Chelsea had been in the middle of the second floor with her friends when the fire broke out. She was clustered with seven others. He showed me the places where some of Chelsea's friends had been found and told me the names of the people just above and below her in the rug. They must have huddled together. Perhaps they had wrapped themselves up in the rug for protection from the heat and flames. What horror!

Up to this point, in nightmares every night. I saw through Chelsea's eyes her desperate search for a way out, running through confusing hallways, pushing on doors that led nowhere. I felt panic rising through my body, silent screams rising in my throat with the certainty I was lost and I was going to die. Blood pounded in my head, and sobs wracked my body until I woke up. Then I would remember Chelsea was dead. She died every night.

Once I learned she was on the second floor with her friends, my dreams changed. That night, I dreamed of others clutching onto her arms, my arms, as she and her friends hid under a rug, reassuring each other they would be rescued. Cries and screams all around the room belied those words. Then, a thunderous crack filled my head. The floor gave way, and I could feel myself falling, the weight of four other people smothering me on the way down.

Instead of sobbing in fear, I woke up choking, my lungs refusing to take in air. Blankets were scattered in a stormy mess all over the floor. The panic I felt must have been a small sliver of what those 36 friends felt when thick, black smoke suffocated them and the heat from a raging fire seared their bodies. Those poor, vibrant young people suffered. I know that.

Prosecutor Quits - March 13, 2019

Imagine my shock when, less than two weeks later, I sat down in my living room at 6:00 p.m. as usual, flipped on the evening news, and learned that Assistant District Attorney David Lim had resigned his post! I had just seen him in his office. The Ghost Ship trial was set to begin in three weeks! Why? Was he fired? He gave the excuse that he was going to start his own real estate law business, but that sounded like a lie. This was going to be a huge trial with national exposure. Quitting this close to the opening sounded fishy. More likely, he was fired. Interestingly, the families of the victims found out about his leaving through TV and print news. Nor had we been notified of a hearing on March 1st when Max Harris' defense team called for a continuance of the trial. Almena's lawyers and the prosecuting team were against any delay. Why did Max's team need more time? What was up their sleeve?

In the meantime, Judge Thompson kept the gag order on witnesses and court personnel in place, which meant I couldn't publicly comment on David Lim's departure. She also made the final decision to ban all cameras, recording devices, and electronic equipment of any kind from the courtroom. The trial was proceeding on silent mode.

Something about that didn't feel right. A creepy feeling of misdirection away from city and county government's responsibility started building in my mind. And what about the owners, the Ngs? Was the district attorney, Nancy O'Malley, any closer to bringing criminal charges against the family? I wondered if the moral and ethical implications of ignoring others' culpable negligence and avoiding holding them accountable had anything to do with David Lim's sudden departure.

David Lim, Judge Stuart Hing. (Courtesy of Vicki Ellen Behringer)

Part Four

The Trial

Chapter 26

The Trial Begins

April 29, 2019

The Trombetta motion was dismissed on March 22nd. The trial officially had begun, but the entire month of April was taken up with procedural hearings and several weeks of jury selection. The public was not allowed to be present when potential jurors were in the courtroom for fear of intimidating or influencing them. Because of the gag order, I couldn't comment until the last juror was sworn in, so there was no sense in my attending what the prosecution attorneys called "boring logistics." I continued to teach each day, rushing home to catch the Ghost Ship TV news updates. There was always something, though usually of little consequence.

One evening in early April, I sat in my living room and watched Kai and Eva Ng on TV, avoiding news cameras just as their mother had done 18 months earlier. A hearing was held that day to determine what evidence should be introduced during the trial, and the Ng siblings were asked about their roles in the management of the warehouse. Eva and Kai Ng each took the witness stand and pleaded the 5th Amendment to every question.

I hit the coffee table with my fist, or rather, I hit my salad plate with my fist, and lettuce flew onto the table, splattering salad dressing everywhere. Why did I delay my leave of absence until official testimony began? I should have taken an earlier leave of absence. This was important information, and I missed it. I wiped off the table with my napkin and groaned loudly. There was nothing I could do at this point but put my faith in the prosecution team. This would not be an easy trial.

As jury selection and preliminary hearings continued, I was determined to focus on my work. Teaching the foundational skills of reading and writing came easily to me; I'd been doing it for thirty years. I felt a little guilty to be leaving the school year a month early, so I scrambled to make sure my students and colleagues had everything they needed to proceed in my absence. That responsibility of organizing materials and lesson plans gave me an urgent sense of purpose, but a feeling of loss hung over the work. I'd miss my little ones.

Being in the company of five-and-six-year-olds gave me a sense of peace, yet not a day passed that I didn't feel the trial was going on without me. The April days passed slowly. Every evening after school, I sat on my sofa in the living room, dinner placed on the coffee table in front of me, and turned on the 6:00 news to catch up on any updates. Nothing much happened, but the Ghost Ship trial loomed ahead, so the reporters would often come on to say the jury was still being selected. Once the nightly Ghost Ship report was over, I could sit back, sigh, and eat my cooling dinner. Aside from the Ngs avoiding cameras and my ever-present nightmares, the month of April was a respite from the drama of the last two years. I was even getting used to the nightly horror dreams. My grief therapist, Debbie, had helped me learn how to tell myself it was a dream even before I woke. Perhaps the trial would progress as smoothly.

Finally, I received an email from the Victims and Witnesses office saying the trial testimony would begin on April 29, 2019. That morning, I wrapped Chelsea's rainbow scarf around my neck and sat on my front step, waiting for my friend, Sioux, who had kindly offered to drive me to the courthouse as often as her schedule allowed. She picked me up at my doorstep. Choking down my awkward discomfort, I walked to her white car and slid into the passenger seat. Sioux handed me a travel mug of coffee and said, "Let's go."

The morning dawned in dull overcast, matching my sullen mood. The drive was long, but Sioux and I said little. Once in Oakland, Sioux parked in the Oakland Museum parking lot across the street from the Alameda County Courthouse, and we headed up the broad stone steps. I'd been there before, but this time, the official formality of pillars and porticoes resonated with the possibility of hope and truth. This was where I would find justice. The massive, block-long square building itself supported me. I may have felt weak and sad, but the formidable size and structure of the courthouse sustained me.

The building carried a nobility that comes with age. I thought of the courthouse as an elegant, older woman—solid hardwood bones, smooth gray and white marble surfaces with a few extra flourishes around the trim, creaky mechanism in the elevators, stone stairs that had sweat-polished wooden banisters, and curved steps worn down from years of one weary foot plodding after another. The setting was solemn and strong.

Inside the heavy glass and polished brass front doors was a security checkpoint. Lawyers and clerks with badges on colorful ribbon ties walked through without incident to the left of the security scanner. Those of us who were not employees placed our belongings on a conveyor belt, which ran into an X-ray scanner. Men wearing belts were stopped and told to remove them and the keys from their pockets. A few women had to be scanned with a wand for unknown reasons. Sioux had a metal hip replacement, and she also needed to be scanned with a wand that whistled as it passed over her hip. Chirps continued behind us as we walked toward the elevators that would lead us to the 2nd floor.

The old elevator doors chunked closed, and Sioux pushed the lit buttons on the panel to the right. I'd received a phone call from my court liaison, Stephanie Lynch, telling me to go to the DA's Office on the 2nd floor and meet with the other families of victims.

Sioux and I left the elevator, crossed a marbled hallway, and entered the DA's offices, where we were led by a neatly dressed young man into a crowded conference room. We sat down at a large, oval, mahogany table that took up most of the room. Black Naugahyde office chairs on wheels tightly encircled it, filled with people who must have been relatives of the victims. Others stood behind the chairs, packing the room. More people sat in tight rows of straight-backed chairs in one corner.

Two pink cardboard boxes of doughnuts sat untouched in the center of the long table. A court clerk brought in a tray with paper cups of coffee, a handful of sugar packets, and a cylinder of white creamer powder. A few of us said thank you and took hold of the cups as something to steady our shaking hands.

We introduced ourselves around the table, said the names of our deceased loved ones, and were introduced to the Assistant District Attorneys who would be the lawyers for the

Prosecution. This time, I wrote down names. Autrey James would continue on the case, joined by his close friend, Casey Bates, who would replace David Lim. Both men were large, convivial guys, one black, one white. They cut imposing figures, and I was glad they were on our side.

A short, officious-looking woman with dark blond pageboy hair stood in the doorway and told us where we would sit in the courtroom, how to behave, and what to expect over the first few days of hearings. In a curt voice, the woman told us, "The proceedings will take place in Department 9." She adjusted her suit jacket. "You are not to speak, make gestures, hold pictures, wear t-shirts, buttons, or give the jury any indication of who you are with the names or pictures of your loved ones. Not only will identifying objects be confiscated but if you violate any of these rules, you will be asked to leave the courtroom." Then she spun on her heel and left the doorway. Family members fell into an awkward silence, shuffling photographs into pockets and purses.

At 8:45 a.m., we were led in a clump to the bank of elevators that would take us to the 5th floor and Department 9. The path would be well-worn in the months to come, but at that moment, a foreign world lay ahead.

The victims' families filled two elevators, and we spilled out onto the 5th floor in a rush, eager to be out of touching distance of such profound grief packed in so tightly I could taste its acrid sorrow.

A crowd of spectators, reporters, and court personnel filled the noisy, wide hallway outside a set of huge, mahogany double doors. A tiny, rectangular window was set in each door at eye level. Standing on my toes and peeking through, I saw another very small vestibule, not much bigger than an elevator. To the right and left were two more sets of double doors embossed with gold painted numbers, eight to the left and nine to the right, that opened into courtrooms.

I moved back into the crowd of people and stood with Sioux near others who had been in the conference room with us. Families. Loved ones. Several men in suits and carrying briefcases rushed past us. I didn't recognize them but assumed they were lawyers. The men entered the inner vestibule and then the inner doorway to the right. Department 9, it turns out, was the name of our courtroom.

As we waited for our turn to enter, a couple approached me in the hallway. David and Kim Gregory had been interviewed on TV the day after the fire. The news was filled with the sweet and tragic story of their daughter, Michela, and her boyfriend, Alex Vega, who were two of the youngest victims. Michela and Alex's bodies were found in an embrace, his body protectively wrapped around hers.

David said, "I'm going to be here every single day." I said I would, too.

Finally, a court security guard peeked his head out of one of the double doors and opened one side, saying, "Families first." A woman from the Victims and Witnesses office guided us through the inner doors and up a short center aisle to the front rows of wooden, pew-like seats in what was called the visitor's gallery.

We settled into our seats, and all eyes turned as the court bailiff escorted Max Harris and Derick Almena into the courtroom. Max wore an ill-fitting suit jacket, and his hair was done up in a bun, which accentuated his neck and face tattoos. He and his two lawyers sat down at one of the forward-facing tables with their backs to the visitors' gallery.

I barely recognized Derick Almena when he entered the courtroom. His hair was also pulled back, and he had gained even more weight in the eight months since I'd seen him at the sentencing. Of course, he wasn't alone in that department. I had found comfort in food after my daughter's death and rarely left my house, a self-imposed imprisonment. I chuckled to myself when I saw Derick. We were both stuck in isolation. I shuddered at the prospect of having anything in common with the man, but there it was - thirty pounds of grief and depression.

Almena and his lawyers took tables on the far right, closest to the bailiff and the door where he entered. Almena was sitting perpendicular to the gallery, where I could see his face.

Finally, the jurors filed into the courtroom from the side door next to the bailiff.

When all were seated, Judge Thompson entered the hall in her somber robes, her dark skin and long black hair shining under the bright overhead lights. The jurors sat in attention as she laid out the rules for their behavior during the upcoming months and gave them instructions on how to let her know in writing if they had any conflicts or difficulties. All jurors nodded, and the trial began. I took a deep breath, trying to calm my nerves.

Opening Statements

The prosecution team, led by lawyer Casey Bates, opened first. An expectant hush fell on the room.

Casey stood in front of the jury box, looking intently at each juror, and laid out the facts in simple, understandable terms. His message was serious. It was all about the 36 victims having no notice, no time, and no exit—no notice via smoke or fire alarms that a fire had started, no time to respond because of the ferocity of the fire due to the highly flammable materials in the warehouse, and no exit. None. They had no hope of escaping because there was no way for them to get from the second floor, where they were trapped, to the single unmarked exit below.

Opening Statement. L-R: Casey Bates, Autrey James, Judge Thompson, Curtis Briggs, Max Harris, Tyler Smith, Brian Goetz, Derick Almena, Tony Serra.

Next, Curtis Briggs, Max Harris' lead defense attorney, opened by standing up behind his table and turning toward the jurors. He appeared tall and fit in a gray, subtle-plaid suit. His red hair and beard looked fiery, but his voice was quieter than I expected as he told the jurors that Max had a "servant" personality, a man who was incapable of saying no to people. He said he was a "Christ-like" figure... "Buddhistic".... whatever that is supposed to mean, and even called him a "Cinderella." It was a rehash of the *New York Times* Sunday Magazine story. Familiar anger surged through my chest. It was as if the paper had handed Briggs a script for his opening statement.

At the end of the day, we were surprised when we walked outside to be met by a crowd of young people carrying signs that read FREE MAX! During the pre-trial hearings, when a few of these protesters showed up, it bothered me a little. But on this day, there were angry shouts. A huge banner hung across the entrance to the courthouse door, and protesters shoved FREE Max signs in our faces, hissing, "He did nothing wrong!" and followed us to our cars.

Sioux and I ran side by side down the sidewalk to her car in the museum parking lot. She jumped in and slammed the driver-side door shut. I rushed into the passenger seat, and we turned to each other, gasping in disbelief.

I gasped, "HOLY COW! Tomorrow is only Day Two! And Tony Serra gets to put on his drama queen shit-show." Sioux raised one eyebrow at me. She didn't swear.

As an afterthought, I said, "Did you notice there are no signs for Derick?"

Sioux laughed softly and shook her head. "Who would want *him* free?"

I sighed and pressed my head back onto the car headrest. "The ugliness has only just begun, Sioux, and I'm exhausted already." Attending this trial each day and knowing I would be exposed to graphic photos of my daughter's death scene was going to be difficult. Layered on top of that was the seething ugliness and confusion surrounding the trial. I was lucky to have a friend on my side who would help me show up each day. I closed my eyes, seeing visions of Chelsea greeting me when I came home.

After a long, silent drive, Sioux dropped me off at my front door, and I dragged my aching bones and muscles up the front steps of my condo. Once inside, I wandered aimlessly from room to room. What could fill this emptiness? I was proud of my little townhouse. It was the place I had lived in longer than any other home in my life, 15 years, and every piece of furniture held a memory. But suddenly, it felt cold.

My dining room was fitted for business. It had been years since I'd served a meal there. The large, rustic farm table was stacked with papers and magazines on one end, mostly about teaching, but a few, like *The New Yorker* and *The Atlantic*, kept me feeling somewhat connected to the rest of the world. On the far end of the table, my laptop computer sat open. I'd been writing notes the night before and never bothered to close it, leaving it ever ready for the thoughts that spilled out unexpectedly.

I wandered down the eight steps to my living room, which existed on a more relaxed level. This area held a soft, tan recliner chair in the corner and the tweedy brown sofa in front of the windows where I read books. It was also the place where I would open the tall, mahogany armoire that housed my TV and settle down with dinner on my coffee table in front of the 6:00 news. Tonight, there was nothing to hold me here; what could the news tell me that I hadn't seen in court? I turned in a circle, feeling lost.

Without thinking, I wound up in the kitchen and pulled open the refrigerator door. I think there was food, but I didn't see it. I grabbed a bottle of cold Sauvignon Blanc and opened it. The effort of twisting out the cork came with a cost. Crying, I poured a glass and sat down at the magazine end of my dining room table.

I stared at a blank space a foot or two from my face and saw the little toddler who lost her father in the fire and asked her mommy, "What happened to the smoke detectors?" Even that one small thing could have saved lives. I imagined that little girl's inquisitive face, and it broke my heart.

Then I pictured the Free Max protestors, who had their own agenda. Some were part of an anti-prison group. Others said Max had saved all his friends on the first floor by shouting "Fire!" and was a hero. Of course, Max took money from the 36 people who were still dancing upstairs to loud music while the warehouse burned. He never gave them a second thought. My forehead hit the hard wood of the table, and I sank into my tears. They were the real victims.

Overwhelmed by grief, Free Max negativity, TV news cameras, and the stilted courtroom culture, I wailed, "I can't do this!" After sobbing a wet spot onto a pile of lesson plans and student profiles, I pried my head up, gulped down the now-warm, white wine, and dragged myself up to bed, knowing the terrifying nightmares would wake me in a few hours. Climbing the stairs, I whispered again, "I can't do this."

Chapter 27

The Families and The Family Room

May 1, 2019

On the second morning of Opening Statements, David Gregory, Sioux, and I walked into the courthouse at the same time and entered the courthouse elevator with Judge Cramer. He was the second of five judges on the case, the one who had listened to the families' impact statements and decided to reject the plea bargain. I didn't recognize him at first because he was wearing a gray suit and not his black robes, but then he smiled at me, and I remembered the warmth of his presence in the courtroom. I smiled back, but I wasn't sure he recognized me. What he said, however, stuck with me. David, Sioux, and I had been deep in conversation about the trial, and I'd said I was there to learn how and why my daughter died. He interrupted us in a gentle voice, "I don't think that's what you're going to get. Trials don't provide all the answers or even a satisfying ending. You may not get what you're searching for." And then the elevator door opened, and he stepped out.

I gritted my teeth and stood motionless as the door closed,

and we continued up to the 5th floor. His words soaked in. I shook my arms as though trying to shake off water, but really, I was trying to rid myself of worry before the elevator doors opened again. Other Ghost Ship parents and friends were waiting for us in the wide hallway.

A young woman from the DA's office, with a brown ponytail and a bouncy gait, met us as we stepped off the elevators and told us to go back down to the 2nd floor. As we all bunched back into two elevators, she said, "You're a large crowd, so we're setting a room aside for you. It's usually our break room, but we think you all need a place away from the press that's private." When the doors opened again, she led us to an employee break room past the district attorney's office.

We were told the lockbox code numbers to enter the room, and the young woman urged us to gather there until the courtroom was open, then she left us alone. The beige room was flooded with harsh, fluorescent light. Four long cafeteria tables were configured in a horseshoe with folding chairs surrounding the tables. A smaller, separate card table off to one side held a metal urn of coffee, hot water for tea, tea bags, sugar, creamer powder, and paper coffee cups. There was no other furniture. It took me a minute, but I realized this was the same room where we had gathered before giving our impact statements.

I looked around the room as the other parents, a few siblings, an aunt, and one fiancé settled around the tables in cold, metal chairs. There were ten of us. I didn't know what to say. Small talk didn't feel like an option; the circumstances were too solemn.

I sank into a chair and leaned toward Cyrus Hoda and David Gregory, who sat across the table from me. They were talking about the charges filed against Almena and Harris. I interrupted, "The term involuntary manslaughter confuses me."

David looked up, "Me, too, so I looked it up online." He tipped his head toward me. "Manslaughter means a death was caused by neglect or just disregard for life." Then he shook his head, "They didn't mean to kill their victims, but it happened."

I still didn't get it. "Yeah, but what does the 'involuntary' bit mean? Isn't all manslaughter involuntary? No intent to kill, manslaughter. Intent to kill, murder."

David hooked his arm over the back of his chair. "Manslaughter means you wanted to hurt someone, or maybe that other person did something to you, and you reacted violently."

He paused to gauge my reaction. This time, I shrugged my shoulders, so he continued. "It means you really did mean to hurt them. Involuntary Manslaughter means you didn't mean to hurt anybody, but your actions led to their death."

That made a little more sense to me. I sat back in my chair, silently wondering about the quest for justice that was beginning to unfold.

Carol Cidlik crossed the room and took the chair next to me. She was the mother of victim Nicole Siegrist and was scheduled as the first witness. We spoke often on the phone. Carol was the glue that held most of the victims' families together. Her bubbly personality kept us smiling when it seemed nothing else could. She was quick to tears and quick to laugh, always trying to stay positive in the face of our shared grief. She called several families each day, sharing news and keeping us connected.

Carol brushed back her dark brown hair from one shoulder and offered, "I was wondering; I know you have a long commute during rush hour. Would you like to share my hotel room with me?"

I knew the prosecution team had flown her in from her home in Hawaii to testify. She peered at me from below her dark bangs, "I really want to stay longer than three days. That's all the court will pay for, but I booked a return flight for two weeks from now. Are you interested in splitting the cost of a hotel room?"

I jumped at it. "Absolutely." I hated that tense drive from Marin to Oakland and didn't like imposing on Sioux to drive me every day. Carol and I opened our cell phones and found an Emeryville kitchenette hotel suite with a shuttle van that would take us to and from the courthouse. Warm relief flooded through me.

The Ghost Ship families who attended the trial nearly every day.

Chapter 28

First Week of Testimony

May 6, 2019

Finally, after a month of jury selection, legal wrangling, and opening statements, witness testimony began. My purpose in life lay in that courtroom. This trial was the only way I would find out how and why my daughter died and find some closure. News accounts didn't have the inside story, and the opening statements on both sides left me wanting more information. Only testimony by the people who were at the Ghost Ship on the night of the fire would feel sufficient.

I felt nervous. Carol and I had stayed in the hotel paid for by the prosecution. She had cried in the hotel room that morning, fearing she would somehow mess up. An investigator for the prosecution picked us up at the hotel, and Carol rallied during the ride to the courthouse, but she fell apart again as we entered the building. I tried to reassure her, but I could feel her anxiety deep within my own bones. Because she was a witness, Carol had to wait with the investigator outside the courtroom door.

I slipped into a seat next to Farzaneh and Cyrus Hoda on one side and saved an empty seat for Carol on the other. Family members began to fill in the seats on the left side of the aisle, and we quietly expressed how grateful we were to see each other. In the back row of seats, I recognized reporters who had interviewed me over the past few months. We nodded hello to one another, and then they looked down at their notebooks. Their presence, at first intimidating, now felt reassuring. The truth would come out.

Feeling the warm camaraderie of the families around me, I felt sorry for the victims' family members who couldn't join us. In a little shudder of belated realization, it occurred to me I could take notes each day for the out-of-town and working families who couldn't attend the trial. I reached down into my tote bag and pulled out the composition notebook and pen I'd brought from home. Connecting with the other parents felt like something positive I could do. Warmth spread from my heart to my hand.

As I watched the attorneys greet each other, I was resigned to the fact that Tony Serra and Curtis Briggs, the lead attorneys for the defense, were doing their jobs. They had to pull out all the stops, cushioning their clients by pointing out the mistakes that were made by others leading up to the night of the fire. Frankly, I was hungry for that information.

Judge Trina Thompson, Max Harris, Curtis Briggs (courtesy of Vicki Ellen Behringer)

Tony Serra, who defended Derick Almena, was the wildman on the defense team. I had first heard of him when I moved to California in 1974, the year Patty Hearst was

178

kidnapped. Serra was a hotshot West Coast lawyer back then. He defended one of the Symbionese Liberation Army leaders, as well as various members of Hells Angels and the Black Panther Party. I didn't give him much thought in those days, but he had a pretty high profile, and I remembered back in the 1980s, he was quoted in the *LA Times* saying, "If you kill a cop, I'll pay to take the case." That's when my opinion of him changed.

Dareld Leite, Judge Trina Thompson, Derick Almena, Max Harris, Tony Serra (courtesy of Vicki Ellen Behringer)

There was some question at the time whether Serra really said it or was simply credited with saying it, but I hardly thought that mattered. Tony's job was to influence jurors, and his histrionics won cases. Period. I would find out more about that later.

It was said Serra took a vow of poverty in the 1960s. His sloppy appearance was a public relations gimmick back then and obviously still was in 2019. The man's wild hair, his gaping yellow teeth, and those disheveled, frumpy clothes were his calling card.

Autrey James, lead attorney for the prosecution, was a large African American man with a steady gaze and a kind but firm attitude. He spoke with authority in his voice, almost like a police officer. I later learned he had spent 20 years as a police sergeant in the San Leandro police department, so that made sense. During four of those years on the police force, he attended law school. I noticed when Mr. James spoke with the families, he was a no-nonsense kind of guy.

Of the two attorneys for the prosecution, Casey Bates was the more affable one. He was chosen to replace David Lim, who had mysteriously quit a month earlier.

Lead prosecutor, Autrey James (courtesy of Vicki Ellen Behringer)

This moved Autrey James into the lead position in the case. During one of their first meetings with the families, Mr. James and Mr. Bates told us they had been good friends for many years, their families often getting together for backyard barbecues. I hoped that friendship would strengthen the prosecution team as a united front. The men looked somewhat alike, sharing the same large build, one black and one white, and their personalities meshed well. Casey Bates had an avuncular bonhomie, which was a foil to Autrey James' pointed remarks. Together, they felt like a solid match for the work ahead.

Casey Bates, Judge Trina Thompson (courtesy of Vicki Ellen Behringer)

On this first day of testimony, Autrey James stood at his full height and, with a strong voice, listed witnesses for the week. These would include a grieving mother, Ghost Ship lease co-signer, two pathologists, an electrician friend of Derick Almena, and several residents who lived at Ghost Ship. That seemed like an odd assortment, but I assumed the prosecutors had a plan that would fit all the testimony into a cohesive storyline. After some arguing back and forth by the defense about Carol's testimony being too emotional, Autrey faced the judge, his voice clear, "The People call Carol Cidlik to the stand." My throat tightened as I waited for her to enter the courtroom.

The bailiff called Carol's name, and she entered through the heavy double doors in the back of the courtroom. I could feel her anxiety as she stepped uncertainly up to the witness stand. She raised her right hand and said, "I do."

L-R: Autrey James, Carol Cidlik, Casey Bates, Judge Thompson, Curtis Briggs, Tyler Smith, Max Harris, Stephanie O'Cloud, Derick Almena, Tony Serra (courtesy of Vicki Ellen Behringer)

I was shocked when they projected the message taken from Carol's phone onto a large overhead screen; it felt so invasive. Nicole's message was highlighted in a gray oval: "I'm going to die now." Carol turned in the witness chair, looked up at the message, and started crying. Carol's text reply to Nicole in a blue oval read: "You'll be okay. We'll talk in the morning." Carol had confided to me on the way to the courthouse that she and Nicole had texted several times that day, and she thought Nicole was just exhausted, but when Carol opened her mouth to explain her response, Autrey shook his head, and she had to stop talking. Her testimony was restricted to establishing the time of the fire.

After that, Carol was excused. I waved my hand at her, and she sat next to me in the seat I had saved. Her hands shook, and tears rolled down her cheeks. Carol leaned over to talk to me, but I pressed a finger to my lips. She didn't know we could be thrown out of the room for whispering.

At lunch that afternoon, The families gathered at the Oakland Museum Cafe. An odd sense of surreal casualness didn't quite fit the sad reality. We all had loved ones who died in the fire, yet there we were, ordering food like this was a social outing. We ordered our food at the counter and then sat at a large table that accommodated all ten family members. Ivania ordered BBQ ribs, and I had to look away. I opted for grilled cheese and tomato soup, my childhood comfort food. At first, our table talk centered on Carol's testimony, but she began crying softly, so we turned to other less sensitive topics.

After the lunch recess, when we returned to the courtroom, a succession of young people, residents and guests, were called to the stand to describe the warehouse and the events the night of the fire. I leaned forward to catch every word, wondering if anyone had seen Chelsea. What was she doing? Was she afraid?

*Testimony of José Avalos. L-R: José Avalos, Autrey James,
Judge Thompson, Max Harris, Derick Almena (courtesy of
Vicki Ellen Behringer)*

One of the witnesses was a resident of Ghost Ship named José. He had fallen asleep in the loft above his RV around 11:00 p.m. He woke up when he heard someone yell, "Fire!" and "Get an extinguisher!" and "Everybody get out!" The young man grabbed his two dachshund dogs and ran toward the front door. He ran into a woman who didn't live there with blond hair and "big eyes, really big eyes" who was wearing a blue shirt. He told her, "Follow me!" and left through the front door.

The young man then started to cry, "I didn't grab her. She didn't make it out." At this point, the counsel and judge decided to call a brief recess. My heart was breaking for the young man who realized the woman he had hoped would follow him had died in the fire. His sorrow hung heavy in the room. Several jurors and family members in the courtroom were also crying. I was one of them.

In The Family Room

Wild speculation about the "Girl at the Door" spread amongst the families as we spilled into The Family Room at the end of the day. Guesses popcorned around the room:

"Could it be Donna Kellogg? She had blond hair."
"What about Amanda Allen? She had blondish hair and wore large glasses, which accounts for her big eyes."
"What about Nicole? She wore wigs when she performed. Could she have been wearing a blond wig?"
"What about Chelsea? She had blond hair!"

I explained to the others it couldn't be Chelsea. I'd seen the photos of her suspended in a rug hanging from the second floor with seven others. She was upstairs on the second floor when the fire broke out. She was nowhere near the front door when she died.

We all left The Family Room together, dodging past the noisy Free Max protesters and hordes of TV cameras, microphones, and reporters gathered on the sidewalk in front of the courthouse. I had spoken on camera in the past and agreed to interviews several times, so I could hear reporters yelling, "Colleen! Colleen!" It was unnerving. Carol and I took the hotel van back to our neat little kitchenette suite. Exhausted, we stumbled downstairs to the hotel restaurant, ordered take-out hamburgers, and ate them at a patio table outside.

Carol enthusiastically said, "We should do something this weekend."

My bones ached, and I really didn't want to do anything, but I knew Carol wanted to see San Francisco. Sunday was Mother's Day, which made the weekend especially fraught.

I just wanted to curl up in bed with the covers over my head. I bit my lower lip. "Can I think about it?"

Carol nodded. "Some of the parents are going to meet in San Francisco for dinner. Nicole loved the Buena Vista Bar, and I want to go there, too!"

That night, Carol sat up on the double bed, hugging her knees. I sat on the fold-out bed propped up against all the extra pillows I could get from Room Service. We were going to have to keep ourselves occupied during the next few days, or I knew I would fall into a funk. We talked for a while and decided to walk around Jack London Square the next day, Friday. On Saturday, we would take the ferry over to San Francisco and meet up with the other family members at Cha Cha restaurant in the Mission District. Sunday was Mother's Day. A group of Chelsea and Nicole's friends had invited us to a backyard party in San Francisco. I wrote an email to Chelsea's friend, Ben Winans, and accepted his invitation.

Sunday was also my Sabrina's birthday. She and Joe were going to be out of town. I think that's what was bearing down on me. Was I losing my other daughter, too? I choked down tears that night. My nightmares came, as usual, but that night, they included Sabrina. She was looking for me while I tried to find my way out of the burning warehouse. I woke up crying, hugging one of the pillows. It was still dark out, and Carol was asleep. I rolled over, curled myself up into a fetal ball, and went back to sleep.

A few hours later, I woke up again and opened my laptop on the tiny kitchen table in the hotel room. Carol was still asleep. It was Friday, my day to write a synopsis of what occurred in court that week and publish it on Facebook for the out-of-town families. I opened my notebook, turned page after page of my sloppy, rushed handwriting, and sighed. The haphazard order of witness testimony didn't make sense. I was looking for a clear storyline, and this was a chaotic mishmash of unrelated topics. By the time I finished writing my post, I was emotionally worn out and disappointed. Nothing felt right. Maybe keeping busy for the next three days was a good idea.

Chapter 29

A Second Floor Witness

May 13, 2019

On Monday morning, Carol and I took the hotel shuttle to the courthouse and slipped through the front door unnoticed. I looked over toward a noisy commotion down a side corridor. There, a bank of reporters and FREE MAX protesters were all busy watching Tony Serra expounding in front of the cameras. His arms were flailing. I couldn't help but smile; he took the pressure off us.

Carol and I climbed the stairs to the second-floor Family Room rather than take the elevator, hoping to counteract the fact that we would be sitting motionless for several hours that day. Carol had brought a box of macadamia chocolates from Hawaii and put them on the coffee card table. Someone else brought pastries. During the previous week, our little cadre of trial attendees had started to feel comfortable around each other. Perhaps that was because we talked about matters that our families and friends avoided. We asked each other about our dead children, what they were like, and we learned how many of them knew each other through friends, bandmates, schools, and mutual interests. In joyful discovery, we realized our children were part of a cohesive community centered on their love of music, art, and each other. As we gathered in The Family Room that Monday morning, I felt the strength of the growing community around me. We began our day together, and I looked forward to continuing our discussions over a communal lunch. Occasionally, we met at the end of the day and rehashed the testimony. Twice that week, the prosecuting attorneys joined us in The Family Room to answer any questions we had. Our children brought us together.

On Monday morning, I sat stoically in the third row of courtroom seats, sandwiched on either side by David Gregory and Carol Cidlik. We all stood as the judge entered, looking equally regal and relaxed in her black robes. Then she gracefully motioned for the visitors to be seated and addressed us, "Standing isn't unnecessary." We stood whenever she entered as a sign of respect and to acknowledge the solemnity of these proceedings. It would be hard to stop; I needed the gravity of the occasion to be grounded by ritual. This was not a casual conversation. Testimony is sworn. Truth is key.

The young resident, José, was recalled to the stand by Tony Serra, who asked him to describe the beauty and camaraderie of the warehouse. I was bewildered. Who cares what the place looked like? Hadn't everyone seen the pictures of the clutter? Those descriptions felt like filler, but one of José's statements stood out to me: "House meetings may or may not have included the discussion of safety issues." Either way, his words were damning. If they had discussed safety and done nothing, they were all involved in those deaths. If they hadn't discussed safety, it was negligence, or maybe just stupidity.

I could feel heat crawling up into my chest, and I wanted to shake anyone associated with that warehouse. I felt like growling and thought to myself, *It's one thing to want cheap housing; it's another to ignore safety. They are not mutually exclusive.*

After José was dismissed, Autrey James questioned a slight, soft-spoken resident named Bob, who talked about what a "beautiful, creative space" the Ghost Ship was. He learned about the place through a Craig's List ad...a common thread amongst all the tenants. Max Harris signed his lease and took him on his initial tour of the place, which refuted Harris' claim that he was just another resident, not a manager. Bob said there was no discussion of house rules except to be "unconditionally awesome."

And I thought to myself, *So, it was just stupidity.*

Bob seemed reluctant to recall anything without having his memory "refreshed" by evidence or a direct question. He said on the night of the fire, two men he'd never seen before were having a private conversation in an area of the Ghost Ship where most of the residents lived. Bob gave them a stern look because he considered this space "off-limits," although no signs were posted, and the paying guests were never told they were not welcome there. Bob said he didn't like the way the two men looked at him as though he were interrupting their private conversation. In fact, he was.

Next, a handsome, dark-haired man, Aaron, was called to the stand. He witnessed the fire developing on the second floor the night of the fire. Derick had invited Aaron to stay at the Ghost Ship as his guest for several weeks, but on the night of the fire, he neglected to tell Aaron about the party. He also neglected to tell his friend that he would be off-premises at a hotel that night. Aaron was not happy. He worried about his music equipment, which was kept upstairs where the party would be held.

That night, as the music got underway and people filled the

second floor, Aaron thought he smelled smoke by Bob's loft near the backstairs. He asked Bob to help him investigate. They unscrewed a flickering lightbulb above the stairs, thinking that was the source of the smell. When Aaron turned on his phone flashlight to inspect the socket, they saw wispy smoke in the air, and the two men left the stairs going in opposite directions.

We had learned in previous testimony that Bob headed down the stairs and through the winding hallways toward the front door. He saw Max and told him about the fire. On his way out, Bob saw another resident, Pete Wentworth, lying on the floor. Pete had broken his ankle and an elbow jumping from his loft. Bob started to pull Pete toward the side door, but the area was almost immediately engulfed in flames. Pete was a large man, and Bob, who was quite slim, had to let go and flee. He ran to the side yard, propped up a ladder, and started to climb and break windows. Bob heard Aaron yelling at a second-story window. By the end of the night, Bob had burns on his hands, arms, and shoulders, and his vinyl vest had melted.

Now, Aaron told us that while Bob ran downstairs, he had run upstairs to alert the partygoers. The music was too loud for him to be heard. He yelled, "Water, water! Don't you see the flames?" Some guy he didn't know must have heard that one word and handed him a small water bottle, thinking he was thirsty.

Aaron yelled again, "Get out, Fire!" The blaring music obliterated his words. Flames started coming through the floorboards. Aaron remembered the window in the kitchen behind a projection screen that had been set up for the party. He yelled, "Kitchen! Window!" Aaron squeezed past the inflated screen and kicked open the kitchen door.

The people behind him didn't know about a door to another room, let alone a window to the outside. Neither Aaron nor the window was visible behind the screen and wall, so no one followed him. Aaron had to hold his breath because of the thick smoke. He pushed a large industrial window out halfway and called, "Please help! Ladder!" Some people below were trying to tear down a chain link fence to get into the side yard. It was too hot to scream, but Aaron managed to call out, "Help us! There are people dying up here!" He put one foot out, then another. Aaron hung on the second-story windowsill by his fingertips and dropped into the soft mud below.

I realized I was shaking when Aaron finished telling his story. I looked down at my notebook, and a tear splashed on the page, smearing the gel ink. I gave a little harumph and thought, *I should have used a ballpoint.*

Next up, two party guests, Ryan and Ivan, were also questioned about the night of the fire. One after the other, they told the stories of their harrowing escapes down a rickety staircase, with a loud, crackling fire and smoke quickly filling the large building. Ryan talked about his friends shining phone flashlights into the doorway, then running to the side yard to help others knock down a chain link fence and break windows. He said nothing about Chelsea.

Ivan was there with four college buddies to see their friend Joel perform. I sat completely still, straining to hear a word about Chelsea. Joel was her friend, too. Ivan said that people who had been casually sitting on couches upstairs and talking started to notice and talk about the smell of firecrackers. He did not hear any firecrackers or fireworks. Then he saw smoke coming up through the floorboards and put the pieces together. He and his friends knew "something had caught fire."

He heard a voice yell, "Exit! Exit! Exit the building!" Ivan and his four friends hung onto each other and looked toward the stairs. People were beginning to congregate there. That's when time slowed down, the lights went out, and the smoke got thicker. He and his friends felt their way to the stairs. Ivan had his eyes closed because the smoke stung, and he had trouble breathing. A silent panic took place, and the partygoers lined up in single file at the stairs. It took about one to three minutes to get to the stairs, and they spent about two minutes on the stairs.

I thought, 'Was Chelsea sitting on the couch with her friends? Did she smell what she thought were firecrackers? Is that when she and seven others stood clinging to each other on the rug in the middle of the room? Were they waiting for their turn to go down the narrow stairway?'

At the Hotel

The testimony was exhausting. Carol and I held our breath as we strode past the TV reporters and camera operators on the sidewalk in front of the courthouse. We hid around the corner, waiting for the hotel shuttle van.

During the ride back to the hotel, my mind was filled with the scenes from upstairs during the fire. As we walked down the hallway to our room, I blurted out, "I can't stop thinking about that guy who jumped out the window. Couldn't he have grabbed a few people or torn down that stupid projection screen? He was the only person upstairs who knew there was another way out!"

As Carol unlocked the door with her keycard, she said, "I felt sorry for him. Maybe the screen was too big for him to move."

I thought about how Aaron had described one of the victims, a young man deafened by the loud music who misunderstood his call for water and kindly handed him a bottle. "Someone gave him water. Why didn't Aaron pull that guy out with him?"

I remembered Ivania Chavarria told me her son, Nex

Iguolo, who died in the fire, and another victim, Joey Casio, brought flats of bottled water to all their shows.

"It was probably Nex or Joey who gave him the water! One of them would still be alive if that guy had just grabbed his sleeve or yelled in his ear that they needed to pull down that stupid projection screen. That room was filled with strong, young adults!"

My head hurt from trying to shut out all the enraged, wishful thinking swimming around in my brain. Carol was saying something nice about Aaron, but I turned her out. I didn't fault the guy for saving his own life; he was smart to get out. I just got stuck in a loop of "what ifs."

I grabbed two aspirins from my suitcase and picked up the bottle of water on the nightstand next to my bed. I looked at it and grunted. A misunderstanding. A bottle of water. Loud music. A hidden window. A projection screen. This trial was a litany of missed opportunities to save those 36 lives.

Chapter 30

Who is on Our Side?

May 14, 2019

The next day, a man nicknamed Dragon was called to the stand. The fire started in his living space, which he shared for eight months with a woman called Swan. He was not at home the night of the fire and didn't find out about it until four hours later. His main point in testifying seemed to be naming the specific make and model of all his audio/video equipment, which he said was worth $100,000. He kept it in his space that had a "dummy lock" on it to fool people into thinking it was locked and secure. On the other hand, he said he gave his rent money to Max to hold each month because Max had a securely locked space. So, he didn't really trust his "dummy lock" after all.

Later, Captain George Freelan, an Oakland fire officer at Station #13, located down the block from Ghost Ship, testified about conditions at the warehouse. He talked a bit about fire inspection checklists, but I didn't see the point. The warehouse hadn't been inspected in over 30 years.

Captain Freelan said he stopped by the Ghost Ship one day when he saw people standing outside. The place was too cluttered to see much, but he walked through and took note of the "fire load," the wood and other flammable products that would add fuel to a fire. He determined the fire load was at a medium to high level, which meant it would take a larger diameter hose to put out a fire there. He called this casual walk-through a "pre-plan."

When asked if it was dangerous to have pianos stacked in a warehouse, he snickered his response, "If it falls on you."

Was this a joke to him?

Freelan only seemed to be concerned about safety codes that applied to Ghost Ship, not the people who lived and died there. He said he could not cite Almena over the fire codes that were broken because he didn't know the official Occupancy Status there. He sent his request to Fire Prevention, but because he never received a response, he didn't warn Almena or anyone who lived or worked there about his fire hazard concerns. He did tell Almena that he liked the woodwork "... because I'm a woodworker, too."

L-R: *Casey Bates, Autrey James, Curtis Briggs, Juge Thompson, Max Harris, Tyler Smith, Brian Goetz, Derick Almena, Tony Serra (courtesy of Vicki Ellen Behringer)*

I was shaking with anger as Captain Freelan testified. In

my mind, he was morally and ethically responsible for following up on the dangerous fire conditions at the warehouse but said nothing to the people who lived there. Nor had he said anything to his colleagues at the fire station even though he determined the building had a "high fire load."

I closed my eyes, feeling the pain of heat and smoke stream through my body. The least he could have done is tell the Ghost Ship residents how to make their space more fire safe. That would have been a kindness. Instead, he did nothing. As the captain left the witness stand, my anger turned to a crushing feeling of betrayal as Casey Bates clapped the man on his back and said, "Thank you for your service." I was stunned. What was going on here? Did Casey really think Freelan had done his duty? Was this man his friend?

At the first morning recess, Carol left for her home in Hawaii. We hugged before her daughter Nicole's friend picked her up at the courthouse. "I'm going to miss you, Carol." She'd been a light to keep me going when the darkness of the trial threatened to overwhelm me. Carol's bounce made me smile.

"I'm going to miss you, Colleen, and all the others, too. I don't want to go. This is my family now." I knew what she meant. We were a family. I was watching my sister leave.

Later that afternoon, the incident commander, Battalion Chief James Bowron, was questioned about the desperate firefight. Casey Bates had come down to The Family Room in the morning, gushing over Bowron's upcoming testimony. He grinned, "You're gonna love this guy!" That confidence left me glowing with anticipation.

I turned to David Gregory as we walked to the elevators after lunch, "Let's hope this guy slams the lack of procedures that led up to the fire."

David put his arm around my shoulders and gave a little squeeze. "He heard what the last guy said. I'd like to see him clamp down on him and all the others who let the warehouse slip through their fingers." David looked down at me. "This has to stop right here and right now." We sat down in the visitor's gallery, waiting for the truth to emerge. I looked over at Carol's empty seat and sighed. Too bad she wasn't still around to hear this.

But that wasn't what happened. That afternoon, as Bowron began answering questions put to him by Autry James, he casually testified that he made the decision to attack the fire rather than rescue the victims. He called it "going from offensive to defensive mode."

Then he said he kept the knowledge of victims a secret from his firefighters. And then, because of the volume of smoke, Bowron said he gave the order to cut a hole in the roof to allow smoke and hot, toxic gasses to escape. He left the location up to his firefighters, who created a toxic chimney directly above the victims, the victims they had no idea existed.

My blood froze. This man was the decision-maker on the night of the fire. I was aghast... staring blankly, blinking into the realization that there was no rescue attempt... none.

Battalion Chief James Bowron, Curtis Briggs (courtesy of Vicki Ellen Behringer)

Defense attorney Curtis Briggs, on cross-examination, said, "You cut the hole directly above where the victims were located, causing the smoke and hot toxic gasses to be sucked out of the building through the victims. They had no hope of surviving that."

Battalion Chief Bowron showed no emotion about the 36 deaths and told Briggs he wouldn't do anything differently. "I stand by my decisions. And then he closed his eyes and said in a monotone, as if by rote, "We regret the loss of those poor, unfortunate victims."

The blood in my body turned from ice to fire. It pounded in my head. I pressed my notebook to my lips to keep from shouting out. David Gregory, sitting beside me, was clutching the armrests till his knuckles turned white. Thirty-six people rightfully expected to be rescued. They were abandoned. Did they mean nothing to this man?

When questioned again about his decision to attack the fire with no intention of using additional personnel from a 3rd alarm to begin a rescue attempt, Bowron started crying and said he had 12 people inside that building who were risking their lives to fight the worst fire of his experience.

Now he cries! I wondered if I jumped up and screamed at him if it would be worth it. He had only 12 people fighting the worst fire of his life. He put them in that danger, and then he cried for those people doing their jobs and not for the dead. My head throbbed; I was burning up.

To his credit, Briggs used the analogy of the 400+ firefighters who died during 9/11 when going into a burning building to rescue people inside. He said, "They believed in service over self."

Bowron was asked again what he could learn and change to make sure this kind of tragedy never happened again. "I stand by my actions," he repeated.

Tony Serra brought up an important point during his cross-examination. He bellowed out into the courtroom, "There is a civil case pending against the City of Oakland. The city attorney is sitting right here in the courtroom!

It was true. I saw the woman frequently in the district attorney's office, talking with the fighters and police officers who would be testifying. When Serra called her out, she stood up and rushed out of the courtroom.

Serra stated that if Battalion Chief Bowron "...admitted to doing anything wrong, or even saying he might do something differently in the future, that might jeopardize the City of Oakland's defense in a civil lawsuit." I caught myself nodding in agreement. This was bad.

Oakland Fire Department First Response Helmet Camera Footage

That afternoon, after Bowron's damning testimony, the courtroom was darkened, and everyone sat transfixed, watching the video on two large overhead screens. One of the first three firefighters to enter the warehouse had worn a camera on his helmet and filmed their entry into the warehouse.

Heather Mozdean, Oakland Fire Department (courtesy of Vicki Ellen Behringer)

The dark, hazy video was lit only by the headlamps of the other two firefighters. They moved forward achingly slowly. I saw the family members around me leaning forward in their seats, straining to see if any of our loved ones were visible, but it turned out that neither we nor the firefighters could see the stairs through the thick, black smoke. In fact, the firefighters didn't know there were stairs or even that there was a second floor.

As the firefighters made their painstakingly slow journey deeper into the building, I silently rooted for them to suddenly notice the stairs on their right and whispered, "Look up! Go that way!" I willed them to run up to the second floor, where they would see the victims passed out and carry them to safety. They would be saved! Instead, our loved ones remained upstairs, silent, except for a low moaning sound in the background of the video. Someone was still alive. When the video ended, I couldn't stand up. The heavy weight of failure held me down on the hard, wooden seat. I didn't warn the firefighters to look to their right. I failed to save my daughter. David took me by the elbow and helped me navigate the dismal halls to The Family Room. "Come on. Casey's going to talk to us."

At lunch, Casey had to face our scorn. He tried to remain positive about the recent testimony and the dark hopelessness of the video, but he couldn't turn the ship of anger around. We were too depressed to air all of our complaints, but I said, "I heard moaning on the helmet-cam video."

Young Grace Lovio's voice echoed, "I did, too." Casey ignored us. After all, if the victims were still alive when the firefighters arrived on the scene, that would have discredited Bowron's testimony that he did the right thing by not mentioning the victims trapped inside to his fire crews or even trying to affect a rescue.

After that, theories about cover-ups and lies started to churn around The Family Room every time we got together. We might have stated our ideas a bit too loudly while sitting blithely in the courthouse a few feet away from the district attorney's employees. Would that hurt us? The families had filed a civil lawsuit against the Ngs and the City of Oakland. I wondered if what we were saying to each other in the "privacy" of The Family Room was being monitored for use in next year's civil trial. An uncomfortable feeling that we were being betrayed by Alameda County officials started to percolate into our conversations.

It was at this point that we asked all the civil attorneys, court clerks, Victim and Witness Department liaisons, and anyone who was not related to the victims to stay out of The Family Room. We wanted our conversations to remain private.

At lunch that day, one of the moms, Farzaneh, spoke up. "Why did the district attorney choose Derick and Max, the lowest hanging fruit, instead of addressing the root of the problem? The Ng's were aware of the state the warehouse was in. What about the fire and police departments? They saw the fire hazards and said nothing. They should all be held accountable, too!"

The helmet video continued to haunt me. Carol was gone, so I drove home alone that evening, feeling tense and uncomfortable. There was something dirty about this trial, something off. And I did hear moaning on the video. I didn't imagine it. I bit my lip to stop from crying and headed off, swallowed whole into the realm of nervous cars and looming tractor-trailer trucks. I dissolved into the flow. Was it Chelsea? Did I hear my daughter's last moan?

That night, I was finally home, sitting up in my own bed, laptop resting on my thighs, my notebook open beside me. What was the point of this week's testimony? I'm not certain what I was expecting the trial to look like, but this wasn't it. Watching the trial during the first and second weeks was akin to watching a tennis match. Our heads swung back and forth as testimony swung from one line of questioning to another. The chaotic presentation, or lack of presentation, continued with the scattershot order of witness testimony. I was starting to get the feeling that this trial was thrown together in sloppy haste. The district attorney wasn't prepared for a trial. The plea bargain had been a cheap, easy out.

Chapter 31

The Last Survivor

May 22, 2019

Sam Maxwell was scheduled to testify as a survivor who experienced the start of the fire on the 2nd floor. He alone had been badly injured and was the last person who made it down those treacherous stairs alive.

First, Tony Serra objected to Sam's testimony because the jurors might be swayed by sympathy for his physical condition and damage to his vocal cords that distorted his voice. Then, Serra said Sam's hands were "tremulous," and his voice was "hollow and ghost-like." He

Testimony of Sam Maxwell (courtesy of Vicki Ellen Behringer)

also implied Sam might have memory issues. The judge overruled his objections and agreed to use a speech therapist, Benjamin Reece, to be Sam's interpreter.

Through Reece, Sam said he was among friends that

night. It's true, Sam's voice was raspy, but I could make out what he was saying and feel the emotion in his voice as he talked about going to Ghost Ship that night to see his friend Joey Casio and the band Obsidian Blade perform. When asked about the front stairs, he described them as poorly constructed, with a dangerous section near the top that was more like a boat ramp than stairs. Upstairs, he saw dim lights, music, and people happily dancing and socializing. The downstairs area was blocked off. Suddenly, the sound of the loud music got quieter, and he noticed smoke from the base of a pillar he was standing next to. The smoke had a noxious smell.

There was only one exit that he knew of. He knew others also noticed the smoke because everyone started to line up at the stairs where a bottleneck of about 80 people formed. The fire illuminated everything. There were flames at the back of the warehouse. Sam waited for the bottleneck to clear and looked to make sure no one had been trampled.

By the time he made his way onto the stairs, Sam thought he was going to die trying to escape. The fire had spread like "spilled milk." He lunged through the flames coming from below the stairs. His hands and nose were burned, but he was wearing a leather jacket that protected him when he thought the flames would envelop him. He said, "I chose death on those stairs rather than the unknown risk of trying to find another way out."

Once outside, Sam went to the only store he saw in the neighborhood, a liquor store, and asked if they had burn cream. They didn't, so he bought water. He walked back to the Ghost Ship and a friend, shocked by the sight of his burns, immediately drove Sam to Highland Hospital, where he was admitted and placed in a medically induced coma. Sam was left with nerve damage to his hands and feet, as well as irreversible brain and organ damage due to smoke inhalation. "Plus, I am in this wheelchair."

Sam said he recognized Max Harris as the person who sat at the booth and "took my money" at the door. When asked if everyone on the stairs ahead of him made it out to safety, Sam said, "I only know my own experience."

Testimony of Sam Maxwell. L-R: Benjamin Reece, Sam Maxwell, Judge Thompson, Autrey James, Max Harris, Derick Almena, Tony Serra (courtesy of Vicki Ellen Behringer)

Chapter 32

Chelsea, My Sweet, Brave Girl

May 23, 2019

On Thursday morning, Autrey James called a resident named Carmen to describe the night of the fire and introduce the 911 tapes. She was a young, beautiful woman with short, wavy, dark hair and large, expressive dark eyes. Her face lit up as she answered questions about sharing the space with 25 other people. Autrey established the excessive electricity use by asking Carmen to name her personal appliances: a small refrigerator, toaster oven, an electric water kettle, computer, a space heater, a hot plate, and lights.

I pictured each of the 25 living spaces filled with similar appliances running off extension cords and shuddered. One spark would cause a fire. The potential for sparks was exponential.

I wriggled in my seat during the cross-examination as Serra asked Carmen questions pertaining to the interior appearance of the warehouse, and she continually echoed Serra's words of "awesome" and "beautiful." Her voice was soft but resonant as she exclaimed over her Ghost Ship home, saying, almost breathlessly, that it was "the most beautiful place I'd ever seen even though I traveled the world extensively."

I wondered what the tack was on this approach. The line "Here we go again" played in my head each time Tony Serra brought up the appearance of the place. Did he honestly think it was possible to justify the deaths of thirty-six people by saying they died in a pretty place? Did he consider what he called "awesome beauty" to be an excuse for skirting fire codes and setting the scene for one of the worst fire disasters in California or even the country? I remembered the videos I'd seen of the filthy, run-down, debris-strewn warehouse before the fire. Why was Serra focused on how nice it looked?

I woke up from my musings as Carmen changed the subject from "awesome beauty" to smelling smoke from her loft. She described lying on her loft bed, her face inches beneath the ceiling of the 1st floor. She saw an "orange glow about the size of a microwave" through the tapestry she used as a wall between the foot of her loft bed and the back of the warehouse. Carmen climbed down from her loft, grabbed her phone and coat, and walked toward the front door. There, she met Max, who was just entering the building and yelling, "Fire!" Everyone downstairs on the 1st floor "sort of shuddered and turned toward the front door." They left the building in an orderly fashion.

When she got outside, she started to pull her phone out of her coat pocket when a girl with blond hair with some pink in it and very thick eyeliner asked her, "Are you calling 911?" When Carmen said yes, the girl pushed past her and went inside the warehouse. She never came out again. This made Carmen cry. Carmen's call to 911 was the first official notice to the Oakland Fire Department.

Testimony of Carmen Brita. L-R: Casey Bates, Carmen Brita, Curtis Briggs, Max Harris, Tyler Smith, Judge Thompson, Brian Goetz, Derick Almena, Autrey James, Tony Serra (courtesy of Vicki Ellen Behringer)

I froze. José had testified about crashing into a girl with blond hair and "big eyes, just really big eyes" who was wearing blue. They collided just inside the front door. He sobbed heavily and said, "I didn't save her. I should have grabbed her and pulled her out!" And I started to get a sick feeling. Could that have been Chelsea, who was safe outside? She had blond hair with pink tips on one side. Her stage makeup included dramatic eye shadow. And on such a cold night, she most certainly would have worn her blue jacket. Was she standing outside the building when the fire broke out?

All the blood in my body turned to icy slush and slid down to my feet as Carmen continued to talk about calling 911. I pictured a girl making sure Carmen was calling 911, and then running inside to warn her friends. Anyone who knew Chelsea knew that was exactly what she would do. Aaron's previous testimony made it clear: Loud music was still playing. People were still dancing upstairs when those who were on the first floor exited the building. Joel saw Chelsea upstairs shortly before the fire broke out, so she would have known who was still inside.

My brain went hysterical, desperate for answers, and I grabbed the picture of Chelsea hidden away in my notebook.

As soon as the judge called for a recess. I burst out into the hallway, my heart pounding, and flew over to Carmen, holding a photo of Chelsea in my outstretched hand. Carmen looked startled when she saw my anxious face rushing toward her, then looked down at the picture and cried, "That's her!" She fell onto my shoulder, sobbing, and I was undone. Carmen saw Chelsea outside, safe and alive when the fire broke out. Chelsea was alive! I tucked my head shaking "no" into Carmen's shoulder. It couldn't be true. A moan started deep in my stomach and spread out to my fingers and toes. I couldn't breathe. I held onto Carmen for support, then looked up to see Max Harris's friends surrounding us and staring at me. Carmen was their friend. I was not. These were the same people who had held FREE MAX signs in my face. I had to get away from their questioning eyes.

I locked my backbone and pushed away from Carmen. Other family members were standing across the hallway near the heavy courtroom doors, but I could barely see them through the welling of tears that spilled over onto my hands and clothes. I walked toward the familiar faces, but my knees wobbled, and my body pitched forward. They were too far away. I aimed my body toward the marble wall near the bank of elevators, stumbling till I placed my palms on the cold stone, turned, and pressed my back against the wall, slumping down to the floor. I sat with legs outstretched, sinking forward, covering my face, and howling into my hands. My body rocked forward and back. This couldn't be real. Chelsea was alive! She was safe! And then she went inside and up the stairs into the fire.

Members of the families, Farzaneh Hoda, David Gregory, Grace Lovio, Ivania Chavarria, Chris Allen, Linda Regan, Sue Slocum, and Mary Vega, ran over and slipped down to the floor with me. They sat with me till I caught my breath and encircled me with love, protecting me from prying reporter's questions. Someone pressed a tissue into my hands. Others put their arms around me.

The security guard at the door called, "Court is back in session." I sucked in a ragged breath, wiped my face with the tissue, and felt gentle hands helping me to my feet. Someone gave me a bottle of water; I think it was Farzaneh. Voices whispered lovingly in my ear. We rose in unison and inched our way back into the courtroom. After two years of unmitigated grief, I was well-practiced in the art of pretending to be fine. I breathed deeply and sank heavily into that hard, cruel, wooden seat. Then I slid the mask of impenetrability onto my face and stared straight ahead. My eyes may have been swollen and red, but I was not going to be kicked out of the courtroom for showing emotion.

Chelsea with "Big Eyes" stage makeup.

Miserable thoughts screamed in my head, but my face was still. We had all speculated about the identity of the girl who was seen near the front door and didn't survive. Now, we knew who she was. Chelsea. My Chelsea Faith. Carmen testified that she was safe outside the warehouse before running into the burning warehouse. José had collided with her inside the front door. She wasn't trying to find her way outside. She was running in!

When Battalion Chief Bowron said he pulled his firefighters out of the building for their safety, he used the words "service over self" as the firefighters' motto. Chelsea was the purest example of Service over Self. I can see her desperately asking if anyone had told the people upstairs that there was a fire. I knew she would be the one to push her way past the people exiting the first floor and run inside to warn her friends. I was furious with her for going back into a burning building, but it's so Chelsea. I had to admit, I was proud of her, too. She did what she thought was the right thing to do, but I wished from the depths of pain that she hadn't done it. If only I could have been there to stop her.

After the break, Carmen calmly strolled back to the witness stand. The judge warned her not to speak to outsiders and warned the visitors in the gallery not to interfere with witnesses. I was appalled by the inequity! I wasn't the only person who spoke with Carmen in the hallway; she was surrounded by Max Harris supporters, but I was the only person held to account. Who turned me in? I looked over at Tony Serra, who stood looking down, busily shuffling papers on the table in front of him. He looked glum. Was my sorrow an obstacle for him? Was Chelsea's act of bravery a problem?

At the end of the day, Autrey James and Casey Bates reprimanded me for stepping beyond healthy boundaries. They said I may be asked by Judge Thompson to leave the courtroom the following Tuesday morning after the Memorial Day long weekend. My defense was, I was traumatized by the surprise of learning Chelsea was alive and safe when the fire broke out.

My reaction was that of a mother. I had been attending the trial every day to find out how she died. The puzzle pieces were falling into place with what I didn't want to hear, but I did want to know.

Chapter 33

Forensic Pathologists' Reports

May 6-23, 2019

Four pathologists reported the cause of death and the percentage of carbon monoxide in the bloodstream for each victim. Some of the victims were shielded from the flames, and some were so badly burned that they were identified by DNA, but it was smoke that killed all of them. Most of the victims had carbon monoxide (CO) percentage readings in the 30-45% range. A reading of 20% is lethal.

The pathologists described what it was like to die of smoke inhalation. I squirmed as they talked about "air hunger," the physical irritation, gag response, cough, panic, vomiting, and disorientation that occur with this type of death. One pathologist said that the time it took for the victims to perish was from seconds to a maximum of five minutes. The brain will not survive, but the victims can keep breathing after losing consciousness. This would account for the CO percentages that in some cases were over 45%. The doctor looked out at the families in the gallery, and I believe the point was to reassure us that our loved ones did not suffer. I was not reassured.

Testimony of pathologist (courtesy of Vicki Ellen Behringer)

In the last afternoon session of the third week, right after Carmen's devastating testimony, a medical examiner gave the final list of victims from the fire. Each time a forensic pathologist or medical examiner was brought to the stand, I held my breath waiting for Chelsea's name to be read aloud. She had to be on this list because it was the last one. My muscles tightened as the carbon monoxide percentages were given for the last eight victims, with the numbers ranging from 33% to 61%, except for Chelsea. She had 80%. A gasp went up in the courtroom. The doctor said that level was unusual. All victims had soot in their airways. I started crying quietly. Did this mean she lived long enough to take in that extreme amount of carbon monoxide? Was it because she ran up the stairs? Would she have suffered longer?

A hand reached up from the seat behind me and caressed my shoulder. I'm not sure who comforted me that afternoon. I was blinded by pain, but I could feel the love in the gentle touch.

The Drive Home

I had to drive myself home that night. Sioux had an acting rehearsal, and I had no idea this would be such a devastating day. I walked in a daze to the Oakland Museum parking lot and just sat there in my car, shivering uncontrollably for a long time, perhaps an hour, perhaps longer. How does one react to the news that their daughter chose to enter a burning building? That she suffered and died when she could have lived? I longed to place myself by her side that night, to grab her by the collar and drag her back from the flames. What could I have done to dissuade her from trying to warn her friends of the danger? Probably nothing.

I shook violently at first, then the tremors softened, and finally, they were spent. I started up my car and pulled out of the parking garage. The rest of the drive was a blur of cars, lane changes, and unspeakable sorrow. My daughter was alive when the fire started, and now she was dead. I held off crying until I pulled into my garage, trudged upstairs, clambered into bed, and stayed there for the rest of the long Memorial Day weekend. Chelsea was alive. She was safe, and she chose to warn her friends. I lay on my side in bed, enveloped in dark thoughts, my breath shallow, my heart leaden, repeating over and over to myself, "Chelsea should be here. I want her back."

From Sabrina on Facebook - May 26, 2019

Ghost ship trigger warning.

From the first few weeks of the testimony at the criminal GS trial, we've gotten a better picture of what

Chelsea's final moments were the night of the fire. To put it simply:

Chelsea was spotted outside the front of the building right as the fire started. She made sure another woman, who had just made it outside, was calling 911. She then proceeded to run back into the building. On her way back in, she ran into a man who was trying to escape. He tried to lead her back outside, but she kept going up the stairs to the top floor. Chelsea had been upstairs not long before being spotted outside, so she knew her friends were upstairs, she knew a lot of partygoers were there, still unaware of the fire.

If you knew Chelsea, this is classic Chelsea behavior. She wasn't being a "hero", she just was prone to rushing in and getting the job done. I don't think anyone could have stopped her from running in to help her friends and partygoers. She always wanted the community of people who were at shows she played at to be well taken care of, safe, and having fun. She would have felt a strong responsibility to get everyone to safety, even though it was not her responsibility at all. She would never have just stood outside knowing her dear friends and music community members were at serious risk. Someone needed to go upstairs and warn everyone to get out, and no one else was doing it, so she did.

There are many more questions, and so many different emotions, and so much more to this complex story. But I just needed to make sure people know this at least. She was a good person.

Thanks.

Chapter 34

ATF Investigation

May 28, 2019

I slipped into the courtroom on Tuesday morning without being noticed. I kept my head down and took notes.

The courtroom felt cold and otherworldly that morning. Sioux sat next to me and whispered, "They're here. I can feel all 36 souls hovering here above us." I looked at her and looked up. Sioux put her hand on my arm. "They're with us."

I wanted to say something to Sioux, to find out more, but just then loudspeakers crackled for a moment and then a woman's voice came on. "911, What is your emergency?" Carmen's voice reported the fire to the woman. Two other frantic voices followed. Then my skin prickled as a young man shouted, "Save me! We're dying! Come save us!" He was one of the victims. I thought I recognized his voice. Was it Travis? In the background people were screaming for help. The fire station was only half a block away. Of course, they would be saved.

No one came to rescue them. Max Harris, who said he ran past the stairway three or four times before retrieving his phone to call 911, was not on the recording.

At the lunch recess, Sioux smiled at me and said, "I could feel their warm presence looking down on us. They were all here." The way she said those words felt like warm syrup on my soul. Was it possible? We walked over to the Oakland Museum Cafe and ordered our meals. Carrying my food on a tray, I walked to our usual table with the others and noticed a white feather on the floor next to my chair. I put my tray down and picked up the feather. Sioux collected them. She looked at it and said, "You keep it. It's a sign. How often do you find a beautiful white feather in a cafeteria?" I smiled weakly. Probably never.

That afternoon, we learned details of the fire investigation and the defense's speculation about the validity of the Fire Origin Report. Because of the extreme heat, all evidence was destroyed and no cause for the fire was determined.

We had already learned how unsafe the building was. A parade of contractors, electricians, firefighters, and police officers had attested to the dangers. On most days, the crushing boredom of back-and-forth questions and answers and the relentless repetition of dull words unhinged from emotion spilled into the room. How could the death of these extraordinary beings be relegated to a dull recitation of leases, squabbles over emails, fire codes, and obvious lies about whether people lived at the warehouse or not? Wasn't there such a thing as stipulation? Almena and Harris lied. That was a given. Why was it necessary to show videos of them lying repeatedly?

In between a few stunning revelations, the drudgery of the trial wore on. I often looked over at the jurors, feeling their exhaustion mingle with my own. Slumped posture, heads resting on hands, notebooks abandoned on laps, they seemed to be drifting off into private thoughts. There were times when I found myself elsewhere, too—Christmas morning watching my daughters tear open presents, or tipping pails of sand into castles on the beach or standing frozen in a parking lot staring at a burning building. Grief never left my side. Words rattled endlessly in the background describing the blighted setting, ignoring the people who died.

ATF Fire Investigation

On the final half day of that week, Barbara Maxwell, ATF Special Agent, and Certified Fire Investigator's testimony filled the entire morning. She talked at length about the Evolution of Fire.

Ms. Maxwell gave a timeline of the fire and, naturally, Tony Serra asked for all testimony related to a fire timeline be stricken. He yelled it was all "...hearsay, double hearsay, and hearsay galore!" Much flailing of arms ensued.

Briggs spent an inordinate amount of time trying to get Ms. Maxwell to identify a picture of a cylindrical item in piles of debris as a broken and scorched bottle. (Remember the Molotov cocktail defense?) Ms. Maxwell kept saying, "It doesn't look like a

(Courtesy of Vicki Ellen Behringer)

bottle to me." Frankly, it didn't look like a bottle to anyone, and even if it was, the picture was taken in the kitchen area. Would a broken bottle really be that suspicious?

(Courtesy of Vicki Ellen Behringer)

Talk moved on to a "clean burn" area, which is caused by a fire so hot and prolonged that it burns away the soot and smoke on a non-combustible area, such as the concrete interior walls of the warehouse. Briggs proposed that the white "irregular shape of a clean burn on the back wall" was caused by someone throwing gasoline on the wall and igniting it. Ms. Maxwell refuted this theory in a lengthy reply.

Tony Serra, stood up and laughed during his cross examination, referring to the Investigative Response Team as "you all." He had four theories:

1. Maybe the point of origin is elsewhere in the warehouse.
2. No one interviewed his client, Derick Almena, about whether he had any enemies.
3. The owners collected 3.6 million dollars from their insurance policy. It could have been them.
4. Men in black hoodies throwing Molotov cocktails present a scenario that no one could have predicted or prevented. Mr. Serra spent at least an hour on his theory that a glass bottle filled with gasoline

could have "melted or evaporated" which would eliminate the evidence of arson.

I sighed. Serra's alternative stories couldn't get any more unbelievable, could they? Turns out, they could.

Chapter 35

A New Low

June 3, 2019

During the fifth week of testimony, Jon, a friend of two other survivors, Ryan and Chris, and two of the fire victims, Alex Ghassan and Hanna Ruax, was called to the stand. He and his friends were on the 2nd floor when the fire began.

Jon described climbing to the top of the stairs where he saw about 40 people talking and laughing. A DJ was at the back booth and Jon's friends, Alex and Hanna, were stretched out on a Bali Bed. To the left, there was a six-foot-tall, bubble-like projection screen.

Jon started down the stairs when he saw a small stream of smoke at the bottom of a pole. At first, he wondered if it was a fog machine. Then, his eyes met Hanna's and he felt sure they both knew it was fire. He yelled at Alex to leave. "... at first, you know, I think he was confused, and I do remember like, you know, one of the last things I saw on his face was some confusion about what we were trying to say to him."

As Jon took a few steps down the stairs, a big cloud of smoke poured up and hit his face. His survival instinct kicked in and told him, 'Just go, move as quickly as you can.' A woman with blond hair "jostled around" him about two or three steps from the top. She was coughing and said, "The smoke is too much." He held his breath and ran down the stairs with his eyes closed.

Jon thought Alex and Hanna were behind him, so he continued down the stairs through the smoke. He held his hands out in front of him and groped his way toward the front door. He pressed on the wall as he moved to help him navigate until it suddenly gave way. It was the door. He had made it outside.

Jon said the stairs made his escape confusing. His footing was uneven, he was disoriented because of the different directions of the stairs, and there was a big drop at the bottom. Jon testified that by the time he got halfway down the stairs, the music grew quieter. By the time he got to the bottom of the stairs, the music was turned off. He didn't know about the lights. It was too thick with smoke.

The girl was Chelsea! Jon's story verified Chelsea's path from outside the front door, into the entryway, and up the stairs. Of course, she kept going past Jon because the music was still playing, and she knew her friends were in danger.

When Jon made it outside, he turned on his cell phone flashlight in the doorway and yelled, "Come this way!" Two or three times. Someone yelled "Get the ladder" on the side lot to the left of the building, so he and a few other people headed over there. Jon climbed on a car and broke windows with a rock until his hand bled. Someone else climbed the ladder.

Finally, the Fire Department showed up. There was a frenzy, and he assumed the fire department would take over the rescue, but they didn't show the same urgency he felt. He told the lead, "There are people up there." She looked surprised. He thought it was 5 to 10 minutes until the fire fighters went inside.

During cross-examination, Serra asked Jon to repeat his story about the woman who pushed around him at the top of the stairs. Jon said, "She had blond hair and jostled past him coughing and saying, "The smoke is too much."

Tony Serra shouted, "Was anyone yelling, 'Don't come down!'?"

Jon quietly said, "No."

Tony Serra stepped closer and asked Jon if the woman he'd run into on the stairs had said, "The smoke is too much," then he yelled, "LIKE IT WAS TOO MUCH TO GO DOWNSTAIRS!" He did not wait for Jon to answer before turning away and storming back to his seat. Obviously, he didn't want Jon to answer. His dramatic indignation was supposed to signal to the jurors that this was a true statement.

Standing behind his table, Serra then made a big point of saying Jon was a hero for stepping back inside the door two or three times. "You must have saved lives!"

Jon answered modestly," I don't know if I did."

Then that old man looked directly at me in the gallery. It felt to me as if he somehow was gloating, like Jon saved lives and Chelsea didn't. He already knew from José's and Carmen's testimony that it was Chelsea who had been seen outside, in the entryway, and then ran upstairs. I ground my teeth together loud enough for me to hear it.

It was Tony Serra's job to find anyone other than his client responsible for 36 deaths, so he implied that Chelsea stopped people from leaving. Stopped them!

The warehouse was a firetrap. Derick Almena ignored fire safety regulations in building out the place. How could arson or even an innocent girl running up the stairs be blamed for

Almena's negligence? Heck, Chelsea was no longer near the stairs when at least 10 others escaped. Not one of them saw her there. She was already upstairs. Would she have run into a burning building to tell her friends to stay upstairs and die? The argument was beyond absurd; it was desperate.

The fire killed 36 healthy, intelligent people, many of whom were found dead lined up in a single file waiting to go down the narrow, illegal staircase. They were overcome by the smoke. Chelsea was one of them. This was a classic case of Blame the Victim. Even better for the defense, she was dead so she couldn't fight back.

These are the Facts

The second attorney for Max Harris, Tyler Smith, ran down the courthouse steps and headed straight toward the TV news cameras during the afternoon lunch break. I watched him smirk into the camera and say, "Some people may learn things they don't want to hear, but these are the facts."

Naturally, the cameras turned to me as I sputtered in the background. Smith was taking a lesson from Serra by blaming the victims, and I wasn't going to let that lie stand. I stepped up to the cameras and told the reporters, "I have something to say to that." I criticized Tony Serra's "smarmy tactics of throwing my daughter under the bus and blaming her for the deaths of her friends." I could barely speak, and my head was pounding so loudly I struggled to find words that would convey the conniving audacity of the lies these men were telling.

I tried to control my anger so I didn't look like a crazy woman on the 6:00 news, and said, "While there are countless reasons the Ghost Ship should never have been built, it was. The fact is Almena built it and Max Harris invited people in.

My daughter tried to save lives. Harris and Almena's negligence caused their deaths."

Finally, on Wednesday, June 5, 2019, the prosecution put together the presentation that The families had been waiting for. They turned their attention to Max Harris, showing he was the only person at Ghost Ship the night of the fire who held a position of responsibility. They wanted to prove he was a manager of the Ghost Ship operation and should have taken care to make sure the event was reasonably safe. He was paid in free rent.

Cell phone messages established Max as the person who made bank deposits at Wells Fargo and signed at least one lease for Ghost Ship. Those were management tasks.

Max's Tinder account on his phone was used to show multiple times Max bragged about his position at Ghost Ship. Three days before the fire, Max said he was the manager and getting ready for an after-hours event on First Friday. There were more Tinder messages of a similar nature. Max wanted the world to know he was in charge that night.

Max Harris testifying about the Facebook invite to the December 2nd show at Ghost Ship (courtesy of Vicki Ellen Behringer)

Max also sent and received emails with Derick and the Ngs

about late rent payments. Obviously, Max was in charge. Most were signed by Max Ohr, Executive Director, Satya Yuga.

The Alameda County inspector who obtained the search warrant for Max's phone said there were some large date gaps in his text messages, which appeared to be erasures. This testimony was stricken.

After Casey had finished the prosecution's audio-visual presentation, he turned to the judge and said, "The People Rest."

(*Courtesy of Vicki Ellen Behringer*)

What?!! My jaw dropped. Sioux and I looked at each other in shock. A stir of voices rumbled through the visitors' gallery. This was the Prosecution's case? David Gregory sat up straight and held his palms up in front of his chest as if saying, "That's all there is?" Other parents were grumbling to each other in disbelief and shaking fists in angry frustration. This was it? What was going on here?

The families left the courtroom bewildered and fuming. We walked back in a disgruntled huddle to The Family Room, still reeling in shock. All around the room questions were shouted:

"What happened? This trial is being thrown away. Something isn't right."

"Didn't they want to prosecute Max?"

"What about him lying about the 911 call?"

Sioux and I left the building and headed toward the museum parking lot. I didn't know what to say. Sioux quietly said, "This was supposed to be Max Week." I knew what she meant. It felt like the prosecuting team wanted Max to go free.

We drove home that evening rehashing all the arguments that should have been used in the trial. We conducted a thorough prosecution of Derick Almena and Max Harris while Sioux navigated the sluggish, rush-hour traffic. We included the Ngs and the officials who hadn't bothered to write up hazard reports in our commute prosecution. By the time Sioux dropped me off, I was convinced something nefarious was going on in the DA's office. This case could have been the means for assuring another tragedy would never happen. Instead, it curdled in a meaningless stew of words, allowing the neglect by city and county agencies to go unchallenged.

Chapter 36

Harris Defense Begins
The Dog Whistle Defense

June 10, 2019

The sixth week of testimony was the start of the defense case. Max Harris's attorneys would go first, and I knew they would bring in witnesses trying to prove Max was an innocent saint. When his defense was finished, Derick Almena's attorneys would try to prove Almena had no idea his illegal apartments and event space had to be brought up to code.

Testimony for Max included character witnesses, a so-called witness to an "arsonist" gang, a befuddled resident, and the return of the Oakland Fire Battalion Chief James Bowron.

Max's professor and advisor at the Lexington Massachusetts College of Art and Design told us Max was honest, giving, charitable, and a good community member. He was especially interested in world religions, ethics, and morality. He "... used music to bring spiritual awakening."

I may have started yawning.

Several more witnesses were brought in to attest to Max

Harris's saint-like personae. I looked over at Derick Almena who was staring down at the table in front of him and seemed depressed. I couldn't imagine Derick would have many character witnesses like this, if any.

Fire Witness and the Gang of "Spaniards and Chicanos"

For over a week, Tony Serra had been shouting about a major witness he had up his sleeve whenever he appeared on TV news reports. He was going Full Arson! This witness was going to "prove beyond a reasonable doubt that arson was the cause of the fire and his client, Derick Almena, was innocent!" Max Harris's attorneys agreed this witness would support the claim that their client also had nothing to do with the 36 deaths. Tony Serra kept up the harangue, "Arson!"

Waiting for Serra's mystery witness to appear, I sat in the courtroom wondering why Tony Serra felt that arson would excuse his client from filling the warehouse with illegal tenants and flammable materials, ignoring warnings of safety hazards from carpenters and electricians, and not bothering to install sprinklers, lit exit signs, fire alarms, smoke alarms, and other warning and mitigation systems. Any spark would be deadly in that place. His client was responsible. Arson would be a terrible crime. So, too, was Almena's deadly negligence. One does not excuse the other.

I changed this special witness' name to Alice as I wrote about the trial because I didn't want to embarrass her further by using her real name. Her testimony was that bad. When she arrived in the courtroom, Alice, a heavy-set, middle-aged woman, seemed barely awake and shuffled her feet to take the stand. She said she lived in Oakland for over 50 years, and currently lived in East Oakland.

Testimony of "Alice"
(Courtesy of Vicki Ellen
Behringer)

This witness' story began on the night of the fire, when she attended a church service and left with her friend, Donna (again, not her real name). They drove home together, but then Alice said she was hungry and "slightly diabetic," so she drove down International Avenue toward the "30s" to go to her favorite taco wagon. She said she saw smoke near the Ghost Ship and drove in that direction.

Tyler Smith for the Harris defense asked, "You said that you saw smoke?"

Alice said "Smoke."

"And so did you see where the smoke was coming from?"

"Yes."

"And where was it coming from?"

"It was coming from the Ghost Ship warehouse."

"And how did you know it was the Ghost Ship warehouse?"

"Because I have been there a couple of times to a couple of their parties."

"So, you were familiar with the name, that it was called the Ghost Ship warehouse?"

"Yes, sir."

"So, what did you do next once you saw the smoke?"

"I kept driving around the blocks between International going to the in-between street. Wendy's is on one side; the Ghost Ship is on the other. I came down that street, and I was continuing to go all the way around the block at least 20 times, and I noticed the fire kept getting worse."

MR. BATES: "Objection, non-responsive."

Judge Thompson for the court responded, "I sustained as to the latter portion after "20 times."

A few minutes later, Curtis Briggs asked, "Did you make any other stops?"

"No."

"So, you went directly from circling around the block to the taco wagons?"

"Yeah. I drove circling 20 times, and I went to the taco wagon."

Tyler Smith stepped up again for the Harris defense and asked, "Did you notice if the Fire Department was responding at all?"

"Yeah. At least—at least five fire trucks had finally gotten there."

"How do you know that?"

"Because I kept driving and driving around until I noticed the fire was getting worse and out of hand, and more fire trucks kept coming, and they were trying to put the fire out."

"Did you notice if they had their sirens on or not?"

"Yeah, they had their sirens on. Yes."

"Did you notice if they were blaring their horns?"

"The sirens I heard."

"The sirens? When you were at the taco stand, could you still hear the sirens?

"They had already lined up trying to put the fire out. They were—there were quite a few fire trucks trying to put the fire out."

"What did you say again that the men were wearing?"

"Everyone had on black, and I noticed they had on hoodies, and when they first arrived—"

Casey Bates for the prosecution objected, "Nonresponsive."

After all this driving, Alice said she needed food, so she

drove to the taco wagon near Goodwill, which is about one and a half blocks from Ghost Ship. She got out and her friend, Donna, stayed in the car. About 14 to 19 men in black hoodies came running toward the taco wagon from either direction. They were happy and loud. The fire was still burning. When the men arrived at the taco truck, they took off their hoodies. She could hear them. "They were "ESTATIC (sic) loud and happy." She repeated this mispronounced word several times as her testimony continued.

Alice described the men to Tony Serra for the Almena defense, "After they pulled their hoodies back, it looked to me they looked like Spaniards or Chicanos, but I did notice at no time no one spoke Spanish."

Serra asked, "And have you seen, for instance—I don't know—criminal types like, you know—I don't know—prostitutes or drug dealers in that area?"

Casey Bates said, "Objection, relevance." He was overruled.

Alice continued, "I wouldn't know."

Serra asked, "Isn't it a fact that you believed, and it caused you great fear, which you still have, that these people in black were a Hispanic gang? Isn't that a fact?

"I thought possibly they might be some type of a gang. Yes."

"And that it's what made you fearful to go directly to law enforcement."

"That is why I drug my feet about getting involved. Yes, sir."

When the owner of the taco truck said his stand was closed, she went to the next taco wagon up the block. The 14 to 19 men in black hoodies ran ahead of her and got into line in front of her. Alice was noticeably irritated as she said this. She said she became suspicious and asked her friend, Donna, to get out of the car and "just listen." The utterances of the "Spaniards or Chicanos" were all in English so she could understand them.

She first reported her suspicions weeks after the fire because she feared for her life and didn't want to get involved right away. She said no report was written up. She also visited the site of the burned-out warehouse and spoke to the security guard there about what she heard.

Tony Serra noted that Alice used the words "They were ecstatic."

Mr. Serra then stated that this meant they were "loud, congratulating themselves, and that it was an emotional state."

"Yes."

Alice said she was shocked at what she heard and could hardly believe it. She delayed reporting out of fear of retaliation because the men looked like criminals. She came forward after two months because someone contacted her.

"I couldn't rest at night knowing those people died in the fire the way they did."

Alice said, "Five of the men were gloating about the way the fire was going. It was like a police report." (I thought she said, Praise Report, but the transcript reads Police Report.)

She never saw these men before and wouldn't recognize them again. When asked if she heard anything about committing a crime or who started the fire, she stated she did not hear them say anything about starting the fire, but she speculated that they might have been involved in setting the fire because of what she heard.

Casey asked her on his cross-examination, "Do you recall what time it was approximately on December 2nd that you noticed the fire?"

Alice answered clearly. "I'm pretty sure it was between—I think around 9:45—9:30, 9:45 when it started."

This was a critical error. The woman had just testified that she observed the fire two hours before it began.

As the woman's story unfolded, I was shocked the Defense allowed her to testify at all. The word *unbelievable* doesn't begin to describe the racist lies and gossipy narrative this woman spewed on the stand.

Alice was excused. I was appalled.

At lunch I knew I shouldn't laugh at the woman, but how could anyone take her seriously? I chuckled, "She circled the burning building 20 times! Two hours before the fire even started!" Everyone at the table started talking at once. It seemed like Derick Almena would find himself in prison for a long time if this was the whole defense case.

Ivania looked serious. Her dark ponytail moved side to side as she interrupted. "No. The jury could still believe her. It only takes one." We all settled down at that.

Someone asked, "But could they really believe that crazy story?"

Ivania shrugged. "One of them could."

After lunch, we all walked back into the courtroom together, subdued. Alice brought some levity at first. Then we faced the reality that justice could hinge on this woman's fantastical testimony. Was there no stunt Tony Serra wouldn't pull to get his client off?

Chapter 37

The Forest Witch

June 11, 2019

It was hard to believe, but Tony Serra brought in another witness whose story even topped Alice's. Their next witness was a resident who moved into a trailer near the front door at Ghost Ship in February 2016. On the night of the fire, he invited an OK Cupid date to come to his place. She arrived around 10:30 p.m. The young man gave her a tour of the upstairs, then they went down to his airstream trailer near the foot of the front stairs.

(Courtesy of Vicki Ellen Behringer)

While watching a movie, he "heard a scuffle" and "two or three people shouting." He couldn't hear what they were saying, but it sounded loud and harsh. He thought it was a fight and that "security" would handle it. The witness poked his head out of his trailer to see what was going on and he saw two or three people running to the front door. Someone said the word "fire." He didn't recognize the people, nor could he say they were men or women.

The witness told the woman with him to run, but he stayed to grab some of his belongings. He thought he had more time. He assumed his date was safe ahead of him.

As he ran out, the young man saw a girl standing by the front stairs, frantically screaming at the top of her lungs, "This is the will of the spirit of the forest! Don't come down the stairs!" Serra then asked his witness to describe the woman who told people not to come downstairs.

I was frozen. Would he say it was Chelsea? Would he say the "blonde woman with the big eyes and blue jacket was to blame for 36 deaths?

Instead, the witness said she wore "a red beanie and a green dress."

I smiled when this description was quite different from the three other witnesses' statements about Chelsea's appearance. I thought back on the zebra-striped tights, black miniskirt, black sequin top, blue and black woolen scarf, and blue jacket I received from the coroner's office. His witch was definitely not Chelsea.

The witness said he was partially blinded by smoke. Things fell and got in his way as he tried to escape. Serra ignored this.

Once outside, the young man said he found his date and put his gathered belongings into the trunk of her car. They watched the fire for a while, and then they went to get something to eat.

All in all, that had to be the Worst First Date Ever.

The Ride Home

Once we got in her car, I was anxious to share something I'd seen with Sioux. "I've seen a picture online of the woman that guy described, I know it! There was a painting at the foot of the stairs in Ghost Ship. It was taken at some other party. I've got to find it. I could send it to Casey or Autrey. It proves that Chelsea wasn't the forest witch."

Sioux looked at me quizzically. "What did it look like?"

"The painting was the head and torso of a woman screaming. Her arms are raised over her head. The background looked like fire. When that guy saw a woman at the foot of the stairs telling people to turn back and stay upstairs, it might have been his confusion with all the smoke." I let out a little laugh. "I'm being generous here. It also could have been drugs."

When I got home that night, I scoured the internet for the picture and finally found it posted on YouTube in the comments under one of Chelsea's songs. Drug use was not unknown at the warehouse. David Lim, the original Assistant District Attorney for the case, had made a point of letting me know that Chelsea had no trace of drugs or alcohol in her blood when she died. Nothing would have colored her level-headed response to an emergency. I couldn't help but wonder, could the same be said for this witness? Could he have seen the painting and panicked before running outside? The unfortunate one-time date was not called to testify. No one else saw the mystery witch or heard someone screaming, "Don't come down!"

I sent the photo to Casey Bates and Autrey James but received no response. It wasn't used in the trial. I suppose this outrageous line of defense wasn't worth a response, but as Chelsea's advocate, it was important to me.

Chapter 38

"Not a Rescue Operation"

June 12, 2019

In the week that wouldn't end, Battalion Chief James Bowron of the Oakland Fire Department was recalled by the Defense.

My body stiffened as Bowron strode up to the stand for the second time. Briggs said he wanted to discuss the timeframe around the survivors and Bowron's decision not to tell his fire fighters about potential survivors in the building.

"What were you hoping to accomplish during those 29 minutes?"

"Over the course of the 29 minutes, as I stated in my previous testimony, it was that the best way to mitigate an emergency is to put the fire out. The men and women, what they did on that scene that evening is we pulled those lines and we made an aggressive interior attack to try to minimize that fire and try to put that fire out. That's what we were trying to do."

"Were you hoping to find victims?"

"I was hoping to find victims, yes, but the reality is, that as the fire got as intense, upon our arrival, with the amount of smoke due to the materials that were burning within that building, I knew as we were carrying on that if we hadn't found any within the first 10 to 15 minutes, that survivability rate was very small."

"So, your window of estimated survivability would be 10 to 15 minutes at that point?"

"I would say, based upon conditions and upon arrival, there was less than that. I was being hopeful, optimistic, but in reality, the smoke conditions upon arrival were so poor that survivability profile that we were looking at was very –"

"But it could have been, if you were being generous or extremely optimistic, up to 10 to 15 minutes?"

"It was less than 15 minutes. When I testified the first time, I stated that what I found upon the scene, how fierce this fire was burning, how much smoke was being emitted out of that building upon our arrival, survivability was extremely low, and that's upon arrival."

"Did you ever tell your firefighters that there were victims in the building, potential victims?"

"I did not."

"Why not?"

"Because announcing a statement like that was not going to change the tactics and the strategies that we were going to employ to put this fire out."

"Well, isn't it true that you have made statements before that suggest the opposite of what you just said?"

L-R: Fire Chief James Bowron, Curtis Briggs (courtesy of Vicki Ellen Behringer)

I sat there with clenched teeth as Bowron testified that he did not regret his decision to not tell his firefighters that there were people inside, nor did he regret his decision to put off raising a third alarm until 17 minutes after the fire started. It was 29 minutes before the additional fire crews and equipment arrived.

Then the theatrics started. Serra stood up and walked toward the witness stand waving his arms and yelling, "You are a disgrace!" He said that if Bowron ever admitted to his error, the city could be sued for millions. Serra raised his voice again, "Twenty-nine minutes and NO RESCUE!!"

Serra was right about that. I was also outraged that there was no rescue attempt at all.

While Tony Serra ranted, the Oakland Fire Department Union Rep and a cohort of five or six firefighters were chuckling and jabbing each other in the gallery when the 36 deaths were mentioned. One firefighter ducked down behind the chairs in front of him like a naughty little boy and gave Tony Serra the finger. These men were sitting right next to family members while they laughed in the courtroom. It was salt in our wounds.

Bowron concluded, "I didn't see people banging on the

windows to get out. There was no reason to use precious resources if no one ..."

He didn't finish the sentence and he was excused.

Here's the thing, the windows upstairs were hidden behind a false wall. Bowron didn't know this because neither Captain Freelan nor any of the other firefighters from Station #13 had inspected the Ghost Ship. Freelan claimed to have filed a request for a change of occupancy form, but it was never found, and he didn't follow up when he didn't get a response from Fire Prevention. A change of occupancy form would have triggered an inspection.

Bowron assumed he knew that if the people were alive, they would be banging on windows to get out. They couldn't. He didn't let any of his firefighters attempt to rescue the victims via ladders to the second floor.

Chapter 39

Max Testifies

June 17, 2019

Television news and print articles began heating up again over the trial. My phone voicemail was filled with messages from reporters wanting to get my take on the testimony. The moment I turned on my phone after leaving the courtroom, it would ring incessantly. Sometimes I would respond, but most of the time, it was too much. I needed time to think.

Each day, more and more TV news camera teams crammed the sidewalk outside the courthouse. They stood close to the stairs where witnesses, attorneys, and the families would enter and emerge each day, hoping for a sound bite. Some days, they simply filmed us coming and going. The courtroom was packed to overflowing with media, families, and other interested parties, so an additional courtroom was opened on another floor to allow for an audio live feed of the proceedings.

The two police officers who were scheduled to appear as

witnesses were not called. In a surprise move, Max was called to the stand.

I was taken aback by Max's high-pitched voice. Smith said, "We finally get to hear from you." After hearing him speak in person, I thought this might have been a mistake.

We heard Max's background, education, many moves, and finally, how he decided to "work on my craft: jewelry, tattoo, stone sculpture and music." He tattooed his own face using designs from nature, religions, artifacts, and designs from science and nature. In this way, he said, he saved himself from ever resorting to a normal job. He described himself as a spiritual person, who practiced Buddhism, but read about all religions. He believed in prayer, and believed he is a child of God, one God.

My mind wandered as he spoke. Most artists didn't have to tattoo their faces to remain true to their artistic dreams; they simply applied themselves to their craft and proceeded with determination.

Max told the story of how he wanted to find his true artistic home. He had a few false starts after graduating from Lexington Massachusetts College of Art and Design before becoming aware of Ghost Ship through an ad on Craigslist. In fact, almost all the residents found their Ghost Ship rentals through Craigslist. It wasn't as much an "artists' colony" as a cheap rental with the promise of something better.

Max moved into the space one door away from Ghost Ship in November 2014, paying $750/month rent and then from early 2016 he paid nothing. Max's duties for his free rent included maintenance and being a mediator for tenant disagreements. He said Child Protective Services came by at least once a month, so the emphasis of his job was on cleanliness.

It bothered me to learn that Child Protective Services

representatives came by at least once a month and said nothing about 25 adults living in the same building with the children. Videos taken before the fire showed their warehouse home was filthy, in disrepair, and a cluttered mess. How could CPS let this slide? Why weren't reports filed to protect the children?

Eventually, Max grew in his role at the warehouse and took on more managerial tasks. He presented himself to outsiders as the Creative Director or Executive Director as he took on the job of emailing the owners and outside businesses. He said he wouldn't use that term in front of the other members of the household because they would have laughed at him, but his embarrassment doesn't mean he didn't take on a managerial role. He was paid in free rent.

Max collected the rent from the other tenants, putting the $4500 in a can in his space until it was all there. He deposited the money on the 3rd of each month. The fire occurred on December 2nd, so the money would still be in his living space the night of the fire. Max said it "burned up in the fire."

During his tenure, there were electrical problems at Ghost Ship. Max saw the electrician the Ngs had hired put in electrical boxes. After that, the problems lessened, but at least once a month the power would go out.

Despite all the overloaded circuits, electrical problems, and a small fire the week before the party, Max didn't think it was going to be a problem to hold an electronic music party planned that Friday. He was more concerned about hosting an Oakland First Friday event. This was Max's big debut.

I thought it was interesting that a unique individual like Max complained about everyone in the neighborhood who didn't live up to his standards. Max complained about prostitutes and drug dealers. He didn't like the young men who rented the space next door and put on loud raves. He said one former Ghost Ship resident who complained about the filthy conditions at Ghost Ship was problematic. Omar, next door, was intimidating. He didn't like Omar's clientele or his employees. With all these complaints about the criminal nature of the people in his neighborhood, it's surprising he didn't think security was necessary for the party.

Max Harris testifies (courtesy of Vicki Ellen Behringer)

Max was asked about his role the night of the fire. He was familiar with some of the musicians who played the night of the fire. He knew it would be awesome. Max was the only person from Ghost Ship who stamped hands and took money from the paying guests. His name was on the flyers. He bragged online about "his" event. Prior to the party, Max cleaned up the warehouse and moved some furniture, effectively blocking the back stairs from view. The money he collected that night was put in a can. The cover charge was $10 per person before 11:00 p.m. and $15 after that. About 120 people attended.

Max admitted he would have been the one person there with the most familiarity with the place. Then he added, "Peter Wadsworth lived there, too." But, of course, Pete was not involved in the event. Max greeted people at the door and stamped their hands when they paid their money. Pete did not. Pete Wentworth was the only resident who died in the fire, so he couldn't defend himself against Max flinging out his name to diffuse his own responsibility.

Before the party began, Max said he went upstairs to hug Micah Danemayer and Jen Mendiola. He saw the projection bubble screen at that time. Then he went back to his space to get dressed. In other words, Max knew the kitchen door leading to an accessible window was blocked.

Max was in line for the bathroom when the fire broke out. Someone said fire and he saw a glow in the back. He went halfway down the hallway and screamed, "Fire!" That's when he kicked in the door to his space to retrieve his large fire extinguisher.

As he ran back to the fire past the saloon doors in the middle of the warehouse, Max saw Carmen headed for the exit. The fire had moved to the ceiling of the first floor and Max's extinguisher was ineffective. He started yelling, "Fire, fire, get out!" to anyone who was downstairs.

Max ran back to his studio again to get his cell phone and his laptop, then ran back and forth between the saloon doors in the middle of the warehouse and the front hallway three or four times yelling, "Fire!" This means he ran past the stairway six or eight times but did not go upstairs. This is when Max could have run up to warn the partygoers on the second floor but chose not to. This occurred when Chelsea saw Carmen come outside.

Max said, "I wish I could have gone upstairs, or put a ladder to a window." He added, "I would have done things differently. Sure, I'm not the only one who feels that way."

Then the music stopped but the power was still on. This is when Chelsea would have made it to the DJ stage on the second floor. Jon and Ryan had already run outside and stood in the doorway shining their phone lights, then they ran to the side yard. Sam Maxwell waited near the top of the stairs for a large crowd to file downstairs before joining the line and making it to safety.

Max said people were coming down the stairs after the music stopped, which would have been after Chelsea ran across the dance floor. Then the lights went out. Max turned on the flashlight on his phone he had retrieved from his space and saw the smoke was increasing.

A voice in Max's head said, "Get out." He didn't need his flashlight because the fire glow was bright enough to see by. Even so, He started yelling, "Use the lights on your phone!" into the downstairs hallway.

Max did not have his cell phone with him. Yet, he assumed everyone else had a cell phone in their hands and the flashlight app on, expecting an emergency. He blamed the victims for not saving their own lives by holding up their friggin' cell phones.

Max knew seven people among the 36 dead. He said all of them had been to the warehouse previously but had to admit the rest of the attendees would be unfamiliar with the layout. He said the guests were not prevented from going into the private lounge areas even though they were difficult to find, and he said the people had access to the back stairs. "Nothing prevented anyone from going there. It was physically possible," though Max said he "never gave a thought" to tell guests about the side door or back stairs.

Max was sure guests knew where the stairs were because they had just come up the stairs to attend the party. He said the exits were clear and there were two doors. He felt it wasn't his place to inform the guests about these things and it wasn't necessary to point out exits to the guests because he didn't expect anything to happen.

Max thought the people who promoted the event should have pointed out exits, but he again had to admit they were not a part of the Ghost Ship community and did not live there, nor would they know the layout.

When Max exited the building, he said about 10 more people came out the front door. Someone else came with a phone flashlight to shine in the front door. There were a lot of people out in front of the building, screaming. Some were breaking windows. Others were in the side yard standing on cars breaking windows. It was a chaotic scene. People were on their phones and yelling "Fire!" and "There might be people inside!" Bob was shining his light in the doorway. Sam Maxwell was the last person to escape.

Max suggested that maybe people stopped coming down the stairs because of the "spirit of the forest woman." He didn't see her, but he said he thought José's description was of that woman. It wasn't. That was a lie.

Max testified that he did not go upstairs to warn the guests because he thought "that would be stupid." He added he might also have impeded the people who would come down. Then he said, "...even though two people could fit on those stairs at a time."

He just had to slip that in because he heard people complaining that EVERYONE would have made it out if the stairs were wide enough for two people. Jon testified that he and Chelsea had to "jostle around each other" at the top of the stairs. Those 36 people died waiting in a single file at the top of the stairs because they could only go down one at a time. Another lie.

Max stayed in the doorway until the fire trucks arrived 10 seconds later, then ran to the side gate because he thought the fire trucks would need to pull into the yard. He saw people in the yard screaming, "Get a ladder!" Darrold, who lived in the side yard, put a ladder up to a 2nd floor window. Max and others tugged at the locked gate and stomped on the chain link fence until it collapsed to the ground. After all that effort, fire trucks did not go into the side yard. It was too cluttered with junk and debris.

Max had been inside the building, knew about the fire, and made sure he and his friends downstairs made it out safely before my daughter ran into the burning building, up the stairs, warned her friends about the fire, and died alongside them. I knew from his Instagram account that Max took videos of the fire in the early stages, since his video showed the fire was raging on the 1st floor but had not yet spread to the 2nd floor. Max stood outside filming on his Instagram. The thought sickens me.

After testifying about his role on the night of the fire, Max was asked about the conditions in the warehouse prior to the fire. He was shown a series of photos of the interior of Ghost Ship before the fire projected on a large screen on the wall directly across from the jurors. Tony Serra asked Max to comment on each piece of furniture or decoration. I wondered at the purpose of this display, but I was also getting used to the defense attorneys pinning their hopes for an acquittal on improbable lines of reasoning.

After Max finished testifying, Briggs brought in a lieutenant from the Oakland Fire Department who showed up in court wearing his full-dress uniform. The officer said he attended a school Christmas party at the warehouse.

This fire official had 17 years' experience as a firefighter and emergency paramedic. He performed many inspections over those years, mostly for small businesses in the area. Even though that was his job, he could not recall one item that was on a fire inspection checklist. Because he didn't bring a checklist to the party, he said he didn't see any fire hazards at Ghost Ship.

This firefighter was either extremely forgetful or

incompetent. Had he reported even a few of the hazards that are on every checklist he used for his job, 36 people would still be alive.

Briggs turned to the judge and said, "THE HARRIS DEFENSE RESTS."

That gave me a start. Finished? It felt to me that Max Harris was his own worst enemy. His tone was alternately whiny and snarky, while his answers were evasive. In my opinion, the last witness, who was supposed to sound like a fire prevention expert, sounded like an idiot.

Chapter 40

Almena Defense Begins
Micah Testifies

June 25, 2019

The eighth week of testimony started off with a mechanical engineer who attended a Ghost Ship party. Serra continued to harp on the "awesome beauty" of the decrepit warehouse. I groaned whenever he started expounding on the drum circles, "all the pianos and organs playing at once," and the museum-like quality of the collected dumpster debris that littered the place.

Then he called Derick Almena's wife, Micah Allison, to the stand.

Micah was lithe and soft-spoken, and Serra made sure it was understood that she was a witness only, not a defendant.

Micah said they had three children and DAMMIT, TONY SERRA PUT UP THAT FAMILY PHOTO POSTER AGAIN! Why are we not allowed to have photos of our children in the courtroom, but Serra keeps putting up that picture? We are forbidden to humanize the fire victims but was it acceptable to humanize his client?

*Micah Allison, wife of Derick Almena, points to photo of
her family (courtesy of Vicki Ellen Behringer)*

Micah told the story of how she and Derick had traveled
throughout Thailand, Bali, Nepal, and India collecting wooden
statues and other art objects with the intention of selling them
in the States. Derick needed a place to store it all.

They lived in Santa Cruz and then a house in Oakland
before finding an ad for a warehouse on Craigslist. It was an
unimproved 10,000 square foot building that sounded like the
perfect place to house their art collection and the small group
of young followers who looked up to Derick as a thought leader.
Derick was twice the age of most of his artist friends. He called
his group Satya Yuga, after the Hindu age of enlightenment.

Micah talked with Derick about the lease and knew it was
"As Is." The warehouse was an opportunity to store their
collected items. At the time of the lease, she and Derick did not
have a steady income, nor did they have good credit.

"We may have reached out to the community for a co-
signer."

They found Nico, who was 18 or 19 years old and born
into a well-to-do family.

"He was our friend. I don't recall if Derick reached out to
others."

Derick and Micah were at least 20 years older than Nico. It

sounded to me like they used a kid for his good credit. I also suspected they used their artists' collective to pay the rent on their homes and storage. Neither of them seemed to have any income to speak of, yet the rent for the newly acquired warehouse would be $4500 per month with a $7500 deposit.

Once the signed lease was accepted, Micah said Derick made significant changes to the warehouse. For some reason, she strongly insisted Derick did not cut a hole in the ceiling, rather he "expanded a hole in the ceiling from 2 feet to 20 feet."

Their collected storage items were moved into the warehouse first, and then more items they had kept in friends' houses were brought in. Derick placed an ad in Craigslist, and residents started to move in almost immediately.

Micah noted there were "significant issues" with the electrical system from the beginning. The landlord knew about it and upgraded the electrical system. The new residents were told to bring their own extension cords to reach each individual living space.

After that, Micah said she couldn't recall much of what went on during those times because she "had a lot going on." Casey asked if drugs were involved. She said she had problems with meth and staying up late between 2014 and 2015. This was around the time of their co-signer Nico's return.

I recalled Nico's mother saying he was "in bad shape" and she was trying to get Nico away from Derick's influence. Meth use could explain a lot of things.

Child Protective Services came into the space about once a month before the Almena children were removed in February 2015 and placed with Micah's family for a few weeks. Then the children were moved to live with Almena's family because Micah's parents "were not fond of Derick."

Micah and Derick stayed in LA for three to four months and returned to the Bay Area without their children in May or

June of 2015. Max was there taking care of things, and the Ghost Ship was "more stable" when they returned. Clearly, the Ghost Ship was managed better by Max than Derick.

On redirect, Casey asked about the rule at the warehouse: no open flames. Was this because the warehouse was mostly wood?

Micah responded, "No, the floor was wood, but the walls were.... There was a huge metal door. The warehouse was not a combustible structure. The walls were stone... concrete."

Casey had to repeatedly say, "The vast majority of the materials used in the interior were flammable." Micah tried to pretend the warehouse was fireproof because the exterior walls were concrete. The interior was packed wall-to-wall with flammable objects.

Micah, the Night of the Fire

Micah said Max made the reservations for her to go to a hotel the night of the fire. She had never done that before. They knew the party would be loud and run late. Micah was with Max when he called the hotel. It was about an hour before they left the warehouse.

It sounded to me like Max oversaw the event and took charge of removing the kids from a large, loud event taking place upstairs in the room right next to the kids' beds. Did he think an event with that many people upstairs could be dangerous?

Chapter 41

Almena Testifies

July 8, 2019

During the ninth week of testimony, the witnesses for Derick Almena's defense included two Oakland police officers, neither of whom bothered to write up reports after seeing the hazardous conditions at Ghost Ship. Also, Darrold, who lived on Ghost Ship property, discussed the "strangers in dark clothes" who ran from the building when the fire began.

Tony Serra tried to show how these men could have thrown Molotov cocktails into the building, though there was no indication that did happen. A more plausible scenario to me was a few partygoers who happened to wear dark clothes running out of a burning building.

Finally, Derick Almena's name was called.

Almena seemed to strut up to the stand, but as Tony Serra approached the witness stand, he quickly slumped down. Almena started fake-crying when he attempted to spell his last name. Serra asked, "How ya' doin' there?"

I cringed and said to myself, 'Oh, give me a break.'

Tony asked: "Are you tired?"

Almena sniveled, "I was in solitary confinement for over two years (He asked to be placed alone for fear of reprisals from this trial.) I'm just so sad. I've never been in jail before. I stopped my meds a year ago. I've gained 60 pounds and I'm unhealthy. I've had no sleep."

Asked about his responsibility for the circumstances surrounding the fire, Almena replied, "I dreamed something. I invited people. I attracted people. I had an idea we could do this."

Again, Serra asked, "Do you take any responsibility?"

"Spiritually, morally. These were beautiful, beautiful people. There's no word for what I feel. I feel death."

He never said he was responsible. I thought about the descriptions of narcissistic personality disorder I'd read in my Psychology 101 days. This felt like a case study.

Testimony of Derick Almena (courtesy of Vicki Ellen Behringer)

In proclaiming his innocence by ignorance, Almena said he had a wife and three children and would not expose them to risk by fire. "I was told it was safe. I was given permission to raise my children there. I wouldn't expose anyone to danger."

Then Serra led Almena through a recitation of his life's

dedication to art. I won't go through his comic book phase or youth camp phase or photography phase. Blah, blah, blah... I was thoroughly bored. It was all "so what" filler.

At the end, Derick responded, "I turned to art to escape a dysfunctional society."

One interesting point—when Serra put a collage of photo portraits on display (yawn) Almena immediately pointed to the picture in the center of the collage and said, "Well, this is me!" Wow, he truly is the center of his own attention. Interestingly, he stopped crying when talking about his artwork and himself.

Almena said this was his third Satya Yuga, describing their devotion to Public Service Work like "rituals, weddings, and altars." This was followed by more blah, blah, blah about Micah and her dancing. Then: "We always have friends staying with us."

And I shrugged to myself, *That means they always had other people paying their rent and expenses.*

Almena believed "Certain art is an endangered species." His artifacts were stored in many places in the US, and he wanted it all in one space... but he quickly added, "But the Ghost Ship was not storage."

While Almena described his "vision of "incorporating doors and windows" into the interior design, I had my own vision. I could see young people pushing on doors and windows trying to escape a raging fire. Some survivors said they felt their way through the smoke pushing on surfaces until one gave way, and I imagined pushing on a door that did NOT give in the fire. How terrifying would that death be?

Finally, Almena said his art's purpose was "living, breathing."

And I nearly jumped out of my seat. Thirty-six people stopped living and breathing because the place was crammed with flammable "art" with no regard for safety.

Almena said he had no agenda for putting on musical events, "they just happened." He didn't make any money, and if he did, "It would go back into the space." It certainly did not go into safety features like smoke detectors, sprinklers, or fire alarms.

Next, Serra led Almena through the state of the warehouse when he moved in. Almena said he "was tricked" into the lease for Ghost Ship.

"There was no electricity, no water, and no 4-inch pipe for toilets." He had described his needs to Eva Ng over the phone.

He told her after the lease was signed, "This is your building. You tricked me into this."

Almena described the landlords' subdivision of the building with a sneer: "They subdivided one building into many separate businesses for as much rent as possible."

Again, I shook my head. That is EXACTLY what Almena did with Ghost Ship–bringing in as many tenants as possible to cover his storage rent to the Ngs.

Casey Bates led the cross-examination and asked Almena if he made any changes to Ghost Ship. Almena said he had a new electrical transformer installed.

When Casey asked how he paid for it, Almena said he paid for it by holding back the rent to the Ngs for two months to pay Ben Cannon $10,000 for those electrical repairs and upgrades.

Almena made other structural changes. He took over an apartment space above Omar's Auto Body shop next door so he would have access to the upstairs bathrooms there for his family's use. In exchange, he built a new bathroom for Omar downstairs.

Almena broke through a brick wall to this second-floor space, which gave him access to a ladder to the roof and a ladder going downstairs to Omar's shop.

At first, I began to picture this upstairs space as a possible escape route if our loved ones had known about it, but then I realized this was the same opening that Micah said was later closed off again. I was left wondering why.

Almena said people in the building were getting along well when he and Micah left for Los Angeles to be with his children, who were taken away by CPS. When he came back from LA, "Everything was changed. No one got along."

I laughed to myself, 'I'll bet Derick's return had something to do with the disharmony.'

The Drive Home

Sioux waited for me as I stopped in front of the TV news cameras at the end of the day. Every reporter was clamoring for a response to Derick Almena's testimony. After I spoke, Sioux took my elbow as we walked to the car.

"That was so great!" We looked at each other and I sighed. It didn't feel so great to me. Then Sioux said, "I'm glad you told the reporters that Derick was a terrible actor. I laughed when you said you'd seen children fake tears better than he did. As soon as the topic turned to him, he perked right up though, didn't he?"

We got into her car and shut the doors. I sank into the comfortable seat. "Derick's habit of BS-ing his way through life has moved into the courtroom, but unfortunately for him, Casey Bates isn't a young, impressionable kid who thinks he's a guru. Derick is a con artist, and not a very good one. He throws words out there hoping one will stick."

Sioux laughed, "Sorry, buddy, your shtick doesn't work in the courtroom."

Chapter 42

Last Full Week of Testimony

July 9, 2019

Autrey James took over the cross-examination and immediately the air crackled with animosity. Autrey stood up tall in front of Derick. His size and posture felt imposing to all of us in the courtroom. Derick scowled.

Almena began by trying to change the questions, "You asked that wrong." And "You're using the wrong word." And "That's the wrong question." True to his nature, Derick wanted to oversee the proceedings.

L-R: *Derick Almena, Autrey James (courtesy of Vicki Ellen Behringer)*

Autrey had the warehouse lease projected on the big overhead screen. He showed Almena that it was signed on October 30, 2013, after Eva Ng sent an email that included the rules about how to go about obtaining proper zoning for Almena's intended use for workshops and other public access.

Almena told Autrey James, "That's what is vague to me." After looking at the email he said, "It was beyond my scope at the moment." So, he didn't read it.

Autrey asked, "You did not take the time to read the whole thing? You signed a 5-year agreement for your valuable objects, where you would put on workshops and build large sets?"

Almena replied, "It was insignificant to me."

Autrey James went over the AS IS lease agreement, line by line.

The document was signed by Derick Almena, Satya Yuga, LLC

Then Autrey asked Almena about Jake and Rodney, two contractors who both said the Ghost Ship was a death trap and dangerous. Almena denied they said it even though both men had put those words in writing.

Almena was then questioned about the illegal "Spider Box" put in by Darrold, who is not an electrician and Ben C., who sent an invoice to the Ngs for $32,000. He said, "This is a batch sent just to Kai Ng. You're choosing the wrong... This is not about me. I've seen all of this, but this is not for me."

Autrey James raised his voice and listed the facts, ticking off each one on his fingers:

- There was never a permit or inspection.
- Almena let people live in Ghost Ship who didn't know it was never inspected.
- None of the residents signed the building lease and all paid rent to Almena.
- None of the residents paid rent to the Ngs.
- Almena was truthfully the landlord for all the residents.
- Almena told the DA he had Max move in to coordinate events.

Almena responded, "I don't know why I said that. I don't remember."

Autrey said, "After the arson fire in 2014 you still didn't get sprinklers, fire alarms, illuminated exit signs, or smoke detectors in common areas."

Derick snapped, "No one told me to get them."

July 10, 2019

The Almena testimony continued the next day. It was clear from the day before that Autrey James and Derick Almena couldn't stand each other. Just the expressions of distaste on each of their faces was enough to read their hostility. The questions and answers felt like a private argument that was about to burst into a physical fight.

Derick Almena and Autrey James (courtesy of Vicki Ellen Behringer)

Autrey James began, "On the date February...."

Almena barked, "You have all the dates!"

Autrey asked, "Do you have a recollection of..."

Almena didn't let him finish, "When you're speaking to someone you don't record yourself."

A video was shown of Almena saying, "No people living here."

Almena responded to the video: "That's a policy Kai had with all his residents. He told me and I said it. Kai saw the kitchens and bathrooms and said, 'Okay, you guys are living here; don't tell the cops.'"

Autrey said, "Eva's email kind of sealed it for civic activities."

Almena snapped, "I've already said that three times. I said the words 'civic activities' without you having to ask me."

Shown a video in which Almena said to the police: "We could even have dwellings in this space." Almena responded, "That statement was made under duress. We could have events, gatherings, and dwellings and we did it."

Autrey asked, "Wouldn't that be an opinion?"

Almena pointed to himself on the screen. "That person was suffering right there. I'm still under duress. That's a very strange way of looking at shock."

Autrey James and Derick Almena were like sparring partners in a boxing ring. Autrey would jab and Derick continually ducked. They argued over what was permitted in the building, what safety features were missing, and whether the RVs would have residual gasoline in the fuel lines.

Autrey James said, "When CPS took custody of the Almena kids…"

Almena blurted out, "They did not. Micah's parents did. The way you're asking the question is incorrect."

The back and forth continued for an hour about Child Protective Services taking the Almena children and the children's eventual return despite Almena's lies about ongoing electrical problems, 25 adults living on the premises, and large parties occurring there.

A line of questioning was introduced about a debauched party. What were they both talking about? I was confused. After a long discussion about used condoms strewn about and who had authorized an adult party, it turned out this was an unsavory story that had nothing to do with the fire or the 36 deaths.

Then there was more talk about commercial zoning. The jump to a new subject and the time taken by the two men arguing about a zoning document was mind boggling. All of this could have been concluded in 20 seconds, but with Almena's long-winded dissemination, it took all morning.

Because Almena still refuted the statement about some wild party, the jury was dismissed for the afternoon. The entire video was shown in full. In the end, the video showed Almena lying about a debauched sex party. Autrey said this goes to "Credibility, Habitability, and Conditions regarding lies to CPS. The subject was finally exhausted, and I was relieved. This segue had nothing to do with the fire.

Finally, in conclusion, Autrey said, "During the KTVU interview, you told the interviewer, 'The whole structure of my defense is pointing and blaming.'"

Autrey James noted that Almena had blamed:

- The Ngs
- Rodney, the electrician
- Maria Sabatini, the fire investigator
- Captain Freelan of Fire Station #13
- Nico
- Kitty, Nico's mother
- Ben, the electrician
- Oakland Police Officer Ocampo

As his time on the witness stand ended, Almena raised his voice, "I'm not blaming anyone!" and the whole courtroom broke out laughing. We had been told the courtroom would be cleared if there were any outbursts, but with this comedy break, the judge just smiled and said nothing.

The Defense Rests

There would still be another week (starting on July 15) of Rebuttal Witnesses to refute statements by the defense witnesses, but the presentation of new evidence was over. The week of July 22nd was taken up with the shuffling of papers and reading instructions to the jurors. I hoped that as many of the families as possible would be able to attend the Closing Arguments which were set to begin on July 29th and continue for three or four days.

I longed for rest after listening to Derick Almena squirm around his answers, trying to bully the attorneys (including his own,) and throwing out a barrage of verbiage in the attempt to cover up his lies. It was exhausting, to say the least. My muscles were sore from holding my tension in check in the courtroom.

On each cross examination, Briggs got in his quick reassurance that Max was not present when the building was modified in 2015. It always seemed to take him a long time to get to that point.

Each time Briggs stood up, I thought to myself, 'Please, can we just stipulate Max didn't build Ghost Ship? He was simply the "Go-to guy" who wanted all the credit and none of the responsibility for events at the warehouse.'

Autrey James led the rebuttal by showing invoices that had Almena's name on it regarding the electrical panels in Ghost Ship.

Autrey said, "This work benefited Ghost Ship?"

After 20 minutes of "explaining" the purpose of the panels, Almena said, "Yes. The way electricity works..."

Oh My God. He's going to explain electricity! What a tool. The judge stopped him.

There were arguments about how much was paid to have illegal work done on the warehouse, and what kind of permits were required and never acquired. Almena was told to get permits and never did. There was more back and forth about zoning. Almena said he only read enough to convince himself that everything he wanted to do was permitted. He never bothered to read the rest.

DA Inspectors Balsouman and Stoddard were recalled backing up facts about Max Harris not calling 911, the Ng emails to Almena, and Harris lying to the police about people living at Ghost Ship.

Oakland Police Officer Hector Chavez said Ghost Ship was his beat. On March 1, 2015, he filed an incident report about alcohol and drugs being sold at a party held in the warehouse.

Officer Chavez said Max shut the door on his leg and became confrontational. Several people were at the door with Max. A video of the incident at the door was shown.

When asked if he reported the violation of city code to the Fire Department or the Building Department. Chavez said, "That's not how the Police Department works." His role is to file an incident report, which he did.

A video of the confrontation between Max and the officer was shown. A female voice said, "Max, back off." Then, a male voice said, "I apologize." Then the female said "Max!" After that, about 50 people left and the party was over.

The video is played, stopped at a still shot of the door and Officer Chavez identified the WRONG MAN as Max. REALLY? We listened to this whole sorry story to find out about Max's nasty streak, and this officer picked out the wrong guy. Ugh!

Max's face was covered by a glare on the video, so the officer pointed to a man who was clearly visible, but clearly not Max.

Curtis Briggs wanted to bring Max back. Would this trial never end? Truthfully, I groaned out loud.

L-R: Max Harris, Curtis Briggs (courtesy of Vicki Ellen Behringer)

Max was practically salivating as he clambered back up to the witness stand and eagerly said, "There was another Max who was sometimes at the Ghost Ship. Max Schultz was the father of one of the residents, Zack Schultz."

Casey Bates questioned this obvious lie. "So, Max Schultz is older than his son, right?" Big laugh from everyone in the courtroom. "Max Schultz must be at least in his late 40s or 50s. He is clearly not the man in the video. In fact, it is doubtful he was there at a rave that night."

And with that, the Ghost Ship testimony ended with pointless testimony and a stupid chuckle.

DONE.

What a monumental waste of time.

So, there we were at last, the court would not be in session until closing arguments were heard on July 30th and August 1st. On August 5th, the jurors would be sequestered Monday through Thursday from 9:30 a.m. to 4:30 p.m. for deliberations.

For the next few days, newspapers and TV reports ran non-stop about the trial. SFGATE reported on the limits Judge Thompson put on blaming others for the fire. KTVU News covered the prospect of landlords being forced to clean up "dirty, disgusting, and dangerous" Bay Area rental homes and apartments.

And, of course, Derick couldn't keep his mouth shut. He told the *Bay Area Reporter*, an LGBTQ newspaper, that the fire was caused by an arsonist targeting a "Queer Event." That's his MO, point and blame. Yes, many of the people attending the party at Ghost Ship the night of the fire were trans, gay, or queer. There was no proof of arson, nor any indication that the party was targeted for any reason, let alone it being a queer event. Pointing and blaming, that's the story of his life. I couldn't help but feel Derick Almena was as desiccated and useless as the clap-trap garbage he collected in that dirty, crumbling warehouse.

Chapter 43

Closing Arguments

July 29, 2019

Prosecution: Closing Arguments by AUTREY JAMES

Autrey stood up in front of the courtroom and took a deep breath. He looked strong and determined. Then in a clear voice he turned to the jurors and began:

The survival of a traumatic event, such as this fire, depends on three things:

1. Notice of danger
2. Time to escape
3. The ability to get out

There were 50-120 people inside the Ghost Ship on December 2, 2016. Thirty-six did not survive. They entered the event expecting to go, enjoy the music and company, and go home. That never occurred. Autrey showed the pictures of the 36 individually and named each of them. Only Peter Wadsworth was a resident of Ghost Ship. The rest were guests, most of whom were unfamiliar with the warehouse.

Autrey James gives closing argument (courtesy of Vicki Ellen Behringer)

There are two ways to conclude Involuntary Manslaughter:

1. The defendant committed a crime or lawful act in an unlawful manner.
2. The defendant committed a crime or act with criminal negligence and the acts caused the deaths.

Was a crime committed?

The nine violations of the Fire Code were committed with criminal negligence and caused 36 deaths.

CRIMINAL NEGLIGENCE

- Act in a way with high risk of death
- A reasonable person would have known that the act would create such a risk.

271

Reasonable people don't avoid safety. They make a good start, a foundation for safety, but that's not what happened. Harris and Almena acted unreasonably and different from any reasonable person:

- They showed a reckless disregard for human life and indifference to the consequences of their actions.

Any of the nine violations of the Fire Code is a crime. Was it criminally negligent?

Analyze the problem: Was it so dangerous that it risked human life or showed indifference to the consequences of their actions? Yes. Thirty-six people died.

1. A permit triggers an inspection.
2. Change in occupancy has new fire requirements, one must put in sprinklers, alarms, lights, illuminated exit signs—all of which would give notice of a fire, time to escape and the ability to exit the building.
3. Permits are not just paper, but everything that comes behind it.
4. Almena could have negotiated with the owners but did not.
5. He could have rejected the building if it was too expensive to upgrade.

Failure to get permits means failure to regard human life or indifference to the consequences.

Almena failed to provide an auto sprinkler system. Is this criminal negligence? Yes. Cesar Avila noted: "Sprinklers are 95% effective in slowing or putting out a fire."

Sprinklers give people TIME to escape. Alarms are hooked up to sprinklers, which means they would also have NOTICE of the fire. Even the water alone is an alarm. You run out of the building when the sprinklers go off.

FIRE CODES ARE WRITTEN IN BLOOD AND ASH

Fire codes are written by using the experience of past fires that caused death.

Codes are designed to make sure it doesn't happen again.

All jurors must agree on which violation (or violations) caused death.

For Involuntary Manslaughter:

- A lawful act in an unlawful manner
- Committed in criminal negligence
- The act caused death

LAWFUL ACTS IN AN UNLAWFUL MANNER

- An event with 50-120 people.
- Narrow stairs.
- Led to bottleneck of 80 people at top of stairs..
- Slow-going to get out, single file exit.
- 2nd floor photo shows the Ghost Ship was not designed for assembly or residence.
- 2nd floor not attached to walls or designed as more than a loft.
- If one is told to "get down low" in case of fire, that would put the guests in the worst possible place. Survivors saw smoke coming up to the 2nd level through cracks in the floor.

- Guests would be suspended in smoke.
- There was a bottleneck of 80 people at the only exit out.
- They had no idea there was any other way out.

Holding that party held on the 2nd floor was criminally negligent.

INADEQUATE ESCAPE

After the fire, the stairs were still in place. They were too narrow and of an abnormal construction.

HIGH FIRE LOAD

The "walls" and "décor" were fuel for the fire.

One resident who lived there testified he had trouble getting out.

The lights went out—and there was no one there to help victims find their way out.

Another resident said he had two smoke detectors, but NOT ONE PERSON THAT NIGHT HEARD A SMOKE ALARM.

THERE WAS NO NOTICE, NO EXIT SIGNS ON THE SECOND FLOOR, NO LIGHTED EXITS, NO SECURITY SAYING "THIS WAY OUT," AND NO SPRINKLERS.

CAUSATION: If the act has a direct, natural, probable consequence of death, and should have been known by a reasonable person, that act is the cause of death.

There may be more than one cause of death. Conduct of each defendant is a cause of death if that conduct is a substantial factor in the 36 deaths. It does not have to be the primary cause.

- Neither Almena nor Harris did anything to ensure the safety of people coming into Ghost Ship.
- Almena was living off the people he brought in to live in Ghost Ship and to attend events there.
- Harris was the coordinator of those events.
- Cause doesn't have to be the only factor or the primary factor, but a SUBSTANTIAL factor... not trivial or remote.

REASONABLE PERSON STANDARD

- Assumes they should have known.
- Presumption of the same awareness as a reasonable person.
- Requires the defendant to do some action with criminal negligence.

FACTS: CREATION OF THE LEASE

1. Almena reaches out to Ngs about building theatrical sets (nothing about residences or parties).
2. Eva sends the CC-2 Zoning email and Almena says he's convinced he can build out Ghost Ship (but says he did not read it).
3. Suddenly remembers it when Briggs cross-examines him in a leading fashion. (But Almena says he didn't look at the Limitations column, only looked to see if he could do what he wanted to do.)
4. A reasonable person would read the document.

5. The conditions and limitations were laid out for him!

6. For the duration of Ghost Ship, Almena did what he wanted to do. Unreasonable Conduct is not reading the Lease before signing:

> Almena signed a Commercial (not Residential) lease.
> No other use permitted without consent.
> For sole use to build theatrical sets and put on community workshops.

THAT'S NOT WHAT HAPPENED

- Alterations without landlord's consent.
- Tenant makes own investigation about applicable laws.
- Almena inspected the building two weeks before signing, saw what he had.
- People moved in right after the lease was signed.
- Nico said he co-signed for an "AS IS" building.

OPERATION OF GHOST SHIP

- People moved in within days (immediate violation of lease and law).
- Almena changed the building without permits in violation of law.
- People lived in Ghost Ship in violation of the law.
- Vehicles stored in building—they were driven in, meaning gas-powered.

WITHIN DAYS OF THE LEASE

- Occupying prior to approval
- No permits for construction and electrical changes
- Failure to abate hazardous conditions
- Stored vehicles indoors
- No automatic sprinklers
- No automatic alarms system
- No exterior alarm

From the first days of operation until December 2, 2016, Almena was in violation.

HAZARDOUS CONDITIONS

The Tenants—25 living there on December 2, 2016—all brought their belongings with them including many electrical appliances, devices, chargers, and instruments. This storage warehouse was not built for use by people as a home.

The Vehicles
Two RVs and two trailers were moved indoors: Vehicle fires give off heavy, black, toxic smoke. The 36 victims died of smoke inhalation.

Construction
Stairs: According to witnesses: "dangerous... narrow... more like a boat ramp...the steps were not consistent... unsteady... descent was slow and single file... 80 people were bottlenecked at the top of the stairs, then the lights went out." When told it would cost $3,000 to bring the stairs up to code, Almena said, "I can do it myself cheaper." (Then Autrey showed a picture of the burnt stairs and said, "This is what cheaper looks like.")

The Side Door
Rodney told Almena it would cost $2,000 for a side door. Almena got Jake to do it for less. Jake started the work but said, "You need a permit." (Clearly, Almena didn't want a permit, which would trigger an inspection and probable eviction of his paying tenants.) Finally, Jake stopped work. He said the Ghost Ship was "a death trap." A reasonable person would make changes, but Almena didn't take Jake seriously. In January 2014, Eva Ng asked for plans and permits for the door. (That was not how he did things.)

Electrical
Almena testified this was a problem from Day One. The power went out, the fuses exploded, extension cords were used throughout the building, and a temporary "Spider Box" used at construction sites was hard-wired onto a breaker box to run the oven... a full oven. This is not something a reasonable person would do. Jake, Ben, and Darrold were all unlicensed, but they were all messing with the electrical in different ways.

Unorthodox Building Materials
Pianos, organs, doors, windows, shingles, tapestries, and siding were all used to delineate walls and walkways instead of fireproof drywall. The 2nd floor was unsealed—in the worst place for a dance floor. When smoke rose, there was no relief for the victims. The 36 died of smoke inhalation.

Floor to Ceiling Construction
Wood, shingles, wooden objects were used throughout. It was not always apparent people lived there. Trailers were hidden with flammable materials, hiding dangerous conditions. The interior was designed to burn. That was not the intention, but it was the effect.

Fire Load

Where flammable materials are positioned and how available they are affecting the speed of the fire. (Capt. Freelan described Ghost Ship as having a "high fire load.") There was nothing in the building to give notice, to give the victims time to exit, and no way to get out.

2013 Meeting with Kitty

If her son could not get out of the lease, she would help make it safe and up to code. She saw the needed work. She went to the City of Oakland website and printed out forms. She told Almena what he needed to do for inspections and how to get money from grants for what they wanted to do. Almena laughed at her. He said she was too conventional, and he wanted to do things his own way. He was a creative type. Nico left after two to three weeks when he saw the alterations. When asked if he had permission for the work, Almena said, "Permission? We're doing it."

September 2014 Fire (The Arson Fire)

It was one of a series of five or six fires that night. There were plenty of flammable items inside. This should have put Almena on notice that fire could happen. He should have moved forward with fire safety. He even said on camera that the "damage was superficial. It could have been horrible." He KNEW the danger two years before the December 2, 2016 fire.

This is another example of "Unreasonable." Creative people know the difference between right and wrong.

After the 2014 fire, Almena was putting more and more people into the building taxing the electrical "system." The Ghost Ship was a residence and they put on dance parties.

HARRIS' DUTIES

By his own testimony, Harris:

- Paid no rent for his duties.
- Collected rent from other tenants.
- Deposited money in Ngs' bank account.
- Gave tours to prospective tenants.
- Signed lease with Bob.
- Negotiated with Ngs for additional space.
- Coordinated events.
- Evicted Shelly.
- Mediated issues.
- Communicated with Ngs for utilities.
- Wrote proposals for festival set-building.
- Changed fuses.
- Called himself the Executive Director when it suited him.

Max doesn't want to use the title, but he was still the manager, not some innocent tenant or bystander.

Max coordinated the event on December 2, 2016. His friend reached out to him. He may not like the name executive director or manager, but "If it walks like a duck, acts like a duck, it's probably a duck."

THE LIES

- A list of all the "Nobody lives here" lies is given... too many to list.
- Almena said, "It's not a venue. I'm not trying to be a bar or a nightclub."

- Almena said, "I got permits. I spent $10,000 for permits."
- Almena lied about the address and the nature of the building.
- Harris said he lied to protect himself and friends from getting evicted.

They were indifferent to the consequences of their actions. The consequence was the fatal fire on December 2, 2016.

FIRE TIMELINE

6:00-7:00 p.m. - Carmen Brito arrives home.

7:00 p.m. - Almena checks into hotel.

10:00 p.m. - Carmen naps.

10:45 p.m. - Jon arrives.

11:00 p.m. - Mike goes upstairs.

11:05 p.m. - Jon goes upstairs and takes pictures.

11:15 p.m. - Jon sees smoke coming up from the floor.

11:15 p.m. - Aaron and Bob investigate smoke smell on back stairs and see smoke.

11:20 p.m. - Carmen wakes up and goes through the front door, calls 911.

11:21 p.m. - 80 people bottleneck at top of stairs.

11:23 p.m. - Nicole texts her friend "There's a fire." Then she texts her mom, "I'm going to die now."

11:25 p.m. - Nick Walrath texts his partner about the fire, "I love you."

12:00 Midnight – Investigators are sent, including ATF Electrical Engineers. Search and Rescue becomes Recovery.

36 Bodies were removed on December 4, 2016.

The carbon monoxide levels considered normal = 3-5%
The carbon monoxide levels considered lethal = or >10%
The carbon monoxide levels of most of the victims = 30-50%
The carbon monoxide levels of some of the victims = 50-81%

The effects of smoke inhalation:

- Coughing
- Gagging
- Increased heart rate
- Air hunger
- Panic
- Vomiting
- Distortion
- Brain death within five minutes

Max could have gone upstairs, but Max made it out.
The 36 victims had no notice, no time, and no ability to escape.

CONCLUSION: THE BOX

Autrey finally explained to the rest of us what had already been explained to the jurors...the mysterious black box on his desk was a metaphor. Frankly, I had never even noticed it until he brought it up, and I couldn't see the box from where I was sitting. Autrey said, "Consider the case by what we put into the container of evidence and law." Ah. His job was to put all the evidence into the box and he expects the jury will do its job and find Harris and Almena guilty on all counts.

THE DRIVE HOME

As Sioux drove the car over the rising overpass, I looked out the window at a brilliant blue sky. The air was clear. It might have been a perfect day, but we missed it. I turned to Sioux, "Okay, I admit I don't really get the purpose of the box metaphor; that was mysteriously feeble. But wow! Autrey James did a magnificent job pulling all the details together today. This was exactly the organized presentation I had been hoping for these past four months. Finally, the story made sense."

Sioux agreed, "I think Autrey did a good job today, but it feels like too little, too late. The jigsaw puzzle approach never made sense to me. Why was every witness brought in like some big surprise guest?"

"I agree, and I still think Chor Ng, the City of Oakland, and Alameda County failed in their responsibilities, but Autrey nailed Derick Almena as the man whose arrogance created the firetrap. And he showed how Max Harris kowtowed to Almena by managing the events, then ran away when it mattered."

Sioux shrugged as we sat inched along in the slow-moving traffic, "I don't know. This whole trial was a mess. I think half of it was just some justification for covering up Alameda County and Oakland's mistakes. Autrey left that part out today and focused on the law. That made me angry, but he did a good job with his closing."

"That was Autrey and Casey's job, Sioux, I get that. They prosecuted the case against Almena and Harris. Period." I looked out the window again and sighed. A perfect day. Would life ever be normal again?

I felt a growl rising from my gut. "I still feel betrayed when they acted so chummy with all the people from Oakland and Alameda County who saw the hazards and walked away."

Sioux said, "That's the part that makes me so mad!" And

we drove the rest of the way home in the disturbing juxtaposition of sparkling sunshine and stony silence.

August 2, 2019

Defense: Closing Arguments by CURTIS BRIGGS and TONY SERRA

Tony Serra produced a rehashing of the racist claim that 14 to 19 Latino gang members threw Molotov cocktails into the Ghost Ship for unknown reasons and ran away to laugh about it at a taco truck. Tony Serra insisted that the cause of the fire had to be arson. He also referred to the story of a witchy woman who sat or stood at the foot of the stairs and told the partygoers to stay upstairs because it was the "will of the spirits of the forest." The supposition was that everyone upstairs who feared for their lives listened instead to this make-believe woman and chose to die rather than oppose those mythical forest spirits. The absurdity of these stories should have been self-evident, but justice lay in the hands of the jurors. Would they buy it?

Closing argument of Tony Serra (courtesy of Vicki Ellen Behringer)

Curtis Briggs spent his time making it clear that "Blame Max" was not a proper course for the Prosecution. His client was not to blame for anything, anytime, anywhere. Max was a saint.

Closing argument of Curtis Briggs (courtesy of Vicki Ellen Behringer)

The Attorneys

The Defense teams exhausted my goodwill. I had nothing left but contempt for the attorneys who felt their only defense was to lie and blame others, and I especially hated the men for blaming my brave daughter. I guessed that Tony Serra had nothing to work with in Almena, so he had grasp at the improbable. That didn't make me feel any better. Curtis Briggs relied on the sob story of "poor Max" for his defense. That wasn't so bad, but his second, Tyler Smith, seemed to relish Tony Serra's fantastical stories more than Briggs' recitations of Max's virtues. It was so pathetic, the whole thing.

I think my opinion of two of the Defense attorneys is clear. Tony Serra and Tyler Smith did not win my respect. Of course, that wasn't their mission. They did what they felt was expedient to win their clients' release. Truth lay flopping on the courtroom floor like a dying fish.

Tony Serra's second, Brian Goetz, was quiet for most of the proceedings. He seemed respectful of the process and kept his head down. I figured he probably did most of the research for Almena's defense.

Curtis Briggs, Harris' lead attorney, was kind. He spoke with reverence for the 36 deceased, and said, "I'm so sorry for your loss," and that he understood my sorrow when I learned about Chelsea entering the burning warehouse from a position of safety. That was in sharp contrast to the conniving ways of Serra and Smith. I liked Curtis Briggs despite his exaggerated descriptions of his client as a minor saint. He did what he had to do by placing Max outside the faulty construction and lack of safety precautions within the warehouse. I might have disagreed with Briggs about his client's responsibilities as an event manager, but he didn't outright lie. He just diminished the importance of Max's role.

(*Courtesy of Vicki Ellen Behringer*)

The Prosecution Team of Casey Bates and Autrey James had one job: prosecute Derick Almena and Max Harris. Discussions got heated in The Family Room when The families protested Casey and Autrey's lack of interest in holding the Ngs, Alameda County, and the City of Oakland partially responsible for the fire. Casey pointed out, and rightfully so, it was not their job to highlight the incompetence and laziness of people in the county and city governments. That didn't sit well with the families. We wanted all responsible parties to acknowledge their neglect and correct it.

The statute of limitations had run out on the Ngs, and they were never charged. Casey and Autrey had to focus, laser-like, on Almena and Harris.

Both prosecuting attorneys have a history in local city and county government. Casey was and still is an Alameda County Assistant District Attorney for over 25 years. Autrey James was a police sergeant in San Leandro for 20 years and an Assistant District Attorney in Alameda County for more than 16 years. It stands to reason they have friends in law enforcement and fire departments. The other family members and I wanted both the Prosecution and the Defense to name the government departments that should have but didn't do their jobs. I reacted viscerally when "our" attorneys patted the Fire Chief and Fire Battalion Chief on the back, but I need to remember they are part of the same community. No matter how despicable I found the fire and police officers who failed to do their jobs, Casey and Autrey were not obligated to condemn them. Just the same, it made me rage inside.

Autrey James was a strong prosecuting attorney, especially in his well-organized closing statements. He was visibly upset when the families complained about the narrow focus of the trial. I can imagine he was exhausted by the effort to maintain equanimity in the face of protests from both the defense and the families. He retired shortly after the trial.

Casey Bates was more accommodating when the families complained about his chummy relationship with the police and firefighters who gave what we considered negative testimony. That doesn't mean he agreed with us. For the most part, he nodded, acknowledged our feelings, and proceeded as he saw fit. Today, Casey keeps a composite picture of the 36 Ghost Ship victims on the wall across from his desk and looks at it often to remind himself of the seriousness of his job.

I liked Casey and Autrey. I also felt middled by the Defense and Prosecution. The family and friends of the victims learned the hard way that we weren't part of the process. We were witnesses to the sport.

At the end of closing statements, a long list of Jury Instructions was read aloud by Judge Trina Thompson. Jurors also received a copy in their binder. The reading was quite specific and took all morning.

The Last Drive Home

On the drive home, I told Sioux, "Wow! It's a good thing those jury instructions were written down. That's a lot to take in. Any one of the statements Judge Thompson named would lead to a guilty verdict." I thought about all the negative testimony we'd heard. "I only wish Max and Derick weren't the only two on trial. They were the easy targets. If Mayor Libby Schaff and Fire Chief Theresa DeLoach Reed had been called in to testify, we might see changes in the reporting systems."

Sioux gave a little huff, "It's obvious there's no coordination between agencies to make sure fire and safety codes are enforced. And it's pretty certain that won't happen now. No accountability means no improvement."

I thought about Sioux's words and said, "You're right, win or lose, exposure of the communication flaws would have led to better fire prevention policies. Instead, all those politicians and government agency supervisors are going to duck behind their desks and pretend that they did their jobs. What a sorry joke."

The rest of the drive, I was lost in thought: The prosecuting attorneys broke my heart with their chummy relationship with errant fire chiefs, police officers, and so-called public servants who failed to protect the residents and visitors in that decrepit warehouse. Then, the defense told idiotic stories and played the blame game. This was justice? This was our legal system? What a farce.

I recalled Chelsea's words she texted to her boyfriend on seeing Ghost Ship for the first time, "I would be impressed if I wasn't so jaded..." She saw through all the inauthentic junk in the Ghost Ship. I was beginning to see through all the inauthentic junk in our legal system. This Ghost Ship trial was a drawn-out game, a disjointed, feeble collection of lies, circumvented laws, and whiny excuses for incompetence. Now I was jaded, too.

Nothing changes if mistakes aren't seen and corrected. In the beginning, I was certain this trial would prevent another Ghost Ship fire from happening. Four months later, I walked away shaking my head. Another Ghost Ship could happen tomorrow.

Sioux was right when she said, "No accountability means no improvement."

Chapter 44

The Jury Deliberates

August 1-19, 2019

I sat at home watching the 6:00 news each night waiting for any word about the jury's deliberations. After just one day, KTVU reported that the Ghost Ship jury posed two questions within the first hour of deliberations. Then, there was no new information for days, only a few reports saying there was "... still no verdict in the Ghost Ship Trial."

During the second week of deliberations, On August 9, 2019, as we waited for the jury to come up with a verdict, I watched in horror as a three-alarm fire in a converted Oakland warehouse flashed on the TV news. It was happening all over again! KQED reported the fire was at the Moxy Art Collective. Thankfully, it wasn't a live/workspace, so no people were hurt or killed, but my anxiety rose through the roof. The contrast with the Ghost Ship fire was heartbreaking. This fire fight went to three alarms immediately and there were no injuries.

For two weeks after that, news reports tried to fill in details about the Ghost Ship trial, but there was no new information.

A few news reports explained the process of deliberation, saying the jurors had to find reckless disregard for human life and indifference toward the consequences of their actions to find the defendants guilty, but this was simply a placeholder for the Ghost Ship time slot.

On the morning of August 19, 2019, I received an email from our liaison in the Alameda County Victims and Witness Department. She said no verdict had been reached, but "something of interest" to the families would occur at 2:00 p.m. in Department 9 of the Alameda courthouse that day. That was short notice.

I drove to the courthouse, curious and a bit nervous, as did some of the other family members. Speculation popped up around the conference room where the families gathered before entering the courtroom.

"Did someone plead guilty?"

"Was one of the defendants injured or sick?"

"Had the case been thrown out on some technicality?"

"Was the jury deadlocked?"

We walked into the courtroom somberly, anxious to find out what happened. The jurors filed in quietly. Several were missing.

Judge Thompson sat for a moment, then told us three jurors were going to be replaced with alternates. Although they had spent 10 days deliberating, the remaining jurors would have to restart their deliberations from the beginning with three new

(*Courtesy of Vicki Ellen Behringer*)

jurors. That was it. No explanation was given for why they were dismissed. Two alternates had already been excused for personal reasons, which meant there were no alternates left.

Any additional juror misconduct would be cause for a mistrial.

Judge Thompson said the jurors' schedule was now in flux because the newly assigned alternate jurors had already made plans that included non-refundable flights and other obligations that could not be changed.

The hearing was short, and the remaining jurors, including the three who had been alternates, left through a side door together.

The next day, August 20, 2019, I turned on the local TV station KPIX and learned that two of the three dismissed jurors could face contempt charges. Judge Thompson was looking at the cell phone history of all three jurors and it was assumed she would be looking for improper use of the internet, or perhaps exposure to media coverage of the case.

News reports on TV and radio continued to speculate about the unusual situation, but all the families could do was wait. For two weeks, we went back to our jobs and our families, trying to forget about the fiasco that was the Ghost Ship trial.

Chapter 45

The Verdict

September 4, 2019

Finally, on the afternoon of September 4, 2019, I received a phone call saying a verdict had been reached and would be read the next morning. My body felt heavy. What would justice look like? The image of those 36 people suffering in the smoke and flames was making me sick with sorrow. The fact that their deaths could have been the product of one man's arrogant deceit and another's reckless event planning infuriated me. The blatant instances of governmental neglect and incompetence made it worse.

Another Fire

At 6:00, I settled into my comfy living room sofa and turned on the TV news, as usual, hoping to see reports with a hint of the outcome. Instead, images of flames and the story of 33 people trapped onboard a burning dive boat knocked me to my living room floor. CNN reported 33 bodies were found and one person was still missing and presumed dead. Goosebumps covered my arms and a cold chill ran down my spine. Not again! I propped myself upon the floor, shivering, elbows on the coffee table, watching the report. The fire that happened over the Labor Day weekend in the cold Pacific waters of Southern California took me back to a cold night in December 2016. Trapped! These poor people were also trapped. The crew members escaped, just like Max Harris helped the people who lived on the first floor of Ghost Ship escape. How could this happen again? I turned off the TV, crawled upstairs to bed, and stayed there, crying.

Early the next morning, I stood outside the courthouse doors waiting for the doors to be unlocked at 8:30 a.m. One by one, family members, friends, and others arrived at the courthouse. At first, we waited in the increasingly crowded hallway outside the courtroom on the 5th floor, but there was a delay of some sort, and the families were sent down to The Family Room on the 2nd floor. More and more people showed up, and the folding door in The Family Room had to be opened to accommodate all the victims' families and friends who had been unable to attend the trial on a regular basis. The tension was palpable. Some people were crying. One person was yelling in the hallway, accusing the families of keeping her out of the room. We clenched our teeth and waited for word that we could go back upstairs.

Who Can Sit at the Trial?

When the court liaisons from the Victim and Witness office stepped into The Family Room and said we could go back upstairs, family members, friends, and other loved ones crowded into the elevators that took us up to the packed hallway in front of the courtrooms.

It's amazing to me how many people feel entitled to sit in the courtroom to watch important moments in a trial just because they are interested. There is a California law referred to as "Marsy's Law" that states family members of victims are entitled to be in the courtroom when the accused are on trial. I had never seen so many lawyers, reporters, neighbors, and courtroom groupies fight their way past grieving family members trying to occupy a seat.

We, the families, joined hands and formed a phalanx, slicing our way through the crowd and into the courtroom. Angry "interested community members" shouted at us. Even a young lawyer from the Public Defender's Office who had nothing to do with the trial told me, "Lines mean something. I've been here since 8:00 this morning," when we pushed past him. Well, you know what? Lines don't mean anything when your child is dead, and I told him that. Most of the family members had been in court every day of the trial and had also shown up that morning at 8:00 a.m. This guy had never shown up once until the verdict was about to be read. How dare he think he had precedence over us?

After the commotion of the crowd and loud complaints when the doors to the courtroom closed some people out, the lawyers, defendants, and finally the jury filed in and took their places. Judge Trina Thompson addressed the jury. "Regarding the defendant Max Harris, have you reached a verdict?" I held my breath.

Yes. One by one, each victim was named followed by the words, "Not guilty." Harris was acquitted on all 36 counts of involuntary manslaughter. A roar went up on the right side of the courtroom. Most of the people there stood up and rushed out of the courtroom. A few remained to hear Derick Almena's verdict.

Max Harris verdict (courtesy of Vicki Ellen Behringer)

Judge Thompson waited while the clerk called for quiet. Then she asked, "Have you reached a verdict for defendant Derick Almena?" The foreman replied, "No, your honor." A hum of surprised voices and quizzical looks spread through the courtroom. I was confused. The foreman of the jury said they were deadlocked, 10 for guilty and 2 for not guilty on all 36 counts. Judge Thompson asked if there was any possibility of reaching a verdict with more time. Again, the answer was "No." Judge Thompson must have anticipated this answer and said, "A new trial hearing will be held on October 4, 2019." She hit the gavel and stood up, stepped down from the dais, and walked out through the side door to her chambers. The trial was over.

I had expected a dramatic reading of the verdict. I thought the pomp of the court would be solemn. Instead, after a few brief statements, it was a slump to the finish.

Judge Thompson (courtesy of Vicki Ellen Behringer)

The families left the courthouse feeling bewildered and angry. This was it? All that time spent in the courtroom. All that time to deliberate, and the jury came up empty-handed. We just kept shaking our heads in disbelief, saying to each other as we walked to our cars: "What happened? How could two jurors let Almena go?"

David Gregory put his arm around my shoulder as we left

the courthouse and said, "Really, Colleen, the only good outcome would be for our daughters to be alive." And I knew he was right. At the foot of the stairs, he spoke to the TV news reporters waiting on the sidewalk with their cameras at the ready. "There was no justice here today. No verdict can make up for the loss of 36 lives, but a guilty verdict would have discouraged other would-be slumlords from operating a living space or a music venue with no regard for human life. Seeing these men in prison would have been justice or at least prevention. Today, there was no justice."

I drove home in a foul mood. Reporters were calling and leaving messages. I could hear the constant ringtone and voicemail pings all the way to the San Rafael Bridge when I finally reached over and turned off my phone. The hope for justice was sucked out of me, but my rage was stoked. I couldn't speak in that state.

Good riddance to Max. He would have to live with the guilt of his inaction for the rest of his life. I brushed his existence off my clothes before entering my house and spit out the words, "Karma, you coward." For me, he was Done.

Almena was another matter. This man had no conscience. He was the kind of person who needed a concrete reminder of his guilt. A new trial was coming, and I would wait for that day. Thirty-six people died because he wouldn't shell out money from the rent that he collected to provide safety measures. Alarms, sprinklers, and safe exits might have saved the lives of the 36 young people who burned to death in his "artists' utopia." He was not an artistic director. He was a slumlord. I rubbed my dark thoughts of this man into an ugly rock and placed it on the ground beside my driveway. Nothing of him would enter my house.

At home, I turned off my phone, sat down in my recliner, laptop resting on my thighs, and began writing down everything I'd learned from the trial. The outcome was almost beside the point. A black depression hovered nearby, waiting to encapsulate me with its dark, weighty sorrow. What was to be gained from this months-long, bone-cracking experience? Four months of testimony had come to nothing. My only hope was to be ruthlessly objective in why I was there in the first place.

My purpose in attending the trial was to gain information about how and why my daughter died. There was still a gem I could salvage from this slag heap of a trial: I found out how brave my Chelsea was. Sabrina was right; she was a good person. Chelsea was my brave heart. Sabrina was my grace and hope. The threatening gloom of devouring depression softened, then melted away.

As I sat writing, a sliver of evening light shone through the blinds in my living room and landed on my hands as I typed. I smiled. In the bleak months of the trial, I'd also learned about friendship. I thought back on David Gregory's support every day of that godforsaken trial. No matter what, I could count on his presence. Carol Cidlik called nearly every day after she returned to Hawaii. And Sioux had driven me to the courthouse and sat with me through it all. She'd listened when I was ranting and offered support when I was flailing. She'd been there for me. The expression Holding Space suddenly made sense. Sioux allowed me the space to learn and grow through this horrible ordeal. There was good in this world. David, Carol, and Sioux proved that to me.

Trudging upstairs to bed, I thought about the long months and years that had transpired since the fiery tragedy. It wasn't my job to carry this anger on my shoulders. It was the weight of the guilty. Shame on Derick. Shame on Max. Shame on the owners, the politicians, and the government agents, including all the fire department, police department, and building department employees who let this happen. They turned joyful artists into ghosts. May they be haunted forever by the knowledge they could have saved the 36 young souls who died that awful night.

I wrote in my journal: "I do not seek revenge; I seek an end to this madness."

Chapter 46

Another Plea Bargain

On December 2, 2019, The Statute of Limitations quietly ended for any additional charges to be filed in the Ghost Ship fire case. Chor Ng, who was a major property owner in the Bay Area, would never be criminally charged for the 36 deaths. For reasons that were never made clear to the families nor to the public, District Attorney Nancy O'Malley let the clock run out. She never gave a statement explaining her decision.

February 26, 2021

After one year and five months of delays, from the initial announcement of a new trial when the verdict was read on September 4, 2019, through countless hearings and delays, came a new announcement: There would be another plea bargain.

I was gobsmacked. Why did Alameda County District Attorney Nancy O'Malley put us through a year and a half of waiting? Why hadn't the trial begun online? Everything else was happening on Zoom. I was teaching on Zoom. Hearings were phoned in or held on Zoom. What went wrong? I suppose it went right for the DA. She got Derick Almena to plead guilty in exchange for a slap on the wrist. He would spend a year and a half at home with his family wearing an ankle monitor. Big deal.

I wrote my third impact statement and another newspaper article, but at this point, any energy I had was depleted. The court system succumbed to the convenient excuse of Covid restrictions. Alameda County and The City of Oakland employees who should have said something about the dangers at Ghost Ship would walk away without being held accountable for their deadly incompetence.

David Gregory said it best a year earlier, "CYA. Cover Your Ass." There would be no reports written or recommendations for others to do their jobs competently. No police or fire training would be enacted, nor massive building inspections rolled out to ensure a tragedy like this never happens again. The people who turned their heads and walked away would never be admonished; they'd just keep on walking. The Ghost Ship fire would be swept quietly off the front pages and forgotten.

Sentencing for Derick Almena was scheduled online for March 8, 2021. After that, I needed to walk away from this putrid court case. It was making me sick.

As the rest of the world emerged from Covid isolation, I felt it was time for me to join them. I had been at home for five years after Chelsea's death in December 2016. At first, I went to work and came home alone every day. Then Covid struck in March 2020, and I remained at home, teaching online. By the time of Almena's sentencing in March 2021, I was ready to step out. So was the rest of the world. My heart was badly bruised; my wings were broken, but it was spring, and I was not alone.

March 8, 2021

Zoom Hearing: Final Impact Statement #3

Zoom hearing (courtesy of Vicki Ellen Behringer)

Sentencing for Derick Almena was held on Zoom. I sat at my dining room table, laptop computer open in front of me, watching the courtroom camera view.

Derick Almena guilty plea (courtesy of Vicki Ellen Behringer)

While attorneys spoke, Derick repeatedly slumped over in his chair, his head falling forward down as far as his stomach would allow onto his lap. He was clearly on drugs. Those of us who were watching the proceedings on Zoom sent desperate Chat messages to the judge and attorneys present in the courtroom. We also sent text messages to each other. Didn't they see him? There was no response. Derick Almena was supposed to be listening to the Impact Statements read by the victims' families.

It crossed my mind that he might overdose on whatever drugs he had taken, his reaction was that extreme.

After a recess, Judge Trina Thompson said that Almena's backpack was checked for drugs, but none were found, and the hearing continued. Of course not. Almena had already consumed whatever it was that caused him to pass out during our statements. The coward couldn't bear to hear what the victims' families had to say, but we spoke on the record anyway. Perhaps he would read the messages later. Probably not. Our words would conflict with his distorted image of himself. My statement wasn't meant for him, anyway. It was for me.

Giving my impact statement (courtesy of Vicki Ellen Behringer)

This was my Third Impact Statement:

Colleen Dolan, Mother of Chelsea Faith Dolan, aka Cherushii.

I come here today in honor of my brilliant, talented, loving daughter, Chelsea Faith Dolan, "Cherushii." And to release her soul from the nightmare circumstances of her death.

I come bearing a blessing and a curse.

My blessing is this: May our 36 beautiful souls dance among the stars. May they know peace and joy forever and ever. I bless the day Chelsea Faith and the other 35 stars entered our lives and surrounded us with their light. May that love bridge the gaping chasm left behind with their loss. May that love overpower the wrong done to them.

Dear Families, my next words describe my nightmares. These words are not for you, only Derick Almena. Please turn off your sound for 40 seconds while I give our cursed nightmares back to him, so that we may be free of them. Please turn off your sound. I will raise my hand <RAISE HAND> when this portion is finished. <PUT HAND DOWN>

My curse is this: May you, Derick Almena, take on the visions I see each day, and feel the pain of my nightmares. My hope is that in giving these visions to you, I may be free. I curse you with intense, burning heat and flames that scorch all the hair from your body and peel the skin away from your face. I curse you with choking smoke saturating your lungs until they bubble and blister, and foam oozes from your mouth and nose. I curse you with the pain in your bones and muscles that comes from clenching in fear, as you face the fury of a firestorm coming to consume you. <RAISE HAND>

I do not need to see you spend years in jail writing and drawing in quiet retreat. I need you to *feel the* *anguish** you caused by strutting and lying to circumvent simple safety precautions in the hellhole that you built. It would have taken so little for you to give up just a pinch of your hipster ego for the sake of others. Instead, you laughed and flaunted your pirate mission to place the importance of desiccated, wooden collectibles above the Awesome and Beautiful Lives of True Artists. You did not take adult responsibility for the tenants who paid to live on the first floor in your home, nor the guests who paid you for the use of your public space upstairs. You did not exercise reasonable care in your actions that foreseeably caused the death of these good people. Your lies helped you slither around your responsibility. Your swaggering ego killed 36 people.

I curse you with the terror and agony those 36 extraordinary human beings felt in their last moments. If ghosts can haunt, I do not wish for their beautiful souls to haunt you, Derick, because they are Innocent. You are not. There is no reason to want their good souls to know the anger and resentment I feel for you, here and now. I give back this nightmare curse you placed upon us all. I curse you with all the power the Universe gives to a bereaved mother. I do not forgive you. I never will. May you burn in the hellish nightmares you created.

And that was it. Other family members read their statements. Then we all signed off Zoom for good. The long trial was over.

Probation Violation

No, wait. Derick continued to behave as if he was above the law. He was released from wearing his ankle monitor in March 2022, but still on probation for another three years. Derick had to report to his probation officer in Alameda County but lived over 100 miles north in Mendocino County. He asked to have his probation moved. Naturally, the Mendocino County Probation Department did a search of his home prior to honoring his request. They found 10 bows, over 50 arrows, a machete, and one live bullet. Probation does not allow weapons of any kind in the home.

Casey Bates, the Assistant DA who had prosecuted the case, filed charges to rescind probation and have Almena sent back to jail for the remaining three years of his sentence. A hearing was held on Friday, September 16, 2022. The judge was unfamiliar with the Ghost Ship case. He was not impressed with the petition to rescind probation and asked if Almena's home was rural, which could account for the bows and arrows. Tony Serra described the machete as a rural "gardening tool."

Derick Almena continued to feel that rules and laws were not made for him. I remembered Derick's testimony about how he used that "gardening tool" as a weapon at a Halloween party on October 31, 2016, a month before the Ghost Ship fire. He was so proud!

Almena bragged on the witness stand about chasing a group of boys who ran into the warehouse wearing masks. Remember—it was Halloween. Derick knew who they were; they lived next door, but he didn't like them. Derick said he "smacked them with the flat side of his machete" to scare them and get them to leave. He chased one boy up to the roof and then locked the door on him, trapping him on the roof.

The young guy yelled down to the people below that the only way for him to get down was to jump. They thought he was threatening suicide and called the police. He was just afraid of a maniac with a machete. That maniac was Derick Almena. The machete was found in Derick's new home hanging artfully on a wall. This was no gardening tool. It was Derick's weapon. He was proud of using his machete to defend his stuff from a bunch of rowdy boys he didn't like.

So, once again, Derick Almena thinks that if he wants to keep and shoot arrows with his family, probation rules be damned. If he wants to keep a machete on his wall, probation rules don't apply to him. It reminds me of his scoffing at fire safety laws because they were "too mainstream," and he doesn't "do things that way." Derick Almena believes he creates his own law. His arrogant attitude killed 36 people. He hadn't learned a thing. This interminable case lingers like a bad smell. Each time I start to feel removed from the ugliness, Derick Almena farts.

Chapter 47

My Plea to Fire and Police Professionals, City Managers, County Executives, and Elected Government Leaders

Year Six After the Fire

Naturally, the hope after a tragedy like the Oakland Ghost Ship warehouse fire is for systems to be put in place that will prevent similar tragedies. I wanted to think the notoriety of the fire would lead to change. The problem with that thinking lies in the nature of the trial. There was no accountability for anyone other than Derick Almena.

Without accountability, there's no incentive to fix what is obviously broken.

Oakland mayor Libby Schaaff and Oakland Fire Chief Teresa DeLoach-Reed never testified at the trial, acknowledging the many illegal residences and performance spaces in Oakland. They weren't asked to explain the disorganized approach to community safety. Even so, the systemic problems that percolated up through the testimony pointed to their own possible solutions.

My Plea to Fire and Police Professionals:

I'm not a law enforcement or firefighting professional. I am an educator. While that doesn't qualify me to advise those professionals in their line of work, it does allow me to comment on the lack of internal and inter-departmental communication systems that led to my daughter's death.

Internal Communications:

Local firefighters are the front line in fire prevention. They have the responsibility of knowing their neighborhoods, or what is known as their first-due area. Yes, the local fire officer who visited the Ghost Ship should have filed a report and followed up, but every firefighter who worked in that station was responsible for educating him or herself on the buildings in their district.

Those 36 lives could have been saved if the first responders had just known there was a second-floor event space. The battalion chief, who took over as incident commander on his arrival, kept secret the presence of up to 50 people trapped inside the building because he didn't see people screaming at the windows. Had he been told about the hidden windows upstairs; would he have made the same decision?

Coordination between City Departments and Outside Agencies:

My hope has been that the death of 36 young people would bring a keen focus on the need for strict fire and life safety code enforcement. I suggest fire professionals make the first move in providing education, communication and coordination between the public, fire, police, building inspection, code enforcement, child support, and other departments and outside agencies.

During the trial, we learned that government agency professionals observed the hazards at Ghost Ship. Easily accessed, open channels of communication between city departments and outside agencies could have alerted the fire professionals of Station #13 to the "firetrap" conditions at an illegal residence and event space in their neighborhood.

Revisit Fire Fighting Protocols:

My daughter was already dead by the time I arrived on the scene half an hour after the fire started. I didn't know that at the time but was dismayed to see no evidence of firefighters having smashed windows or effecting a rescue attempt of any kind. I wondered that night: Did that mean there were no victims?

During the trial, I learned from the forensic pathologists that toxic smoke from building fires like these kills people within five to seven minutes. Those minutes are precious. Now I wonder every night: Had firefighters immediately tipped ladders up to the second story windows, would even a few of those 36 victims have been saved? One resident jumped to safety from an upstairs window. He knew where it was hidden. Survivors were standing on cars and climbing a ladder trying to break windows and rescue victims. Didn't their actions indicate victims on the second floor? Don't second-story windows indicate the location of a second floor?

The first responders arrived before dispatch even announced the first 911 call. They were in the building within 3.5 minutes and could have saved lives, but they were woefully ignorant of the layout of the building. The first crew didn't know the upstairs windows were blocked off. They didn't even know there was a second floor. Firefighters didn't listen to bystanders who told them there were up to 50 victims upstairs. They followed protocol and went inside the front door. The second crew followed them inside the front door. None of them climbed ladders to the second floor.

The incident commander said he would do nothing differently despite 36 people dying in the fire because he followed protocol. He claimed it was "a firefighting operation, not a rescue operation" because he didn't see people "screaming at the windows." He assumed the victims were already dead, so he didn't tell his crews that there were people trapped inside. He waited 17 minutes to call in a 3rd alarm to avoid too many vehicles and firefighters on the scene. Thirty-six people died, but the incident commander said he would do nothing differently in a similar fire in the future.

The unwillingness to attempt or even imagine a better outcome set my teeth on edge. In the past, I was awed by the heroic aspects of firefighting, especially after the fall of the Twin Towers on 9/11. Multiple deaths with no rescue attempt at the Ghost Ship fire left me smoldering with resentment.

Inspections, Inspections, Inspections:

Just two weeks before the fire, inspectors knocked on the Ghost Ship door in response to complaints about trash outside and illegal construction inside the warehouse. No one answered the door, so they walked away. Twenty-five people lived there at the time, but no one opened the door. They were probably hiding, knowing that uniforms at the door meant likely eviction.

The Ghost Ship warehouse hadn't been inspected in 31 years. The confusion around who is responsible for reporting building changes that trigger inspections must be revamped.

Neither building owners nor tenants who make structural changes to a building want to be financially responsible for expensive safety upgrades. The result is an adversarial relationship. While they argue, inspections slip through the cracks.

The Ghost Ship building had no working smoke alarms, no fire alarms inside or out, no illuminated exit signs, and worst of all—no fire sprinklers. ALL COMMERCIAL BUILDINGS SHOULD HAVE FIRE SPRINKLERS. According to the National Fire Prevention Association website, "...sprinklers have proven to be reliable in reported structure fires considered large enough to activate them. From 2015 to 2019, sprinklers operated in 92 percent of such fires and were effective at controlling the fire in 96 percent of the incidents in which they operated... Fire sprinklers are widely recognized as the single most effective method for fighting the spread of fires in their early stages—before they can cause severe injury to people and damage to property."

The fire code in effect in Oakland, California, in 2016 required sprinklers for new construction. It was not required when the Ghost Ship building was first constructed in 1930. The Ghost Ship warehouse was never retrofitted. The owner, Chor Ng, and the master tenant, Derick Almena, argued about who was responsible for safety upgrades. Neither one would pay for sprinklers. New or not, how could this out-of-compliance building be allowed to exist as a storage building, let alone a live/workspace?

I learned at the trial that Oakland does not require storage buildings to be inspected. That sounded crazy to me. Warehouses don't ever catch fire?

It turns out, a storage facility would only be inspected if its status was changed to residential or assembly. That whole idea felt oddly antiquated, almost Dickensian, as if storage buildings were unimportant and not worthy of fire protection.

Wouldn't that omission put the surrounding communities at risk? Fire safety seems simple to me. Since the Triangle Shirtwaist Factory Fire in 1911, safety laws regarding better access and egress, fireproofing requirements, the availability of fire extinguishers, and the installation of alarm systems and sprinklers have been on the books. Occupational Health and Safety (OSHA) laws were passed in 1970 requiring fire safe construction, fire alarm and communication systems, stair capacity, and other building features that would prevent injury to firefighters. We assume any building today would have minimum safety standards. Not so.

The lack of fire and life safety inspections confused and angered me. I needed to know more, so I turned to an expert. My friend's husband, Eric Nickel, had spent his life as a fire service guy, serving as battalion chief, deputy chief and fire chief for over thirty-five years. Then he became a senior advisor in the project management service group of a public agency that serves the consulting, administrative, and project management needs of local governments. I figured he would have some answers.

And he did. On a chilly February afternoon, we sat down at his dining room table and Eric told me what I wanted to know about fire code enforcement in Oakland.

"Eric, what's with the inspection of some of the most dangerous buildings being left off the schedule? I mean, isn't it likely a warehouse could be filled with flammable materials? Shouldn't that be a priority?"

"No, that's not how we look at it, Colleen. Storage is considered a simple, low risk use. But most modern fire departments set up comprehensive annual or bi-annual inspection programs. Storage buildings, at a minimum, should be inspected bi-annually."

We just sat down and already I was flabbergasted. "Wow! From inspections every year or two in some locations to thirty years with no building inspection in Oakland. That's a big gap." I sat back and folded my arms.

Eric continued, "Well, there are two types of inspections—Company inspections and Fire Prevention Bureau inspections. Company inspections are led by the fire crews assigned to that area. They inspect storage and low-risk businesses every two years. That would have been Station #13 crew if Ghost Ship was being used as originally intended."

"You mean as a storage facility."

"Right. Fire Prevention Bureau inspections would include gas stations, auto shops, like the one next door to the Ghost Ship, and assembly occupancies. The Ghost Ship was being used for assembly. These would be high hazard inspections done annually with highly trained fire inspectors whose sole responsibility is fire inspection."

"Okay, Eric, I'm starting to understand. Using those modern standards, the Ghost Ship initially would have been identified as a low-risk building and the local fire company Station #13 would inspect it every two years."

"Right, then, Station #13 crews would see that it was not being used for storage, but rather as a residential and assembly building, which would have triggered a referral to the trained fire inspectors and a high-risk annual inspection by the Fire Prevention Bureau."

"I see two problems with that whole scenario. Think of Ghost Ship: No organized inspection or communication programs were in place. And something else, an officer from Station #13 testified that he conducted what he called a "pre-plan walk-through" of the Ghost Ship with no records to back him up. I unfolded my arms and leaned forward, "Is that really a thing?"

"He could have been referring to a company inspection."

"Okay, let's give him that. But then this fire officer said he sent numerous Change in Occupancy forms to the Oakland Fire Prevention Bureau, only the records were never found online, nor in hard copy files. He received no response after several attempts to communicate and eventually gave up. And eventually 36 people died."

Eric carefully placed both hands palm down on the table. His face told me he was going to tell me something difficult. "Colleen, had a standard reporting process been in place, a full-time fire inspector would have come in and begun an enforcement action with the building department, code enforcement department, and city attorney's office to enforce compliance with the original occupancy."

Eric paused and took a deep breath. He flipped one of his hands over. "The only other option would have been to require the owner to complete a change of occupancy process that would have triggered significant and expensive building improvements. In particular, it would have required exit, electrical, and fire and life safety upgrades."

I sighed heavily. "Welp, that never happened. Eric, everyone knows about the converted warehouses in Oakland. The Mother's Cookies conversion, the Vulcan, and a myriad other unauthorized live/work lofts are well known. What I don't understand is how they evade safety inspections. Mayor Libby Schaff and Fire Chief Teresa DeLoach-Reed were never questioned during the trial, so we never got those answers."

Eric frowned and said, "Here's what you might have heard from them, and it's the truth. In a lot of California cities like Oakland, the city managers, county executives, and elected officials face a slew of fiscal priorities, and they may decide to not fully fund fire department personnel budgets. A lot of suburban and urban fire departments are underfunded and understaffed due to escalating personnel costs from pensions and other benefits. You won't like this answer, but that means fire department support functions, including Fire Prevention Bureaus, must be cut to keep fire stations open and staffed."

I could feel my eyes squint in anger. "What? You mean it was money? My daughter died over a budget dispute?"

Eric said. "I understand your frustration. But you should know things are changing. There's a new focus on fire and life safety growing among fire professionals. Let me show you this."

He opened his laptop and showed me *The Guide to Community Risk Reduction* on the website www.strategicfire.org. Then Eric pointed to one sentence: "As with any organizational culture—particularly within the fire service—there tends to be substantial resistance to what's new, and a strong investment in the old ways of doing things."

Then Eric said, "This is what I do. It may be a slow process, but we're working on educating policy makers and fire officials on the benefits of prevention."

The memory of the Oakland fire fighters snickering up their sleeves and giving Tony Serra the finger at the trial came to mind. "It seems to me there's a conflict between Community Risk Reduction and the cowboy art of firefighting. No offense to you and other firefighters, Eric, but that's what it feels like to me."

Eric looked at me seriously. "You have to understand, for the most part, public policy, and that includes fire safety, is expressed through the local budgets. The necessary personnel to improve communication networks, inspections, training, and other prevention measures are not up to the firefighters."

"Huh." I grunted out a cynical laugh.

He shook his head, "No, really. Local government executives set and implement public policy. Fire and police chiefs and building officials then carry out the policy. It is the duty of cities and counties to acknowledge there are competing interests for limited budget money but realize public safety must be their top priority."

I shrugged, "You don't think the Oakland Fire Department was fully staffed?"

"I can't say that, but most fire and police chiefs and building officials ask for additional personnel in the budget process. Often these new positions are not approved by the city executives or the elected city council." He leaned forward. "And this can happen in closed-door meetings."

I thought about Fire Chief Deloach-Reed who served as both Oakland fire chief and fire marshal. No doubt, she asked for a budget inclusion of funds for an Oakland fire marshal to address public safety needs. It would be impossible for her to do both jobs. I wondered how many other budget requests for additional staff, including qualified fire inspectors, are quashed in closed, internal meetings by city managers or budget directors.

Eric said, "Here's the thing, community risk reduction saves money. Look at that Community Risk Assessment Guide again. For every dollar spent reducing community risk, it would take $10 to achieve the same result with fire engines, fire stations, and firefighters."

I sighed and shook my head. "Maybe one day all the budget-people will begin to demand prevention as a cost-cutting measure."

I drove home after my conversation with Eric in a depressed funk. The problem felt insurmountable. Most likely, Chelsea and her friends were squeezed out of the budget. Inspectors and communications systems fell through the cracks. I learned from Eric that many budgets are decided in closed door meetings.

The fiscal decision-making process that led up to a weak fire inspection program in Oakland was never explored during the Ghost Ship trial. Oakland and Alameda County government officials ducked quietly behind their desks and hid from responsibility.

My Plea to all City Managers, County Executives, Elected Councils, and Board of Supervisors:

The Bay Area has some of the most expensive housing in the United States, but it is not alone in the proliferation of sites like Ghost Ship, non-residential structures converted into living units and performance spaces. They are largely ignored unless, like Ghost Ship, they garner multiple complaints about blight or, also like Ghost Ship, they become the scene of a tragedy.

During the trial, I wondered how the Oakland mayor and other city and county officials could ignore this growing problem of uninspected buildings and lack of standardized reporting systems. Was it neglect? Slow moving governmental bureaucracy? After listening to Eric, it felt more like a budget decision.

It is time to cut through the inertia of local governments. When I got home, I reread in the Community Risk Assessment Guide: "It is important that fire service leaders, their firefighters, and other staff begin to shift their thinking towards reducing and mitigating risks, as this will ultimately be expected by their communities and elected officials. This will probably not be a simple or immediate change."

I put the pamphlet down and sighed. The change must happen now.

Elected officials must take note and convince old school firefighters to adopt Community Risk Reduction as their main priority, if for no other reason than budgetary concerns. More importantly, property and lives will be saved. Fortunately, a new wave of firefighting professionals emphasize prevention. Eric restored my faith in firefighting professionals. It isn't just about putting water on fires. Prevention is the work of the future. Prevention would have saved my daughter and her friends' lives.

Our sons and daughters were martyrs to incompetence and systemic failure at all levels of local government. The battalion chief who said he would do nothing differently was wrong; there are lessons to be learned from the Ghost Ship tragedy. We owe those victims the simple changes to fiscal priorities, policy, and communication systems that could prevent future fire tragedies.

Part Five

The Ongoing-ness of Grief

Chapter 48

Swedish Death Cleanse

Hopeless Attempts at Moving On

Around 5:00 a.m. one Sunday morning, six years after the tragic fire, I was awakened by Chelsea barging through the front door. She was talking loudly and laughing with someone else. My first thought was, 'What the heck is she doing here so early!?' I smiled as it crossed my mind that Chelsea and one of her Marin County friends must have been out all night and she didn't want to drive back to the city. My home was always a safe haven. A second thought made my stomach roil, 'That's not Chelsea!' My third thought was a little gentler, 'She was here, no doubt in my mind.'

That's just the way she would arrive, the front door banging on its hinges, boots clunking up the steps, laughing with her head thrown back, walking through the door mid-conversation with a friend. I woke up fully and started crying, "I want her back."

Each morning I begin again.

Don't let anyone tell you grief proceeds in five well-regulated stages. It doesn't. I've likened it to navigating a maze blindfolded. Good luck following that path. What works to help one person get through the day could be devastating for another. I've heard dozens of stories in the various grief groups I've attended, and not one is ever the same. We come and go through this ugly journey without guardrails. For me, a fire truck siren, a child playfully screaming on the playground, or smoky air from a distant wildfire, can send me running for shelter. Other bereaved parents see clothes, smell food or perfume, or are just struck with a memory, and they are sent back to Day One of their grief.

After the trial had concluded, I visited my friend, Patsy Murphy, at her home on the wild Northern California coast. She was the person I'd called 33 years earlier when 3-year-old Chelsea asked me, "Mama, do you remember our old house? You know, the big

Patsy and Colleen on the bluffs of the Pacific.

white one that burned up in the fire." Patsy was going through some difficult health issues, her life was at stake, and I didn't want to burden her with my emotional pain. I just wanted to visit my friend and make sure she was okay, but as we walked along the bluffs above the Pacific Ocean, she expressed concern about my health and mentioned Broken Heart Syndrome. This, from a woman who had just had a pacemaker implanted in her chest.

Always one to listen to dreams, I told her about Chelsea barging through my front door, and Patsy started to cry. She took my hand. "How are you going to heal from this? The trauma of standing outside that burning building shook your foundations. Then you had to deal with Chelsea's death. And the trial. The reverberations of your loss haven't ended. Maybe they never will."

Patsy hugged me warmly. "I'm not asking when you're going to move on, Colleen. Chelsea was your beloved daughter. You can't pretend her death and the trial never happened. I'm asking, *What are you doing to heal your physical, mental, and emotional pain?*"

I was taken aback by Patsy's question. My quick response was, "This wasn't about me."

My quest had been to find out how and why my daughter died. The trial answered those questions. Patsy's question turned my whole experience on its head. She was right. The question remained: *Now what?*

I stepped back and took in the wholeness of my friend. Illness had stripped her tall frame of 30 pounds, but her thick, dark hair shone, and her eyes were clear. She had found a way back to health. Could I? I didn't even know I was sick, but Patsy could see it in my nervous tics, pale skin, and flaccid muscles. I had lost myself in grief.

When I returned home from Patsy's house, I decided to clear out the debris of my former self, knowing I would never be the same person I was before. Since I'd pretty much talked myself out with my therapist, I decided to follow the "move your hands, mend your heart" maxim. Serendipitously, I heard about the Swedish Death Cleanse on a National Public Radio program. The idea is for late-middle-aged adults to get rid of all the clutter in their homes, so their children or partners won't be stuck with the chore after we elders die. Sabrina had the task of cleaning out Chelsea's apartment. She brought along a burly friend, but it was still emotionally and physically overwhelming for her. I couldn't put her through that again.

I began to pare down closets and cupboards, ruthlessly discarding and donating items that no longer served my new life. On the other hand, I couldn't bear to discard Chelsea's things. What she saved held meaning and brought me a little closer to her, each piece a touchstone to her thoughts.

I recreated her bedroom in my garage, placing her purple velvet sofa and mirrored side table on a fluffy white rug. There, I touched her DNA on journals, saved scraps of paper, colorful clothes, jewelry, and even her orange, life-long stuffed lovie, Crab. Vivid memories came flooding back. She didn't collect much, but what she did save was precious to her. Chelsea's life mattered.

In contrast, my stuff was mostly simple accumulation. While ridding my bookshelves of books I'd already read or would never read, I filled a large packing box with grief books and donated them all to my local hospice thrift shop. Maybe someone there would get some use out of them. The pat advice never hit home for me. If I were audacious enough to give advice to someone who is grieving, it would be to do what feels good and brings you comfort. Don't let others bully you into smiling and fake cheerfulness. The false front doesn't serve you; it serves them.

My advice for friends and families of grievers is based on the food-train fellow teachers at my school set up for me. It was perfect: Prepare a meal and leave it on the front doorstep in a cooler, then leave without waiting for thanks or acknowledgement. Text when you're gone to say the food has arrived. Maybe the griever will welcome you next time, but don't force your goodwill on them. After a while, the griever will emerge, blinking in the bright sunlight. Be there without gushing. Talk about their loved one who is gone. They are not gone to the griever. Those who are suffering will need to make their own meaning in their own time. It isn't your job to fix them or push them into "moving on."

Chapter 49

Pentimento

Pentimento is the discovery of an original drawing or painting which was later painted over by the artist. The original art is often uncovered through scratches caused by some disaster or mishandling. I am reminded of pentimento as I conclude this story. Layers of sensational news accounts and the lawyers' "alternate stories" kept me from seeing how my beautiful daughter died. Fortunately, sworn testimony from trial witnesses left scratches in the cheap surface overlay, and allowed me to peek into Chelsea's last moments. She was a beautiful work of art. This is the picture I found:

Chelsea Faith Dolan aka Cherushii.

The party upstairs had just started, and the music was so loud Chelsea and Travis couldn't hear each other speak. Darn! Her ear plugs were in the car. She got up from the couch and left Travis and the others upstairs for a minute so she could save her hearing and get some fresh air. It was 11:20 p.m. Chelsea found her sparkly custom earplugs in the glove compartment, put them in her purse, and then leaned against her little Honda Civic parked under the streetlight. It shone blueish silver in the light from above and the neon glow streaming across the street from the Wendy's hamburger joint.

Chelsea looked and felt incongruous in the scrappy neighborhood. She was lucky to have parked right in front of the entrance. This was a neighborhood where one might expect to find their car stolen or the windows smashed in. It had happened to her before, and she knew enough to park where there would be light and people. The run-down warehouse beside her had piles of scrap wood and trash stacked near the front door, two tiers of dirty metal-grated windows, and a graffitied screaming pirate skull painted on the front of it. Otherwise, it was a nondescript, old, white hulk of a warehouse on 31st Avenue in the Fruitvale District of Oakland, California.

Chelsea's performance outfit made her stand out. She wore mid-calf black boots with large buttons up the side, zebra striped tights, a black mini-skirt, black sequined top, a long, cobalt-blue faux-leather jacket with a blue and black checkered scarf wrapped loosely around her neck. Chelsea's long platinum blond hair was tipped with hot pink on one side, and turquoise blue on the other. She wore large, silver-wire spiral earrings that brushed against her shoulders. Her sparkly eye makeup made her look especially out of place. Sharply formed wedges of shimmering blue eyeshadow completely covered her eyelids from her eyebrows out to a point at her temples. Her glittering appearance was an anomaly standing next to the grimy building.

Chelsea stared off into the night sky, her arms wrapped around her middle like a hug, shivering a bit from the cold and thinking about home and warmth. She could almost taste the leftover pizza from dinner waiting for her in the refrigerator. A voice made her wake up from her reverie. A word. What did he say? She stood up straight and faced a steady stream of people emerging from the front door. She cocked her head to one side, straining to hear. There. She heard it again. "Fire." No one seemed panicked. No fire bells or smoke detector clamored for attention. Everyone walking out was calm and dry, so no sprinklers had gone off. The music upstairs was still blasting. It couldn't be too serious. She searched the faces for her friends. So far, none had walked out the door. They were still upstairs where she had just left them. A knot formed in her stomach. Something wasn't right.

A dark-haired girl in a black wool coat pushed through the front door and pulled a cell phone from her coat pocket. Chelsea pointed to the phone and demanded, "Are you calling 911?" When she heard the word yes, Chelsea tugged open the heavy metal door and rushed into the dark, loud, beat-throbbing space. Most of the lights had been turned off for the party and her eyes had to adjust to the hazy darkness. Just inside the front entryway, she collided with a young man and .... a dog! No, it was two dogs! Chelsea backed away. The man was carrying two dachshunds, one under each arm. Her blood turned cold. This was an evacuation.

The young man winced at her frightened face and yelled, "Follow me!" He rushed through the open door. When he got outside, he turned around. Chelsea was not behind him. She was still inside. He cradled his dogs as he stood waiting out front on the sidewalk, but she never came out.

Chelsea looked back and forth inside the cluttered labyrinth of RVs, trailers, partitioned living spaces, and walls of organs and pianos stacked high with junk and draped with hanging fabric. It suddenly occurred to her that all the tchotchkes, wooden statues, bicycles, and other random collectible debris strewn about or hanging from makeshift walls and wooden rafters might topple. A few more strangers pushed past her toward the door. What was wrong with these people? Didn't anyone warn the people upstairs? Some guy ran toward her yelling "Fire!" He poked his head into makeshift bedrooms and seemed to be looking for someone downstairs. No one upstairs could have heard the commotion over the music. Hell, it was almost impossible to hear that guy yelling right next to her.

She looked up the stairs. No one was coming down. She'd have to go up and warn them herself. Chelsea shook her body from head to toe to rid herself of her growing fear and took a deep breath. It tasted like smoke. She looked around and tried to orient herself to the layout she'd seen when she first arrived, and the lights were still on. Pianos in the way. A huge, wooden statue somewhere around the corner. Two chairs positioned in front of the stairs The staircase itself was almost a U shape with two sharp turns. She remembered a few uneven steps up with a bathroom on the landing to the right. More stairs to the left. Stupid ramp with wooden slats near the top. A last turn to the left. She could do this. She took another deep breath. More smoke stuck in her throat, and she coughed.

As she grappled her way around the obstacles in her path, an ominous orange glow flickered in the distant back of the warehouse beyond all the wooden posts and paraphernalia. Fire. She froze, stunned, as a thick black wave of smoke rolled along the ceiling of the first floor headed straight for her. It bellowed toward the front of the building and engulfed

Chelsea in toxic, black fumes that smelled like burnt plastic. She ducked low and her heart pounded till her ribs nearly broke free of her chest. She felt her way around the piano that blocked the hallway, her head even with the keys, and groped in the dark for the stair railing. She tried not to breathe again, but soon had to suck in more poisonous smoke. Her nose and throat burned. Her breath bubbled and rasped. Her tongue felt heavy. A massive, rasping cough shook her body, but even that couldn't clear her lungs. She could barely see; streaming tears blinded her as she bounded up the stairs in giant leaps. Near the top, on the swaying "pirate ship" ramp, Chelsea jostled her way around a young man who was cautiously starting down the stairs. She choked out at him, "The smoke is too much." He blinked at her, took a deep breath, held it, closed his eyes, and continued down the stairs.

The music was still blaring. Chelsea looked in horror at her friends dancing, smiling, and gesturing to each other. She flailed her arms, hoping to catch their attention and start back down the stairs, but no one paid attention to her. She ran toward the DJ stage. Chelsea had been there early enough to help set up the stage and knew exactly where the master volume control was. She reached across the deck and grabbed the knob.

She gasped out the word, "fire." A wave of people moved toward the stairs. Immediately, a line formed trailing behind a massive crowd at the top of the stairs. Chelsea pushed back toward the stairs and got as far as the middle of the room, standing with Griffin and Ara Jo. They and others huddled together, anxiously facing the slow moving, single file of frightened people stumbling down the smoke-filled stairway. She thought, "Go, go, go!" Then a thunderous crack filled the building. The floor! She felt herself falling. Fade to black.

Chapter 50

The Afterlife, Psychics, and Mediums

I have longed to believe that Chelsea's spirit lives somewhere out in the Universe, but I've always been a skeptic about psychics, having read stories through the years of scam artists and fakes who emptied the bank accounts of the bereaved. Just the same, I went to see a man who was a semi-famous medium with two other mothers who had lost their young adult children to sudden death. I didn't go as a true believer but wanted to support my friends who had seen this man before and wanted me to experience the wonders of spirit communication.

We drove together to a hotel in San Francisco and joined about thirty other people in a conference room sitting on straight-backed metal dining room chairs lined up in rows. The medium stood at the front of the room and explained how he would go into a trance and call out the initials of the departed ones who wanted to contact us in the room. His first call-out was from a "young woman whose name starts with C." There was a reference to music, darkness, and a terrible, accidental death. He felt something around her neck and throat... upper respiratory... but she was not sick. It was a sudden death. He said she knew her mother was trying to find out what happened during the last moments she was alive.

So, you can imagine, I felt this was all about Chelsea. I raised my hand and acknowledged that it was my daughter. The medium said she wanted to tell her mother that she did not suffer... and she was not suffering now. Later, as a story was unfolding about a man's son who wanted his dad to start writing down his feelings and keep a journal, the medium threw up his hands and asked, "Who's Chelsea?!" No initials this time. I said, "She's my daughter. I was told she wouldn't stop interrupting, almost shouting, and she was insisting I should continue writing. It could be a book or a movie, and she knows I stopped, but she wanted me to start up again. He said she will be with me and help me write. It may not be what I initially intended to write, but that's because she will be writing it, too. Then the medium said, "Didn't I already speak with you?" I said yes, and he moved on. I thought, *Isn't it just like Chelsea to barge right in when she had something to say?*

Coincidence?

Shortly after Chelsea died, I received a package from a clothing store. I hadn't ordered anything, but it's a store where I have an account. When I opened the plastic bag, I pulled out a slinky, colorful, sleeveless top and laughed. It was gaudy with primary color swirls and not anything I would ever wear, let alone  order for myself online—especially in the middle of winter. The silliness of it made me say out loud, "This is something Chelsea would wear." Then, I thought, *Why not try it on?*

I went upstairs to change and looked at myself in the

bathroom mirror, hoping to glimpse a little memory of Chelsea before sending the top back to the store. Suddenly, the overhead fluorescent light fixture started blinking off and on wildly with a loud blinky-blink-blink sound that filled the room. It was the sound you might hear if a fluorescent bulb were burning out. Of course, the timing was impeccable, so I looked up at the light and shrugged, "Do you like it, Chelsea?" It was just a joke, but the blinking sped up even more. Then, I said, "Okay, okay, I'll keep it!"

The blinking and noises stopped abruptly. The light shone steadily.

I shrugged, put the top on a hanger and reverently placed it in my closet. That was several years ago. The light bulb never burned out and it has not blinked since. The top was never billed to my credit card. It's still not something I would wear, but it is something Chelsea would want me to wear. She used to tease me, "Oh, Mother, you're so monochromatic." Then, we'd both look at her flamboyant outfit of the day and laugh.

Something else happened early in 2022. I kept Chelsea's phone on my AT&T service. They helped me find her messages that I'd deleted just before she died, and I thought Sabrina and I might need to access something on her phone for her music or a picture or whatever. I also sent Chelsea occasional messages just because I wanted to pretend she would receive them. I sent her a text message one day, "I miss you, sweetheart. Please send me a sign." Two days later, I received a letter in my mailbox. It was from a woman named Theresa who said she speaks with the dead.

The woman said a girl named Chelsea told her two years ago that she didn't do what she was accused of, she wasn't burned, and to let her mother know that she was okay. It was two years earlier that Tony Serra had accused Chelsea of being a mysterious witchy wild woman who sat at the foot of the stairs in Ghost Ship and had told her friends not to come down because it was "... the will of the spirit of the forest."

Well, Chelsea would know I'd never fall for that garbage, but it was odd this woman was sending me the message now. Theresa explained in her letter that she had tried to find this Chelsea girl's mother for two years. She didn't live in the Bay Area, but somehow had just seen a Ghost Ship anniversary article in an old newspaper that mentioned my name and Chelsea's. She looked me up immediately and sent me the letter. It arrived in the mail two days after I asked Chelsea for a sign.

I once told my friend, Sioux, that if Chelsea ever wanted to contact me it would be through electricity. That was her creative medium; she was an electronic musician. Of course, I don't think Chelsea reads text messages or sends orders online to clothing stores, but there's something just so odd about the electronic connections. I want to remain open to the possibility that an entity of Chelsea-ness still exists on some other distant shore with the same sense of humor, purpose, and connectedness intact. I see her as swirling multi-colored sparks in the Universe, emanating love.

From Chelsea's photo collection.

Chapter 51

Greece — The Release

May 31 - June 21, 2022

Writing has been my solace and my therapy. Sometime during late summer, 2021, I started looking online for classes or seminars. Writing can be a lonely endeavor, but in the company of others there is the dual comfort of focus and friendship. I scouted around the internet but kept coming back to The Writing Room. Two women put on a writing retreat in Greece. Sarah Bullen is a writer, agent, and writing coach from South Africa. Kate Emerson is a writer, life coach, and organizational genius who lives on a remote island in Scotland. Together, they inspired me to expand my Facebook musings and newspaper articles into a book.

The first week of June 2022 at the Greek beachfront village of Skala Eressos was deliriously productive. I put the final touches on my first draft of this book and began the editing process. The easy camaraderie of our small cadre of 11 writers was deeply satisfying. I felt at home in their company.

Friday, June 10, 2022, was a day of rest between the first

week of workshops and the following intensive residency. Sue from South Africa, Karin from the Netherlands, Suzanne, my compatriot from California, and I decided to fill the day by squeezing into a little blue rental car and heading up the mountain to the Petrified Forest National Park. The winding road was treacherous and sometimes seemed more like a dusty, unpaved path, but Sue drove like a pro - calmly and carefully. I laughed nervously when we passed one of those diamond shaped, yellow caution signs that depicted a car falling off a cliff. Yikes!

At the top of the mountain, a crushed stone path led from the tidy parking lot to an open-air stone hut. One man, dressed in a green guide's uniform, leaned his hip against a low stone wall. He greeted us with a smile and *"Kalimera,"* as we entered the building. Under the open-air roof, another man sat at a folding table, took our money, and issued tickets. Five or six more workmen sat on a wooden bench or stood next to it, smoking, and chatting amiably. The guide led us in the direction of a beautifully paved flagstone path that wound downhill around glossy stone tree trunks. They lay in manicured dirt displays encircled with smaller, round-stone frames as far as we could see. The view of distant, surrounding rocky outcrops and soft green valleys was breathtaking.

Our first tree off to the right of the path was quite large, about 30 feet long and broken into 5 segments. It was impressive. There was an informational sign in Greek and English next to the path. I leaned forward to read it, not paying attention to the 1-inch step in front of me.

Here's the spooky part: I felt someone shove me with what felt like a huge hand covering my back or a hurricane force wind, but there was no one behind me. The shove was forceful but inexplicably smooth. I pitched forward in slow motion, giving me time to decide to sacrifice my hand, rather than crush my face or, even worse, crack open my forehead and risk losing cognitive function. My left hand took the force and snapped back touching my forearm. I heard the crack and braced the remainder of my fall with my other hand and left foot. They both fractured, as well.

Once I came to a standstill, time returned to normal speed, and the absurdity of the pratfall made me laugh. I couldn't be upset. Something pushed me, and I was pretty sure it was Chelsea. I heard her say, "Mother, get out!" in her sweet, smiling voice. That weird impression wasn't something I wanted to share with my new friends. They came running over as I sat up and dragged my already swollen, lifeless left hand onto my lap. It hurt like heck, so I sat for a minute to collect myself before they tried to help me to my feet. My left foot collapsed under me. Stunned, I sat back down on the offending tiny stair step. How were we going to get back down the mountain if I couldn't walk up the slight incline to our car in the parking lot? I couldn't move.

Kostos and his crew came to the rescue. He was the manager of those men we'd seen who maintained the site. They were big, strong, and Kostos kept us smiling as they half-carried me back up the path to the parking lot. Then Kostos gave Sue directions to the nearest medical clinic, jumped into his own car, and led us all the way there. Thank you, Kostos! Suzanne, Karin, Sue, and I didn't get to see much of the park, just one fallen tree and one fallen woman, both fractured.

The doctors and nurses at the local medical clinic spoke no English and the four of us spoke no Greek. Nevertheless, I had X-rays taken, and through gestures and body language we understood that the broken bones in my wrist were too complicated to be set in their small clinic. They wrapped my hands and ankle in yards of gauze, sending us off with the words "Hospital. Mytilene."

As I was being wheeled out the door, I asked, "Money?"

"Ohi, ohi, no, no. Public Health."

Sue, the self-assured driver, took the four of us to the only hospital on Lesvos, which was in the capital city—the Mytilene Hospital. We kept ourselves distracted on the 90-minute drive with medical and metaphysical adventure stories. We took turns describing impossible journeys, absurd accidents, misdiagnosed diseases, ghosts, haunted houses, and other mysteries. That's when Sue dubbed this *The Fracture Tour.* Believe it or not, we laughed the whole way to the hospital.

Once at the hospital, we looked a little like a comedy team. Suzanne became my buddy and wheelchair driver. Karin took charge of intake papers and the packet of X-rays. Sue parked the car and ran inside with her iPhone set to Record. Then a green garbed, bossy angel appeared. Young, handsome Dr. Marc Heller spoke English! Although nurses tried to tell us in Greek and hand signs that I was only allowed one visitor, he tsk-tsked them away. We laughed when he explained to us that he told them we were foreigners who didn't know any better.

Thank goodness. We all had our well-defined roles at this point.

Then Dr. Marc told me what was wrong with my misshapen, throbbing hand. The gist was that my left wrist was badly broken, and the bones were dislocated. Karin took detailed notes. Sue recorded what he said. Suzanne stood beside me and kept me smiling with witty commentary under her breath. I don't think I ever felt this nurtured. More X-rays ensued. Finally, Dr. Marc told me I needed to be admitted to the hospital to have a metal plate inserted into my wrist as soon as possible, probably on Tuesday. I could be admitted that Monday, but since it was a holiday, the operation would take place the following morning. But first—he would realign the bones that were dislocated.

I stopped smiling. He whisked me off in my wheelchair to a dimly lit private room where I was told to lie down on a flat, vinyl-padded examining bench. I was getting a cold, ominous feeling. While his male assistant held my elbow out in the air at a right angle from my body, Dr. Marc dusted his hands with chalk and chuckled, "Like a gymnast. So I don't slip." I thought he was kidding and tried to smile. Then he pulled on my hand and fingers while his assistant pulled steadily on my elbow. I screamed and cried and begged him to stop. A nurse, who had been holding down my merely fractured right hand, stuffed a soft paper towel into my fingers and Dr. Marc said gruffly, "For your eyes."

Okay, wiping away tears was the last thing on my mind. The pulling went on for hours. Well, actually about 3 or 4 minutes, but it felt like hours. Then a half-cast was quickly applied to the underside of my forearm while the assistant held my bones in place. The top was left open to leave room for swelling. From there, I was sent back to my hotel with painkillers, which by the way only cost €2. When I asked Dr.

Marc about the bill he said, "Bring your Medicare and insurance cards, but this was an accident. Probably no charge." My friends and I drove back to the hotel at Skala Eressos, though this time I was on drugs, and we'd used up all our stories. It was quieter in the car on the long return to the hotel.

I spent the weekend propped up on pillows and painkillers. On Monday morning, one of my new writer friends from London, Ruth, who was a physio-carer and held a doctorate in communication, accompanied me back to the Mytilene Hospital. She guided me through the registration process, and I was escorted by a young, chirpy nurse into a room with three elderly women. I struggled to understand any of them, but they spoke incessantly all at once, in rapid Greek. All I could say was, "Ven katalaveno Helinicá." I don't understand Greek. They talked to me anyway.

On Tuesday morning, I was wheeled to a bright operating room where Dr. Marc and another, older surgeon drove a metal plate with eight screws into my unstable, broken wrist bones. I was numbed but awake the whole time. A drape was secured to hide the sight of my split-open wrist. Nurses and doctors circled and spoke to me, but I didn't understand what they were saying. Finally, after three hours, when the whining of the drill ended and I was sewn back together, Dr. Marc stood smiling next to my head, gave me a thumbs up, and declared, "We did an excellent job!"

That night, back in the room with my three chatty neighbors, I was given a bowl of lemon soup with bits of fine pasta swirled in it called avgolemono. That soup was the most comforting thing I'd ever tasted. Sated, I looked out my hospital window at the Strawberry Full Moon hovering over distant Greek mountains. As pain and poignant beauty intertwined, it dawned on me that something significant had occurred that weekend. Chelsea had set me free. For five and a half years, I witnessed the Ghost Ship fire through Chelsea's eyes in recurring nightmares. I felt her panic and pain, and every night she died again. Since my fall, I haven't had the nightmare once.

During the long months of the trial, it helped to see the events from her perspective, but that advocacy ended. I laughingly told everyone in Greece, and later at home, that my broken bones were an offering to the Greek gods in exchange for letting me keep my brains intact. But I knew in my secret heart that it was Chelsea shoving me out of her body and back over the dark threshold into the world of the living.

On Wednesday afternoon, I checked out of the hospital and was only asked to pay a room charge for three days. All medical services were covered by Public Health. Then I returned to the hotel to recuperate. My Skala Eressos friends, Sue, Suzanne, Karin, Ruth, and others watched over me like angels. Ruth fashioned a sling for me out of a rainbow-hued beach wrap, and we had long talks about grief. She had recently lost her husband. For the rest of the week, my new writer friends brought food and kept me company while I recovered in bed. Living alone for years, I'd nearly forgotten what it felt like to be cared for in this way. Chelsea chose the right time and place to push me back into my own body. I was in good hands.

Whether the broken bones brought me back into my own body or Chelsea did, the result was the same: We both blessed the release.

Chapter 52

Facing Forward

S ix years is too long to remain angry or spend the rest of my days in grief-driven isolation. I have mourned my daughter's death and the loss of a community of creative souls long enough to know this: There is no lesson or meaning to be gleaned from their deaths. Nothing good came from their loss. They should still be here.

*Kim Gregory, me, David Gregory, and Carol Cidlik
celebrating our girls on the fifth anniversary.*

Somehow, I must learn to reconcile this depressing reality with my daughter's warm, effervescent joie de vivre. And she was not alone. The 36 Stars filled their lives with creativity and purpose. I never met a kinder group of young people. The brevity of their time here on Earth was countered by their joyful exuberance for Life while they were with us. No wonder they were friends. It wasn't their deaths that taught us a lesson, after all, but their brief, full, beautiful lives.

Linda Regan (Amanda Allen Kershaw), me, Carol Cidlik (Nicole Segrist) scattering ashes of our girls on the fifth anniversary.

When I think back on that cold December night in 2016, while a burning warehouse seared my soul, I remembered how a brief, cold salve washed over me. Chelsea had softly whispered in my ear, "I see you and Sabrina, Mother, but I have to leave. I have work to do elsewhere." And then it felt like she whooshed away into the far reaches of the Universe.

(Courtesy of Jeremy Danger)

Standing before the fire that night, I chalked up the sensation to some complex psychological gymnastics my brain conjured to soften the awful possibility of her death. But little by little over the years, my skepticism has receded. Maybe the psychic was right, after all. Chelsea might be helping me write her story, but I cannot keep living my life through her eyes. I must let her go. She has work to do elsewhere.

I am reminded of the story of the mother orca whale pushing her dead calf to the ocean's surface for two weeks, or the mother monkey Sabrina told me about in the crematorium. That mother was begging for help from her fellow monkeys, desperately trying to bring her baby back to life. The mother orca believed she could create a miracle.

Like that whale, I've tried to keep Chelsea alive by pushing her to the surface through dreams, the trial, and my writing. By holding onto her so fiercely and living my life through her eyes, we both remained in the tragic loop of my denial. It has taken me all this time to realize I did get my wish that awful day in the crematorium. For Chelsea's story to live within me, we had to trade places. I had to die.

Now, I must learn to live again. I accept now that Chelsea will not take another breath, but a part of me still waits for her return.

Even if there is no afterlife as I want to envision it, Chelsea lives on in a very real way: She has inspired her friends, family, and even complete strangers to believe in themselves and follow their dreams. I can put one of her Cherushii vinyl albums on the record player, sip a mimosa in her honor, and feel her thought patterns evolve through the music. She taught us to relish this gift of life, and that's almost enough for me. But if you're listening, Chelsea, a little visit would be nice. Call your mother.

Composite picture of Ghost Ship victims.

Acknowledgments

One year after my daughter, Chelsea Faith, died, I attended a writing workshop with Zen poet and essayist, Roger Housden. I sat cross-legged on the floor of a lovely yoga retreat, writing about small incidents in my life that I thought would distract me from my grief. Roger listened kindly and patiently. Finally, he acknowledged my sorrow over Chelsea's death and gently offered, "This is what you want to write about but work so hard to avoid. Why not just do it?" And so, I have. Thank you, Roger.

One year later, this book came together through the encouragement of Sarah Bullen and Kate Emerson, my writing mentors and moral support. They led The Writing Room retreats in Skala Eressos, a tiny beach town on the island of Lesvos in Greece. There, with a cohort of hopeful authors, I learned how to "stop mucking about" and get the book done. I am grateful to my Greek island friends, Susan Casamento, Karin Giphart, Sue Adams, and Ruth Parry, who nurtured me when I fell, breaking both wrists, one ankle and my will to keep writing. My bones and my heart have healed, my friends, and I am grateful.

Beta readers Susan Casamento, Sioux Krings, David Gregory, Carol Cidlik, Karin Giphart, JK Stenger, Ingrid McCartney, Ted Holzman, Roman Bodnar, Eric Nickel, Cynthia Leir, and Lesley Miles all read critically and with heart. Thank you to my editors, Dorothy Wall, Katherine

Abraham, and Sarah Bullen, who helped me pull out unnecessary details and add my own experiences and emotions to each chapter. Nisha Zenoff inspired me to use their expert advice and keep going until my book was published.

I owe Stephanie Larkin of Red Penguin Books my heartfelt thanks for taking on the hard business of publishing my book. Writing flows easily for me. Getting this emotional story out of my body and onto the page felt essential. But getting *The Ghost Ship Fire* published and promoted felt impossible. Like most first-time authors, I faced the impenetrable wall of literary agents and publishers. I bought books on how to write a query letter and sent out dozens. I attended conferences and workshops on how to present book proposals and received kind responses from agents but no offers. Finally, as I was about to give up, Stephanie said, "We can do this!" And here we are. I am proud to have Red Penguin Books publish this work and grateful for Stephanie's enthusiasm.

Some of the photos in this book include the work of Nazar Vojtovich and Julianna Brown, both of whom generously allowed me to use their pictures of the fire and Chelsea's memorial. Other photos were donated by my family and the victims' families and friends. Thank you all. The courtroom sketches are the work of renowned courtroom artist, Vicki Berringer. I sat behind her each day of the trial, looking on with amazement as she captured the heart of each moment.

Special thanks to Sioux Krings, who drove me to the Ghost Ship trial each day and listened to my rants on the way home. Your insights kept me sane.

I'm grateful to my dear friends Patsy Murphy, Gary Gunsel, Steve Kopp, and Susie Baker who stood by me during the dark years without giving unsolicited advice and nudged me toward the light when I was ready. And where would I be without my ZF Tribe, Marianna Nickel, Margie Schwartz,

Evelyn Howard, Debbie Fraschetti, and Tina Guterman, who provided the warm camaraderie and laughter I needed so desperately when I had zero Fs left to give?

The friends and families of our loved ones stood with me in solidarity when I needed to speak out during the trial and beyond. May we honor the memory of our 36 Stars by living our own lives as fully as they did and sharing their gift of exuberant joy. Most of all, I am grateful to my daughter, Sabrina, her husband, Joe, and my grandson, River, who remind me to keep facing the future. I love you.

Throughout her life, Chelsea inspired many people to follow their dreams just as she did. Nearly everyone who knew her has a silly, inspirational, or poignant Chelsea story to share. There were too many to include them all here. My sisters, Leslie Buchman and Marcia D'Alba, brother Jim Dolan, and their families all keep her childhood memories alive. Chelsea's oldest friend, Josey Duncan, who threw a disco party for her memorial, still checks in. It sustains me to hear Chelsea's name spoken aloud in the present tense. Thank you all.

The statements in *The Ghost Ship Fire, A Mother's Search for Answers* are true based on my best recollection, confirmation from victims' family members mentioned in the book, my 11 journals filled with notes from the trial, and the full transcripts of the trial, which I purchased from Gerald Nachman and Kathleen Lyons, Alameda County court reporters.

Photos

Ariel image of the Ghost Ship building post-fire was taken for California Fire. The photographer is Josh Edelson. Purchased from Getty Images.

About the Author

Colleen Dolan is a writer, Certified Grief Educator, and retired Educational Therapist.

Her daughter, Chelsea Faith Dolan, was a well-respected electronic musician and producer known professionally as Cherushii. Chelsea died in the Ghost Ship fire, one of 36 talented young friends who attended a party on the second floor of the warehouse.

Colleen witnessed the fire on December 2, 2016, attended every day of the trial two years later, and has written several articles about her grief experience. *The Ghost Ship Fire* chronicles her journey from the night of the fire to her eventual acceptance of grief as an ongoing part of her life. This book is written for bereaved parents searching for the How and Why of their children's deaths. You are not alone.

The statements in this book are true based on my best recollection, confirmation from victims' family members mentioned in the book, my 11 journals filled with notes from the trial, and the full transcripts of the trial which I purchased from Gerald Nachman and Kathleen Lyons, Alameda County court reporters.

∼ Colleen Dolan

Printed in the USA
CPSIA information can be obtained
at www.ICGtesting.com
LVHW070511091024
793248LV00018B/319

9 781637 776360